HD
2755.5 Ledogar, Robert J.
.L43 Hungry for profits : U.S. food & drug multinationals in Latin America / Robert J. Ledogar. New York : IDOC/ North America, c1975.

xiii, 209 p. ; 22 cm. (IDOC/international documentation)

NjTeaF FDU*po 75-39985

Hungry for Profits

U.S. Food & Drug Multinationals in Latin America

Hungry for Profits

Robert J. Ledogar

IDOC/North America, New York

Hungry for Profits

Published by IDOC/North America, Inc.
235 East 49th Street, New York, New York 10017

Introduction

ISBN 0-89021-034-9 *cloth*
ISBN 0-89021-038-1 *paper*

Library of Congress Catalog Card Number
75-39985

Printed in the U.S.A.

Issued as No. 70 in the monographic series
IDOC/International Documentation,
published by IDOC/North America, Inc.,
under the general editorship of
Pat VanHeel Gaughan

CONTENTS

INTRODUCTION

This is a book about the impact of multinational food and drug corporations on consumers in Latin America. It is a fact book, bringing these companies down from the abstraction ladder of conventional theorizing to ground level where human beings suffer the consequences of their capital and marketing strategies.

The realities described by Ledogar and his associates are drawn from observation in the countries as well as from a range of studies that have received too little attention in the United States. Sample the following corporate-induced or corporate-produced conditions:

•U.S. and European drug companies in Brazil push over-medication of the upper classes. Yet needed drugs are priced beyond the means of the masses. This is done in the familiar context of corruption and gross underregulation by the government.

•Gulf+Western in the Dominican Republic draws more and more acreage into sugar cane at the expense of land devoted to growing domestically consumed food. The sugar is exported for foreign exchange that is significantly squandered among the political and economic elites. At the same time, land availability to meet local needs of hungry, undernourished people is reduced.

•Ralston Purina builds up the chicken industry in Colombia by expanding feed producing lands. While food production for the majority who are poor lags, the upper classes consume chicken and eggs directly or in processed products such as mayonnaise.

•Brazil exports 97% of its orange crop to companies such as Coca-Cola, while U.S. soft drink companies vigorously press to sell vast amounts of zero-nutrition soft drinks to Brazilians, many of whom suffer from a vitamin C deficiency.

•Nestlé, the giant Swiss conglomerate, strives to secure replacement of breast feeding with bottle feeding using its infant milk formula. Pediatric nutritionists term this shift, induced by clever psychological appeals, a health disaster for infants. These children are deprived of safer, more nutritious mother's milk and exposed to expensive milk formulas that are easily contaminated through dilution and unsanitary preparation.

As recent disclosures in the media show, multinational corporations often buy their way into country markets by buying government officials. In addition, differences between consumer protection laws in the United States and Europe, on the one hand, and Latin America, on the other hand, have led to marketing products for uses which would be prohibited in the home country of these companies. Ledogar describes some of these double standards by drug companies in this report.

The insinuation of foreign multinational enterprises throughout poor countries calls for a broader framework of analysis and resolution than the customary approaches of development economists. Pressures for this broader look are coming from several directions. Corporate nationalists in developing countries are demanding greater equity ownership in multinationals or outright purchase or displacement. President Alfonso Lopez Michelsen reflected this constituency and the Colombian government's belief that more self-reliance and less direct foreign investment and foreign aid will bring faster economic growth, benefitting more people, as well as fewer economic and political problems between his country and the United States. Under the terms of the Andean Pact, Colombia, Venezuela, Ecuador, Peru, Bolivia and Chile have pledged to eliminate foreign control over their domestic economies.

Another movement that may provide a powerful critique of multinational companies is the small or intermediate technology school, whose intellectual leader is the British economist E.L. Schumacher. In his book, *Small is Beautiful,* and his group's publication, "Intermediate Technology," Schumacher argues, from many case studies in poor lands, that highly capital-intensive, complex technology—the kind pushed by worldwide corporations —is harmful to the economic well-being of these countries. Labor-intensive technology that is distributed geographically where people live and that uses local resources, local skills, and local currency is what builds stable and just economies, he contends. Such scaling down of technology is more efficient and less conducive to the distorting effects of foreign reliance for equipment, spare parts, and other supplies.

There is substantial historical support for Schumacher's thesis. It is hard to find any poor country, even ones very receptive to foreign investment, where multinationals have contributed to a pattern of intensive job development and base-broadening economic growth. Instead, these companies contribute to single-cash-crop type development and the buildup of elite classes and authoritarian regimes which neglect the vast majority poor. Some observers believe that the ill effects of multinational companies reveal structural divergences between their immediate profit maximizations and the economic, health, and safety needs of developing lands. One analyst concluded that "no amount of good will on the part of corporate executives can change that."

It is clear that Ledogar's material can be interpreted as supporting this argument. It is easier and more profitable to sell Coca-Cola in Brazil to fewer, *relatively* better-off people than a nutritious drink to a large number of people. So that's what Coca-Cola, Inc., does. This does not mean that nutritious drinks are not around to promote; it's just that they are not as "patented" and not as profitable. Meanwhile a great opportunity to contribute to the diets of tens of millions of impoverished human beings is forsaken. The point is that there are markets and products that multinationals have little or no interest in making or identifying for alternative institutions to meet. These companies are quite able to adapt to the reality that Brazil, a land of 105 million people, is a market of about 20 million customers for their products. The needs of the rest of the people, the expendable economy, do not affect the policies of these firms. They are not organizations of distributive justice, decentralized initiatives, or longer-range concerns and indigenous investments. They are not interested in public health, public education, consumer or producer cooperatives, land reform—all generally recognized to be requisites for solid economic well-being for the deprived and disadvantaged.

Some countries, particularly Japan decades ago and China in the postwar period, chose comparative economic isolation to build their capital and their other resources in an internally recycling manner rather than an externally exchanging or draining one. This was easier to do in those countries than in Latin America. For south of the border the multinational firms have long had the active backing and guarantees of the U.S. government and the U.S. taxpayer.

U.S. government insurance, loans, guarantees, grants, commercial contracts, tax preference, and diplomatic, intelligence, and even military support have bolstered the position of these private corporations—at taxpayers' expense—without, as one of Ledogar's sources notes, "any demonstration of benefits to the economies of the less developed countries involved."

Perhaps that is Ledogar's central point—a humanistic one. How does the behavior of multinationals really affect the people in these countries, and how can Americans learn more about such behavior which, whether as stockholders or taxpayers, is often done in their name? Before that detailed awareness is developed, the range of choices and changes will be left to a few corporate managers to decide for millions of human beings.

Ralph Nader
Washington, D.C.
October 1975

PREFACE

In writing this book, we have tried to keep rhetoric to a minimum and to avoid, wherever possible, the shrill tones of moral outrage. But in planning our investigation and reporting the results, we were equally determined to steer clear of any false journalistic "objectivity" which would require balancing every adverse statement about a company with something positive. Since the companies themselves spend millions of dollars every year to tell us how much good they are doing,* it hardly seemed necessary or wise to spend any of the modest budget available for this study on corporate image-building.

A balanced assessment of multinational corporations can be achieved only when the essential data on them are in the public domain. Right now these data are well-guarded corporate secrets. There are some very good reasons why corporations maintain secrecy over their accounts, production figures, marketing analyses, and other information; but without public access to such data, we know for the most part only what corporations want us to know—or cannot avoid telling us—about themselves. Under such circumstances, a balanced view of corporate activity is, for the outsider, impossible, and a superficial attempt to give "both sides" on any issue would simply compound the imbalance of information that now exists.

The case of ITT, though not a subject of this book, is enlightening. In 1974 the company spent $6.4 million in an effort to improve the image tarnished by such events as its involvement with the CIA in Chile. In one year's time, as a result of this advertising campaign, the number of people who believe that ITT "cares about the general public" more than doubled, from 20% to 43%. Such is the power of corporations to influence public opinion.[1]

On the other hand, we did not set out to "get" any one particular corporation. Many corporate names are mentioned in this book. Whole chapters in some cases are devoted to the impact of a single company. But the intention was never to damage the position of any one company in relation to that of its competitors. Similarly, our intention was not to damage the position of U.S. corporations vis-a-vis their competitors from Europe or elsewhere. Though our focus was naturally on the activities of U.S. business, we included available information about European multinationals and national companies within Latin America wherever appropriate. We found no evidence to indicate that the business practices of U.S. corporations in Latin America are notably different from those of their competitors.

This book was not written to urge a change of behavior within companies or groups of companies (even though this would be desirable in certain circumstances). Instead, its purpose is to illustrate some of the human consequences of a distinctly modern phenomenon called multinational enterprise.

Although the ultimate responsibility for this book and its contents is mine, the work is essentially a team effort. The original working drafts of the several chapters were prepared as follows: "Pushtherapy in Brazil" and "I'd Like to Buy the World a Coke" by Bernardo Kucinski; "Promoting Health" and "Formula for Malnutrition" by Laurie Kramer; "Sugar Republic" by Alan Howard; "One Man's Meat" and "The Protein Business" by Rick Edwards; "The U.S. Government's Helping Hand" by Susan Gross who, from Washington, did investigative work for other chapters and assisted with the editing. "Ambivalent Hosts" was put together by me with pieces supplied by Rick Edwards, Bernardo Kucinski, and Susan Gross. Laurie Kramer contributed greatly to the overall editing of the final manuscript.

There are many more people who assisted as consultants, resource persons, critics, researchers, typists. Several specialists, well known in such fields as pharmacology, nutrition and agricultural economics, reviewed the manuscript. I owe thanks to them all, but were it not for the team of Kramer, Gross, Kucinski, Howard and Edwards, this book would not be.

* * *

The author gratefully acknowledges the financial grant from CONSUMERS UNION OF UNITED STATES, INC., which made this book possible. The findings and conclusions of this book are solely those of the author, who assumes all responsibility for its contents.

Robert J. Ledogar
New York, August 1975

Note: Unless otherwise indicated, statements made herein generally reflect conditions as of September-October 1974.

1/OVERVIEW

It is only within the last few years that multinational corporations have become a topic of broad public interest in the United States. In Latin America, however, multinational firms, especially U.S. multinationals, have been a highly visible part of everyday life for more than a quarter of a century, their power and influence widely discussed in newspapers and books, coffeehouses, and political caucuses.

There are those in Latin America who believe that even many of their so-called "national" corporations, whose major stockholders bear the most respectably indigenous names, are really controlled by foreign capital. But even if this claim is totally discounted, the public record is startling enough. A recent list of the 422 largest corporations in Latin America revealed that Latin Americans had controlling interest in only 182. The rest were under foreign control. One third were wholly or substantially owned by U.S. investors.[1] In 1968, U.S. multinationals were responsible for 40% of all manufacturing exports from Latin America.[2] By 1971, multinational corporations accounted for 70% of total net profits in five major sectors of the Brazilian economy: rubber, motor vehicle, machinery, household appliance, and mining.[3]

The pharmaceutical industry in Latin America is one of those most deeply penetrated by North American and European capital. U.S. and European firms control over 84% of private-sector drug sales in Brazil and reportedly an even larger share in Venezuela.[4] In Colombia, it was found in 1970 that foreign firms controlled 70% of antibiotic sales,

65% of analgesics, 80% of vitamins, 45% of hormones, and 70% of antacids.[5]

In the Latin American food industry, U.S. firms still trail behind the Swiss giant Nestlé, but they are expanding rapidly.[6] The degree of market penetration varies from country to country. In Brazil, for example, foreign companies, including several from Argentina, control about 37% of the food industry.[7] A 1974 government survey of the food industry in Mexico, on the other hand, discovered areas where U.S. takeover is nearly complete. There, three quarters of the soft-drink market is in the hands of Coca-Cola, Pepsi-Cola, and Crush; three quarters of the canned fruit and vegetable industry is shared by Heinz, Campbell Soup, and Del Monte, with McCormick and United Brands holding an undetermined share of the rest; Kellogg's sells all but 5% of breakfast cereals; Gerber sells 80% of all the baby food; and Carnation sells 85% of evaporated milk.[8]

It is impossible to determine precisely how much money U.S. multinationals are making in Latin America. The Department of Commerce estimates that U.S. investors, in 1971 alone, earned about a billion dollars in dividends, interest, and branch earnings from Latin America and the Caribbean.[9] But these estimates are admittedly rough, and they make no allowance for the devices used to mask the true source—and size—of a company's profits (some of which will be discussed in Chapter 4).

While the U.S. public has had little to say about multinationals until recently, its government has, for many years, aided and encouraged the expansion of U.S. industry into Latin America. Arguing that multinational investment is a remedy for underdevelopment, the United States has provided tax incentives, political risk insurance, loans, and the representation of State Department officials to help make names like Coca-Cola, Ford, and Pan Am household words in Spanish and Portuguese.[10] These efforts have succeeded remarkably well.

In recent years, however, voices have been raised in

the United States, joining those in Latin America that question the impact of multinational corporations on less developed regions. For the most part, the debate has centered about the issues of national sovereignty, transfer of technology, currency manipulation, and economic development. Important topics, all of them, but too remote to evoke much participation from the people whose lives are directly affected.

This book tries to look at some of the ways in which corporations have a direct impact on people. It is a collection of micro-studies—a complement, we hope, to the necessarily more general picture offered by a book like Barnet and Müller's *Global Reach*.

This is the work of a small team of investigative reporters. Our resources were very limited. We followed the leads which came to our attention. We looked for case studies that would illustrate corporate impact on people. We chose Latin America because it was closer and because U.S. investment has been heavier there than in other developing areas. We chose food and drug companies because they produce goods which are needed by everyone, rich and poor.

The result is no scientific thesis, no definitive indictment; it is a collection of facts which suggest that all is not what the companies would have us believe and that there is indeed cause for concern.

Starting with the more homogeneous drug industry, we looked at Brazil as an example of a country whose pharmaceutical market is almost totally controlled by multinational firms. We found that although three quarters of the people die before the age of 50, the pharmaceutical industry makes most of its money selling large quantities of drugs to the rich and the urban middle class—the minority which needs them least.

We found evidence that the drug companies take advantage of a weaker regulatory situation in many parts of Latin America to pursue labeling and advertising policies of a dangerous kind.

We found cases in which companies have taken

advantage of their multinational status to manipulate the prices of raw material imports so that consumer prices are kept artificially high and taxes to the host government as low as possible.

We found that there are forces within the governments of Latin America trying to control the effect of multinationals on their people; but because of their governments' dependence on foreign investment and the multinationals' monopolies over technology and raw materials, they are often left powerless.

In the area of food, which is much more complex, we concentrated first on industries that are sometimes held to be models of what business can do for underdeveloped countries.

• Sugar in the Dominican Republic, like bananas, coffee, and cacao in other parts of Latin America, supposedly uses land that is little suited to other crops in order to earn valuable foreign exchange for a developing nation on the world market. With it, the nation is supposed to buy the machinery and technology with which to industrialize, create jobs, and raise its standard of living. But from what we learned in the Dominican Republic, where Gulf+Western is responsible for 30% of the sugar production, the system does not work that way. Land for local food production seems to be going into sugar and other export crops, and while the foreign earnings obviously benefit the company and the government, the people are still hungry.

• The poultry feed industry in Colombia, led by Ralston Purina, has successfully increased the production of two important sources of animal protein, chicken and eggs. But the poor of Colombia still cannot afford to eat chicken and eggs. Moreover, the shift to using additional land for the production of animal feed has meant that a nation in need of more protein is getting less.

• The hope was raised during the 1960s that U.S. technological know-how could be put to work to develop high-protein foods and market them to malnourished populations in developing nations. The U.S. government encouraged the food-processing industry to try its hand at such an effort, but the record up to now, as illustrated by two case histories in Colombia, has been failure.

Unhappily, the most successful U.S. food enterprises we found in Latin America were soft drinks and cornstarch. It seems to be the least nutritious products that have been most extensively—and most successfully—promoted to the poor.

We also found some very questionable practices connected with the marketing of infant milk products to low-income mothers.

The overall impression left by these case studies, both in food and drugs, is that the benefits of multinational activity in Latin America have accrued to a minority, while the majority—those who most need the food and drugs that the multinationals produce—gets little of either.

Failure of business to deliver food and medicine to people who need it, coupled with extraordinary success in delivering what people do not need, happens not only in Latin America. We know it in the United States as well. The biggest difference is that in the United States the desperately poor are a minority, and in Latin America they are a majority.

There is much to be learned from observing how corporations behave in countries where power and wealth are even more highly concentrated—and government regulation of business is even weaker—than in the United States. Among other things, it teaches us a good deal about the limits of "corporate responsibility."

This book is an exploration of those limits.

2/PUSHTHERAPY IN BRAZIL

There are 110 million people in Brazil—twice as many as in the next largest country of Latin America. Multinationals from the U.S. invest more money there than in any other developing country.[1] For Brazil is the land of the "economic miracle." Its GNP rose at an average of nearly 10% per year between 1968 and 1973.[2]

The multinational drug industry does a very good business in Brazil. It sold an estimated $650 million worth of drugs in 1974[3] —but not to 110 million Brazilians. Most of the people, though they suffer from many diseases which can be treated by drugs, cannot afford to buy them. The industry makes the bulk of its income selling to less than one quarter of the population.[4]

Panorama

From São José dos Campos (in Brazil) comes a wide range of products—more than from any other Johnson & Johnson company outside the U.S.—that help to meet the medical and health needs of the nation.

Richard B. Sellars, President
Johnson & Johnson, Worldwide[5]

For most of its 270-mile length, the São Paulo-Rio highway is lined with factories bearing familiar multinational names. But pharmaceutical plants are distinctive. The Johnson & Johnson plant near São José dos Campos is clean and elegant, surrounded by lawns: it looks like a university rather than a factory. The building gives the impression that within its walls medicines are indeed being created and produced "to meet the medical and health needs of the nation." Nearby is the Pfizer plant: red-brick buildings and a large garden encircled by enormous trees. Over 1,000 employees work in this plant.[6]

These and other familiar corporations dominate Brazil's pharmaceutical industry: 69 multinational drug companies (of which 29 are North American) are responsible for more than 84% of the total sales volumc in the private sector and 72% of all drug sales in Brazil.[7] The 20 largest drug firms in Brazil are all controlled by multinational capital:[8]

Johnson & Johnson	American Home Products
Hoechst	Sandoz
Hoffmann-LaRoche	Rhone Poulenc
Lepetit (Dow Chemical)	ICN
Squibb	Schering
Ciba-Geigy	Parke-Davis (Warner-Lambert)
E. Merck	Merck Sharp & Dohme
Sterling	Roussel
Carlo Erba	Montedison
Bristol-Myers	Lederle (American Cyanamid)

The industry, with multinationals in the lead, is a model of financial skill and industrial management. In 1972, the 56 largest companies in Brazil were operating at nearly 90% of their capacity, and investments for expansion increased by 41.3%.[9] In 1973, their capital investment grew by more than 61%.[10] Financially, the industry is in an excellent position, well above the average for Brazil: after investments, remittance of over $3 million to parent companies for "technical contracts,"[11] and payments of more than $50 million (mainly to parent companies) for the import of raw and processed materials,[12] enough money was left in 1972 for a good profit. The 56 largest firms averaged 16%.[13]

An estimated $900 million worth of drugs was sold in Brazil in 1974. Nearly three quarters of that amount represent sales of foreign-owned firms.[14]

Meeting the Needs of the Nation

May 1973. In a makeshift camp called the Arraial do João Pezinho, 20 miles west of Altamira along the Trans-Amazon Highway, 50 families are waiting to be transferred to their own plots of land under a program to colonize the Amazon. The road is fairly busy for such a remote place; every 10 minutes a jeep passes, carrying some government official, technician, visitor, journalist, or social worker. But in their temporary lodgings, the 50 families just wait.

At the door of one of the houses, Mr. and Mrs. Sampaio are watching their baby die. They lost their youngest son when they arrived from the Northeast six months ago. It was measles. The baby Mrs. Sampaio is holding in her arms was born at the Arraial only a month ago. The infant is sick with diarrhea and looks as if she is going to die in a day or two.

"What did the doctor say?"

"He said to bring her back to the hospital if she gets worse, but what for? She only got worse at that hospital."

"Did the doctor give you any medicine or a prescription?"

"He gave me a prescription all right, but how can I buy the medicines? We don't have any money left. . . . They used to give us the drugs, the cheap ones, but now there isn't much of that."

"Aren't you afraid she might die?"

"Yes, I am; no one wants to lose a child. But . . . she is in the hands of God. If she is to die, there is nothing we can do."[15]

Mrs. Sampaio's fatalistic attitude to illness and death is shared by millions of Brazilians all over the country. Among the 50 families in the Arraial do João Pezinho alone, 20 children died in two months in early 1973.[16] In the Northeast, where they came from, it was the same: in the town of Amaragi, about 50 miles from Recife, all of the 72 children born in 1970 died before the age of one.[17] Fatalism is born of generations of destitution, with no way to get expensive drugs when they are needed.

Statistics for the general population are equally depressing. Of every 1,000 Brazilians born, 720 (compared to only 200 in the United States) die before the age of 50, 105 of them before their first birthday.[18] The majority of these premature deaths are caused by communicable diseases, aggravated by malnutrition. Many of the killing diseases—intestinal infections, measles, diphtheria, whooping cough, tuberculosis, and other respiratory infections—can be prevented by vaccines or treated by various drugs.[19] But there is no money to buy medicine.

Brazil's Ministry of Health estimates that there are 126,000 new active cases of tuberculosis every year.[20] In 1972, 48% of all army draftees and 12% of all children entering school were infected with TB bacillus.[21] Each year deaths from tuberculosis amount to 27.5 for each 1,000 inhabitants.[22] In 1971, a Brazilian Senator estimated that the recommended drug therapy for tuberculosis, combining Dow Chemical's RIFALDIN with Lederle's MIAMBUTOL, would cost $650 for three months.[23] The average São Paulo worker was then earning about $100 a month, and 20% of Brazil's population in 1969 was earning less than $75 per year.[24]

Besides the diseases which kill directly, there are those which debilitate: malaria, parasitic worm infestations, leprosy, "Chagas disease" (a tropical fever for which a cure has not been found), and schistosomiasis (a severe parasitic disease marked by blood loss and tissue damage).[25] It is estimated that 20 million Brazilians are infected with roundworms and 10 million with hookworms.[26] In towns near Belo Horizonte, capital city of Minas Gerais, the Ministry of Health found recently that 69.52% of children examined were infected with worms.[27]

The majority of people afflicted with these diseases live in rural areas. But not all of them. During the last 15 years, millions of people have moved from impoverished rural areas to the industrializing cities of Brazil in search of work. They brought their diseases with them. If they found work, it was for very low wages. They settled in slums and on the outskirts of the large cities in conditions of overcrowding and inadequate sanitation.

In São Paulo alone, Brazil's richest city, two million people out of a population of 7.2 million are now classified as "marginals"[28]—people with less than a subsistence income. As a result of these conditions, infant mortality in São Paulo, which reached a low point of 60 per 1,000 births in 1961, has been steadily on the rise since then. By 1973 it had climbed to 93 per 1,000.[29]

Poor sanitation and malnutrition contribute a great deal to all this misery, but much of it could be alleviated and many deaths prevented if drugs were obtainable.

But in the areas of Brazil where disease is most prevalent, the North, Northeast, and the Amazon basin, many people could not afford to pay for drugs if they were offered to them at cost. They certainly cannot afford the prices charged by the drug companies.

It is in the rich areas of the south, in the states of Guanabara and São Paulo, plus half a dozen of the biggest cities, that over 80% of pharmaceutical products are sold.[30] When asked why the poorest and largest section of the population had no access to medicine, the President of Pfizer in Brazil, Roberto Schneider, replied: "Well, it is because they are not economically active. Only 20 million Brazilians, in a population of over 100 million, are economically active; all the rest of them do not lead an active life; they just vegetate; they suffer from diseases induced by the environment, by lack of basic consumption; they do not buy clothes, shoes, and least of all medicines."[31]

Meeting the Needs of the People

When buying a drug you might be saving the life of your child. That's the plain truth, no exaggeration; you know that. What you probably don't know is that each drug is a result of a complex process, of lengthy and constant research. High investments in machinery, precision equipment . . . permanent quality control, to assure the same safety, tranquility. Because the drug must not fail. Think about that when buying a drug and remember always that no price is too high when saving a life.

advertisement by ABIFARMA, *trade association of the Brazilian pharmaceutical industry, May 1974*

April 1974. In the basement of the Santa Casa da Misericordia Hospital in São Paulo, Dr. Claudio Daffré operates a pharmaceutical factory. The whole basement is occupied by laboratories, storage, and processing rooms. In one month alone, January 1974, this factory saved the hospital more than 210,000 cruzeiros ($33,000) by producing drugs at a fraction of the cost charged by the commercial pharmaceutical companies. In one fiscal year, it saved $400,000 for Santa Casa, which is run as a charity and provides medical care for the poorest section of the population.[32]

Dr. Daffré speaks quietly but with some emotion. He remembers the days just before the Second World War, when every hospital in Brazil had its own laboratory to provide "compounded" prescriptions issued for individual patients. This is how the local pharmaceutical industry was born in Brazil only a few decades ago—in the basements of the hospitals.[33]

These basement laboratories did not last long. Factories were soon set up outside the hospitals as normal commercial enterprises, to capitalize on this new market by offering mass-produced standardized drugs. Doctors soon began to prescribe drugs by brand names rather than by the generic names of active compounds. Most hospital factories were shut down. In most medical schools, drug preparation was taken out of the curriculum as an outdated specialty, and pharmaceutical schools began to prepare technicians for work in industry or analytic laboratories.[34]

But after a few years, charity hospitals like Santa Casa da Misericordia, which serve the poorest and largest section of the population, realized that they could not afford the drug prices charged by the industry. The basement laboratory was revived on a modern basis.

Now Dr. Daffré can offer low-cost drugs to the various sections of his 1,200-bed hospital and to the medical college attached to it. His aspirin is 1/10th the market price; his vitamin C, 1/5th; and his IODETAL, which costs 2.90 cruzeiros in the drugstore around the corner, is offered for only 0.78 cruzeiros. Dr. Daffré's prices reflect not only the cost of raw materials—which he usually must buy from the drug industry itself—and other production costs, but also his share in the general operating expenses of the hospital. (Without this contribution to overhead, his prices would be even lower—by half.) Even when he is forced to use the expensive technique of extracting from finished products certain compounds unavailable in bulk—as in the case of a compound that he extracts from large amounts of Johnson & Johnson's DROPERIDOL—he can still effect huge savings.[35]

While there may be as many as 30,000 brand-name products on the market,[36] the hospital has found that it can operate from a basic list of 600 generic drugs. Dr. Daffré's factory provides nearly 300 of them.[37]

Charity hospitals named Santa Casa are very important institutions in Brazil. In every large city, they provide medical care for that section of the population which—because of unemployment or other reasons—cannot even rely on the precarious service provided by the compulsory social security system. The Santa Casa hospitals are not alone in their desperate search for inexpensive drugs. Universities and research centers have been engaged for decades in the production of serums and vaccines used in government-sponsored health campaigns, as well as a few other drugs widely used by the social security hospitals. Army laboratories have also been engaged in drug production.[38]

In a 1971 speech to the Parliament, Senator Benedito Ferreira compared prices of drugs produced by government institutions and therapeutically similar drugs produced by the pharmaceutical industry. He found differences of up to 2,500% (for neomycin sulfate with sulfadiazine) and 1,700% (for piperazine adipate). HIDRAX, a drug which combats dehydration and is one of those developed by Johnson & Johnson specifically for the Brazilian market, sells for 2.15 cruzeiros, while state-sponsored laboratories were charging one ninth the price for similar products.[39]

With prices too high for the great majority of Brazilians, how did the drug industry manage to do $900 million worth of business in 1974?

The Market

Copacabana, in the fashionable southern district of Rio de Janeiro, has the largest concentration of wealth per square mile in Brazil and one of the larger in the world.

Copacabana is the paradise of the Brazilian elite. It is also the paradise of the Brazilian drug industry. In Copacabana, there is a drugstore on almost every block, and frequently more than one. These neighborhoods, the citadels of the upper-middle class, together with the more pedestrian middle-class areas, provide a lucrative market for the pharmaceutical industry: first, because drugs can be bought without prescription, like chocolate bars; second, because the Brazilian elite now has more money than it ever had, Brazilian executives having replaced North Americans as the highest paid managerial class in the world.[40]

In downtown Rio, at number 35 Rua Senador Dantas, a self-service drugstore called Drogaria do Povo is open 15 hours a day, seven days a week. Anyone walking in will see several specialized display counters. One counter has 30 different kinds of analgesics. Another has a large display of antibiotics. The more expensive drugs must be asked for, but to obtain most of them there is no need to show a prescription. A pharmacist is on duty, but he is more worried about potential shoplifters than about people buying drugs without a prescription.[41]

Because they offer people so little opportunity to get advice from a pharmacist, drug supermarkets like these are the ultimate stage of a system called *self-medication*, the practice of buying medicines without a doctor's advice or prescription.

This system flourishes in many Latin American countries, but in order to understand what it means and how it developed, one must think of it not in the context of huge self-service drug supermarkets, but rather in terms of the small neighborhood pharmacy.

"The small pharmacy," said Senator Ferreira in a 1971 speech to Parliament, "is an advance outpost of the Health Department, especially for the less favored class which doesn't have the money to buy medicines, much less pay for a doctor's consultation. And often people don't have enough time, while struggling to make a living, to spend a day on line at the welfare hospital. . . . It is the small pharmacy with its trained professional who tells them what medicine to take and sells it to them on credit, gives injections and applies small dressings to wounds. In the big self-service drugstore, the poor person can't even talk to a salesclerk, and there is no credit."[42]

A study published in 1974 of purchasing power and spending habits among working-class families in São Paulo showed that Brazilian workers, whatever their income, spend about 3 1/2% of it on "health"—including doctors, dentists, and drugs. The study further found that families with incomes of more than $100 a month, who spend at least $3.50 a month on health, spend the greater portion of their health budget on doctors and dentists. But the many poorer workers who earn less than $100 a month, and thus are unable to come up with even $3.50 a month for the health needs of their families, spend more of their tiny health budgets on drugs than on doctors or dentists. Unless they have time to spend waiting at government or charity hospitals, they must do without medical attention. They can afford to buy a few drugs only because a doctor's prescription is not required.[43]

The argument used to justify self-medication is that a strict system of prescription control, such as in the United States, would force these people to spend their health money on doctors, with nothing left over to buy the drugs the doctor prescribes.

In Brazil successive governments have winked at and given *de facto* legitimacy to self-medication. One authority estimates that 75% of all drugs sold there are bought without prescription.[44] This means that there is a kind of two-tier health system. The lower-income population gets little or no medical advice; their access to drugs is limited by cost rather than need or safety controls. The upper-income population has access not only to doctors but to all the drugs they want with or without a doctor's advice. To them the system is an open invitation to consume more than necessary.

By custom among the upper and middle classes and by necessity among the poor, Brazilians, like many other Latin

Americans, purchase and consume without prescription some very potent and potentially dangerous drugs. If they go to a small drugstore where there is a pharmacist, they may or may not get some good advice on how to take the drug and what danger signs to watch for. Otherwise, they consult relatives and friends or the directions given in the package leaflets. Drug purchasers in the United States seldom see these leaflets because they are kept by the pharmacists. But in Brazil, as in many other Latin American countries, a customer gets a leaflet with the drug. It is often written in hard-to-understand medical jargon, but if the customer forgets what the pharmacist said, the leaflet is there to give information about the drug. In Brazil this leaflet is called a *bula*.

When executives of drug firms in the United States are questioned about the marketing of their drugs in Latin America, they disclaim all responsibility for sales without prescription. "We market that product [CONMEL] under the same conditions as in the United States—by prescription only," says Dr. Monroe Trout of Sterling.[45] When asked about a drug (CINCOFENO) we purchased without prescription in Venezuela, Dr. J. L. R. Barlow, International Medical Director of Abbott wrote, "Presumably you obtained it on prescription from a physician who knew of the drug's uses and adverse effects."[46] The CINCOFENO package is indeed marked "by medical prescription," and similar wording can be found to accompany most ethical drugs sold in Latin America.

But the fact is that pharmacies do not sell such drugs by prescription only and the pharmaceutical companies know very well that they do not. Even within Brazil's Ministry of Health it is admitted that "the habit of self-medication plays an important role in this country."[47]

Whatever its justification, the habit of self-medication makes it easier to sell more drugs, and the inducement for companies to exploit such a habit must be very strong, especially in countries where government regulation of the drug industry is weak.

Control

In 1972, Brazil's National Service for the Control of Pharmaceutical Products (SNFMF) received 5,415 applications of various kinds. Among these were 2,316 applications for new products to be produced, registered, or marketed; 1,015 applications for license revalidation (a license is valid for 10 years and is renewable); and 195 applications for drugs with formula modifications to be licensed for marketing.[48]

Expected to deal with this situation is the SNFMF staff of only about 60 public servants, including inspectors, clerks, and administrative personnel. About a dozen are doctors and half a dozen pharmacists. The budget amounts to only 50 cents for every $1,000 worth of drugs consumed in Brazil. In the whole of Latin America, only Paraguay and Guatemala spend less than this on drug control.[49] These figures are from data collected in August 1970. But little has changed in Brazil since 1970. In fact, little has changed since 1946, when the current drug regulations were issued.

* * *

The SNFMF is housed in a narrow seven-floor building in a side street of Rio. In a very small room inside the building, a doctor, seated behind a huge pile of files, slowly examines one of them.

"In this pile in front of me," he says with an expression of great boredom on his face, "I have more than 2,000 applications to be examined: new drugs, old drugs with new formulas, modifications of names, packages, trademarks to be registered. How do you think we can cope with this? We have no equipment, no personnel, no budget, no laboratories. We have to rely, many times, on the industry's laboratories. They are the best in the country. But this doesn't mean that we examine the drugs. All we can do is check the labels, the formulas, the literature, the *bulas,* and reports from other governments as given to us by the applicant.

"Every drug," the doctor continued, "must have a certificate showing that it has been in use for at least one year in its country of origin. And for the most popular drugs, like the antibiotics, for instance, there are some standard warnings that must be put into the *bula*, so we see that it is done. But you see, it is too much work to be done by too few people. Sometimes, someone comes from above, or even a colleague, and asks for a particular application to be speeded up. We speed it up because, otherwise, it would be waiting on this pile for who knows how long. No one wants any trouble. Do you know the basic salary for a doctor at the SNFMF? It is 1,700 cruzeiros ($180) a month. Of course, most of the people leave very soon. The drug industry itself takes care of them, offering better salaries."[50]

* * *

A small number of drugs, mainly psychotropics and hallucinogens, are subjected to strict legal control. (Contraceptives are regulated also, but the law is not enforced.) Controlled drugs are divided into five government lists, each with a different degree of control, ranging from the obligatory presentation of a prescription at the drugstore to a stricter proceeding in which the doctor is issued numbered prescription paper which is registered with the police. But this latter regulation has little to do with the mainstream of the pharmaceutical market; it is a police mechanism to curb narcotics traffic.[51]

Sources within the Brazilian Parliament recently called for an investigation into the compromising relationship between multinational pharmaceutical firms and the nation's drug control agencies. A parliamentary investigating committee was reportedly given an internal document of the Swiss firm Ciba-Geigy containing a list of 135 public officials in the SNFMF and other licensing agencies who were to receive small "gifts" and "donations" from the company.[52]

São Paulo's leading newspaper recently quoted, without naming, the director of the research department of a large pharmaceutical company as saying: "The SNFMF is composed of half a dozen bureaucrats and a few specialists who lack the time, the organization, and the knowledge of research methodology sufficient to analyze the products submitted to them. Anybody can get a drug licensed, and very quickly."[53]

Within the industry there seems to be a split of opinion as to whether the SNFMF should be strengthened along lines similar to the United States Food and Drug Administration (FDA). The large multinational firms tend to emphasize the need for "quality control" rather than labeling and advertising control.[54] Though stricter quality control might be more expensive for everyone, it could make things even more difficult for the beleaguered local firms. Consequently, some doctors believe that stricter quality control would only serve the interests of the large foreign firms.[55] But quality control is only part of the problem.

Drug Pollution

A large drugstore in Brazil may stock from 50,000 to 70,000 different items, including cosmetics and sanitary products.[56] The number of strictly medical products licensed in Brazil is near 30,000, if different forms or concentrations of the same drug are counted separately. Even if different presentations (pills, solutions, injections, etc.) are not counted separately, there are over 10,000 pharmaceutical products for sale in Brazil.[57]

Each year, every major drug company in Brazil tries to launch at least three new products.[58] But new chemical compounds with therapeutic properties are not discovered that easily. And so, to make up for the lack of truly new medicines, the industry uses Parisian *haute couture* methods: a new look is given to old products that are not selling well enough. New variations in size, concentration, and form are developed; combinations of two or more well-established medicines are introduced as new products; finally, products are recommended for the largest possible number of symptoms. Some drugs are recommended for so many problems that they sound like veritable panaceas.

The best new dress for an old drug is a vitamin. "As

soon as sales begin to fall," says Dr. Daffré, "the same drug is relaunched in association with a vitamin."[59]

The second-best new dress for an old drug is chloramphenicol. There are dozens of anti-infective drugs in the form of ointments, suppositories, pediatric compounds and solutions, all containing chloramphenicol.[60] "Chloramphenicol," says Juarez Bahia, an editor of Rio's leading daily newspaper, "is recommended abusively by the layman, the drugstore sales clerk and the free-sample-dispensing salesman to cure every little cough. . . . It is not rare in pediatric clinics to encounter fatal cases of aplastic anemia due to unnecessary use of chloramphenicol."[61] (See page 46 for a discussion of chloramphenicol's dangers.)

Chloramphenicol is also an excellent example of how broadly a drug can be recommended. AMBRA-SINTO, a combination of chloramphenicol and tetracycline marketed by a Dow Chemical subsidiary named Lepetit, is indicated in the package insert for the treatment of more than 80 different conditions.[62]

Antibiotics provide the most ample opportunities for manipulation and variation in mixtures, forms, and concentrations. Carlo Erba do Brasil, subsidiary of an Italian multinational, may hold the record for the number of variations of one compound. It markets 13 presentations of its chloramphenicol product, QUEMICETINA, offering it in syrups, ointments, pills, suppositories, etc.[63] TETREX, a tetracycline marketed by Laboterápica Bristol (Bristol-Myers) which is the most widely sold ethical drug in Brazil, is sold in seven different forms.[64]

In a typical upper-middle-class hospital in Rio, Hospital Ipanema, a study on resistance to antibiotics was conducted during the first half of 1973. It was discovered that the antibiotic on which the most money was being spent was also the least effective. Ampicillin, which accounted for 32% of total hospital expenses in antibiotics (over $50,000), was encountering a rate of resistance of 70%.[65]

Simply and succinctly, "People are being induced to

an irrational form of drug consumption in this country," said Representative Jaison Barreto, himself a physician and President of the Health Committee in the Brazilian Parliament.[66]

The Drug Pushers

Success, high success, is what we all wish you in the promotion of this extraordinary product of our company, developed after top level scientific research made by scientists closely linked to our family—the Johnson & Johnson family.

from the sales manual for NOVULON "S"[67]

Self-medication is a system so widespread in Latin America that it opens up a huge potential market for the indiscriminate sale of drugs. But a particular drug's success in that market is best assured by a carefully orchestrated campaign directed first at the professionals—physicians and pharmacists—who will ultimately influence consumers. Prescriptions provide the initial thrust. When a drug is prescribed by doctors to their patients, these patients with prescriptions, like carriers of a disease itself, will spread the word about the new drug to relatives and friends. If, at the same time, pressure is put on pharmacists to stock and also recommend the drug, then it has a real chance to become a hit.

The pharmacist's role is crucial. He can arrange his stock to display the new drug conspicuously and keep other drugs in less accessible places. He can suggest the new drug to the hesitant customer at the counter. And he may also recommend the drug to customers who have prescriptions for similar drugs, because he might have a special discount on the drug that has just been launched.[68] His incentive may be a personal premium given him by a drug company, an old practice which, though frequently denounced, has not disappeared. According to one participant in this bribery system, "There is a constant war among salesmen; corruption is widespread. In dealings with large hospitals, honesty is rare. Where large amounts of money are involved, the salesman checks back with his boss."[69] Senator Ferreira claimed in 1971 that drug companies were unscrupulously promoting birth control pills to pharmacists and salesclerks—offering them television sets and portable radios as incentives to buy their products and recommend them to the public.[70]

The end result of such influence—the whole process of a pharmacist's pushing a drug which a customer has not asked for—is now so widespread that a new word has entered the language to describe it: *empurroterapia* —"pushtherapy."

But while "pushtherapy" was coined to describe only the particular pressure exerted by the pharmacist on the customer, in fact the whole system of drug marketing in Brazil might be characterized by the same expression. And the principal "pusher" is the drug company salesman, the detail man.

The salesman's manual issued by Johnson & Johnson in 1965 for launching the birth control pill NOVULON "S" suggests what looks like the typical strategy: to push the drug upon the consumer through doctors and pharmacists, until it becomes accepted in the world of self-medication. The approach to doctors is outlined where the manual states that NOVULON "S" is to be promoted to every medical specialty, "particularly to obstetricians, gynecologists, clinicians, . . . cardiologists, psychiatrists, neurologists, etc."[71]

The company's intention to exploit the self-medication habit via the pharmacist is shown in the section on sales: "When visiting pharmacists to introduce NOVULON "S", give them, as you have already done with NOVULON, all the basic data on the product, with the objective of having it *indicated* [emphasis in original]. As we know, a product of this nature is continually sought after by customers and they might become, in their turn, an excellent source of indication for the products."[72] The strategy, clearly, is to persuade the pharmacist to recommend NOVULON. This recommendation could not possibly be solicited if Johnson & Johnson honored what it printed on the NOVULON box: "for sale under medical prescription."

Not surprisingly, NOVULON and NOVULON "S" are

among the top-selling contraceptives in Brazil.[73] "We sell all we can get of this contraceptive," says the buyer for a large São Paulo drugstore.[74]

* * *

It is nine o'clock in the morning. The Santa Casa Hospital in São Paulo is in full swing. Near every large building, patients are waiting to be seen by doctors. The hospital, with its dozens of clinics, a medical school, and hundreds of doctors and nurses, serves thousands of patients every day.

There are benches on both sides of the hospital's main entrance, where more than a dozen young men sit chatting and watching. They are not patients. They look healthy, and they carry large briefcases. They belong to the army of company salesmen, and the Santa Casa Hospital is their main target every morning of every day. A doctor is coming in and stops to talk to one of them. He is given a free sample of a drug and some leaflets. Soon after, he is encircled by four other salesmen. Each in his turn, with care and respect, hands the doctor drug samples and exchanges a few words. Then one of them produces a plastic bag and gives the bag to the doctor with great courtesy. More free samples and leaflets are handed over; the doctor fills up the plastic bag, exchanges a few more words with the salesmen, and leaves.[75]

* * *

Senator Ferreira, who is himself a doctor, decided to investigate the intensity of the sales activity directed at doctors. For 21 working days he kept track of salesmen's visits to his clinic. He was visited on 18 of the 21 days by a total of 69 salesmen. He was given 452 free samples of drugs (after refusing extra quantities so as not to distort the counting); he received 25 gifts, including coffeepots, notebooks, plastic bags.[76] "It has become a plague," said an official of Santa Casa. "I issued an order forbidding them to enter the hospital. This is why now they have to sit and wait for the doctors at the entrance."[77]

The drug industry association's own breakdown of production costs for a drug shows that 3.3% is spent on free samples and 2% on publicity, the sponsoring of medical congresses, and similar activities.[78] Salesmen's wages are not included in these figures. If salesmen accounted for only 1/10th of the wage bill of the industry (in Argentina they account for 25%),[79] their salaries would add another 2% and bring promotion costs to a total of 7.3%.[80]

This is five times what the industry claims to spend in Brazil on research and development.[81]

But the industry's expenditure for promotion is certainly higher than it admits officially. During a 1961–63 congressional inquiry on the drug industry in Brazil, Valfir da Rocha, ex-president of the Drug Industry Association of the State of Guanabara, stated that promotion and publicity costs accounted for 31% of total expenses in the drug industry.[82] The Brazilian government's Master Plan for Pharmaceuticals (see page 67) shows that, for foreign companies, 40% of the value of drugs sold is accounted for by "commercial expenses."[83] In 1970, Senator Ferreira claimed that in free-sample distribution alone, the industry was spending 135 million cruzeiros a year ($30 million) —which is 8% of the value of sales for that year.[84] Comparable data from Argentina support these higher figures.[85]

The distribution of free samples, a common promotional practice of the pharmaceutical industry, has special importance in poor countries. The well-intentioned doctor, particularly in small villages in the hinterland but also in big-city charity hospitals and neighborhoods inhabited by the poor, will often prescribe a drug because he can give the patient a couple of free samples. "But the quantity given to doctors is almost always sub-clinical," says Dr. Herval Ribeiro, "sufficient to give a start to the medication, but not to sustain the treatment. The result is tragic. A poor patient, for instance, suffering from pneumococcic pneumonia, can be treated cheaply with penicillin. But it so happens that the doctor has some free samples of ampicillin and he hands some to the patient together with his prescription. But the man has to buy the remaining quantity. He will have to pay 30 times as much for the ampicillin [as he would have for the penicillin].''[86] Dr. Mario Migliano agreed and added another possibility: ''It might happen that the man will be unable to buy it. In this case, he will take what he was given and will interrupt the treatment before due time. Instead of being cured, he will develop a resistance to that particular antibiotic.''[87]

* * *

Free samples, detail men, unnecessary duplications and combinations, and massive publicity efforts are standard promotion techniques of the pharmaceutical industry the world over. But in the context of Brazil, with its affluent minority, struggling workers, and destitute masses, these sales practices help keep the cost of drugs generally out of reach of the majority, while encouraging irrational overconsumption among the well-to-do.

And there is another dangerous side of drug promotion: the exaggeration of therapeutic claims and minimization of risks in labeling and advertising—tactics helpful to drug sales, but particularly harmful to the self-medicating middle classes all over Latin America, as the following chapter explains.

3/PROMOTING HEALTH

A pattern of promotion designed to increase sales—even if it means that human beings are frequently exposed to unnecessary danger—emerges from a collection of drug labels and advertisements gathered throughout Latin America.*

Indications

The incidence of disease cannot be manipulated and so increased sales volume must depend at least in part on the use of drugs unrelated to their real utility or need. . . .

Dr. Dale Console, former medical director of E.R. Squibb & Sons, 1961[1]

Since the days of patent medicines, it has been the natural temptation of drug salespeople to over-recommend. Obviously, the more diseases for which a drug is recommended, the more occasions people will have to buy it.

***Note on the methodology of "Promoting Health"**
The materials on which this chapter is based were gathered as follows: A basic list of about 130 drugs was first prepared with the help of experts in Washington, D. C. The list contained some drugs which had never been approved for marketing in the United States, some which had been withdrawn from the U.S. market, and many which are available in the United States but, because of potential side effects, can only be marketed with specific warnings and contraindications. All are "ethical pharmaceuticals"—that is, drugs which, if available at all, can only be sold in the United States by medical prescription—and most are taken orally rather than by injection or by superficial application as lotions or ointments.

With the help of this list, drugs were then obtained over the counter in Latin America. (In a number of cases friendly pharmacists simply made the package inserts available instead of asking us to buy the drugs, but—with the possible exception

(continued on overleaf and facing page)

The diseases for which a drug is recommended are called its *indications*. In the United States, indications for prescription drugs are carefully regulated by the Food and Drug Administration (FDA), according to intertwined standards of efficacy and safety. A drug may not be promoted by the manufacturer for use in a certain disease unless it has been proven to the FDA's satisfaction that the drug is in fact effective in treating that specific disease. Even if the drug is effective, its benefits must be weighed against its possible toxic effects, and consideration must be given to other therapeutically equal agents (if they exist) with a higher benefit-to-risk ratio. Manufacturers may not label or advertise a drug in the United States for any indication which has not been specifically approved by the Food and Drug Administration.[2]

Elsewhere in the world, however, American drug companies' enthusiasm for their products is not hampered by FDA restrictions. As a result, manufacturers will often recommend the same drug for a much wider variety of conditions in Latin America than they are permitted to do in the United States. In fact, some drugs which are considered too toxic for all but the narrowest indications in the United States may be promoted for quite broad and sometimes trivial indications in Latin America.

---

of pentazocine—all the drugs could have been bought without prescription.) The drugs were directly obtained by members of our team in Brazil, Colombia, the Dominican Republic, Guatemala, and Panama. Interested persons in these same countries as well as in Venezuela and Argentina supplied us with additional samples, copies of package inserts, promotional brochures, and advertising. We also obtained copies of Latin American reference manuals which compile drug information supplied by manufacturers (equivalents of the *Physicians' Desk Reference* in the United States) for Mexico, Colombia, Ecuador, Argentina, and Brazil. For advertising we also consulted the collection of Latin American medical and health journals in the library of the Pan American Health Organization in Washington.

The materials were then compared with the labeling currently approved by the United States Food and Drug Administration (FDA) as found in the most recent edition of the *Physicians' Desk Reference,* as well as with the entries in standard reference manuals such as *AMA Drug Evaluations,* Goodman

The extent of a drug's indications is no academic question. If, for example, a drug is recommended and used for a disease against which it is not effective, then the disease, perhaps serious, will be left untreated. In addition, and despite the ineffectiveness of the drug, the person using it still runs the risk of its toxic effects. Even if the drug is effective, the person may be subjected to unnecessary risks if a less toxic drug would do the job as well.

The following are some examples of "indications" accompanying drugs available over the counter in Latin America:

Anabolic Steroids

Among those drugs classified as anabolic steroids is a group of synthetic male sex hormones which have the general effect of promoting weight gain and a feeling of well-being. One of these is marketed by Winthrop under the brand name of WINSTROL. In the United States, WINSTROL is considered too toxic for all but the narrowest indications.[3] It can cause serious disturbances of growth and sexual development if given to young children: in both sexes, premature stunting of growth; in boys, premature enlargement of the penis and increased frequency of erections; in girls, an increase in body hair, male-pattern

---

and Gillman's *The Pharmacological Basis of Therapeutics,* and *The American Hospital Formulary Service,* as well as with *The Medical Letter, Drugs and Therapeutics Bulletin, Side Effects of Drugs, Martindale: The Extra Pharmacopoeia,* and the World Health Organization's *Drug Information* circulars.

A draft of this chapter was then prepared on the basis of comparisons. The entire draft was reviewed by three expert consultants. Simultaneously, each of the companies was contacted, one by personal interview and the others by letters from the author. Enclosed in these letters to the companies were copies of the material obtained from Latin America on their respective products. The companies were asked to explain the discrepancies we had found in dosages, indications, contraindications, and warnings of adverse effects between those discussed in standard references and/or approved by the FDA and those used in both package inserts and promotion distributed in Latin America. The draft was then modified on the basis of the consultants' comments and the companies' replies.

baldness, deepening of the voice, and clitoral enlargement.[4] The disturbances in girls "are usually irreversible even after prompt discontinuance of therapy. . . ," according to the FDA.[5] These effects are not rare idiosyncratic reactions. *The Medical Letter,* an independent nonprofit publication on drugs and therapeutics, warns that "every child who takes the drug in the recommended dosage for a long enough period of time will demonstrate these effects."[6]

WINSTROL is approved in the United States only for use in the treatment of aplastic anemia and pituitary dwarfism, and as a supplement in treating osteoporosis.[7] Although drugs like WINSTROL are sometimes given to children for specific growth disorders, the American Medical Association warns that these drugs "should not be used to stimulate growth in children who are small but otherwise normal and healthy."[8]

But in Latin America, Winthrop promotes the drug widely as (among other things) an appetite stimulant for underweight children.

A two-page advertisement for WINSTROL COMPOUND (WINSTROL plus vitamins and iron) carried in a Mexican medical journal in July 1972 showed a picture of a healthy-looking boy about seven years old. The ad recommended WINSTROL COMPOUND "if he complains of poor appetite, fatigue, or weight loss."[9]

William J. Brooks, director of communications for Sterling Drug in New York City (of which Winthrop Products Inc. is a subsidiary) denied recently that this 1972 ad from Mexico typified company promotion of WINSTROL. He called the ad a one-time mistake by the company's advertising agency.[10] But the most recent edition of the Mexican *Diccionario de Especialidades Farmacéuticas,* a drug compendium distributed to doctors and based on company-supplied information, recommends WINSTROL "in states in which weight gain in children and adults is necessary, for loss of appetite no matter what the cause, for beneficial action to increase strength, interest, and general well-being. . . ."[11]

Similarly, boxes of WINSTROL tablets purchased in Brazil in 1973 and 1974 carry the statement that "in states of appetite loss and malnutrition, [WINSTROL] stimulates appetite and improves protein anabolism" (i.e., protein buildup). The manufacturer's package inserts, tucked inside the WINSTROL boxes, add "thinness," and "alterations in nutrition and growth in children," as well as many other indications.[12] Despite the known harmful effects of WINSTROL on young children, Winthrop even markets a special pediatric version of the drug in Brazil. When this product was purchased in 1974, the package insert recommended it for, among other things, appetite loss, malnutrition, and thinness, specifying "alterations in nutrition and growth in children of preschool age."[13]

A package insert for WINSTROL purchased in the Dominican Republic in 1974 uses quite technical language to describe the drug—terms like "anabolic androgenic coefficient," "nitrogen and mineral retention," and "hemoglobin levels." But one sentence will be clearly understood by anyone purchasing the drug and reading the insert: "WINSTROL frequently improves appetite, vigor, and the sensation of well-being."[14] In the Dominican Republic WINSTROL is recommended for use in eight wide-ranging conditions. Just one of the eight encompasses "nonmalignant chronic diseases (renal, cardiovascular, gastrointestinal, arthritic or chronic infections)"; another of the eight conditions is "retardation of growth in children."[15]

Winthrop is by no means the only multinational manufacturer encouraging the wide use of synthetic male sex hormones. Swiss manufacturer Ciba, for example, promotes DIANABOL in Brazil for (among many other indications) "thinness," "underweight," "appetite loss," "lack of strength," "general weakness," and "growth disturbances in nursing infants, preschool children, and schoolchildren. . . ."[16] DIANABOL can cause the same effects as WINSTROL, and in the United States its only indications are osteoporosis and pituitary dwarfism.[17]

Many other drugs considered too toxic in the United States for all but the narrowest indications are also promoted for broad indications by American companies in Latin America. Here are just four more examples.

Dithiazanine Iodide

This drug was introduced in the United States in 1958 as treatment for a wide variety of parasitic worm infestations in humans.[18] As evidence of the drug's toxicity became apparent, its indications were gradually restricted to severe cases involving those parasites for which other drugs were not available.[19] The government of France, followed by the government of Chad, banned dithiazanine iodide in 1965.[20] By August 1966, at least 10 deaths had been associated with the use of DELVEX, the Eli Lilly brand of dithiazanine iodide.[21] Lilly discontinued marketing DELVEX in the United States in 1967.[22]

One other company—Pfizer & Co.—also marketed dithiazanine iodide in the United States. Pfizer marketed the drug in continental United States for 14 months in 1959–60 before discontinuing it,[23] and in Puerto Rico and the U.S. Virgin Islands until 1964.[24] In March 1964, FDA Commissioner George P. Larrick wrote to Pfizer, informing the company that it would have to revise its dithiazanine iodide labeling, because of recent reports of deaths associated with the drug, and send a "Dear Doctor" warning letter to physicians in Puerto Rico and the Virgin Islands. Commissioner Larrick instructed Pfizer that dithiazanine iodide's indications would have to be sharply narrowed because of the drug's hazards.[25]

Presented with these new labeling requirements, Pfizer decided to stop marketing dithiazanine iodide in areas under FDA jurisdiction. In an April 1964 letter signed for Pfizer by S. Lidsky, the company stated that "In our view, these restrictions on the indications for use of dithiazanine iodide would not support the continued marketing of the drug in Puerto Rico and the Virgin Islands. Therefore, we advise that we are deleting dithiazanine iodide from distribution by the Pfizer International subsidiary in these areas."[26]

As far as warning doctors about dithiazanine iodide deaths, Pfizer claimed that since stocks of the drug in Puerto Rico were already depleted (the letter does not mention any checking of stocks in the Virgin Islands), there would bc no point in sending out "Dear Doctor" letters:

> In view of the fact that our warehouse and customer inventories have been entirely exhausted, and since we do not propose to continue marketing the product in Puerto Rico or the Virgin Islands, we see no useful purpose in sending a "Dear Doctor" letter to physicians in the areas where our drug is no longer available.[27]

In the areas outside the jurisdiction of the FDA, Pfizer's marketing tactics have not been interfered with in the same way. Under brand names like NETOCYD and DILBRIN, the drug was being promoted in many countries of Latin America as late as 1974 as a broad-spectrum anti-parasitic agent.

The package insert that accompanied a bottle of NETOCYD tablets purchased in Panama in July 1973 describes the drug as "a significant advance in the treatment of the most common kinds of parasitic infestation" and as a "vermicide of broad spectrum" which is effective against the "most frequent worms in human parasitism."[28] The package insert does not attempt to restrict NETOCYD's use to severe or life-threatening infestations. Although the insert gives instructions on how to avoid the possibility of intestinal absorption, it fails to mention that the consequence of such absorption may be death.

In an October 1974 letter Pfizer stated that the "international product document" for this drug had been changed to restrict recommended usage to the treatment of only one type of parasitic infestation.[29] In September 1974, however, we purchased over the counter in Venezuela a bottle of DILBRIN. It is described on the box as an anti-parasitic agent of broad spectrum and the package insert gives dosage for use against four types of parasites.[30]

Dipyrone

This painkiller, which occasionally also kills the person who had the pain, is very popular throughout Latin America. Many companies, both multinational and local, promote it in Latin America to treat trivial complaints for which much safer drugs are available.

Dipyrone is an effective analgesic (pain reliever) and antipyretic (fever reducer), but it may cause some fatal blood diseases, of which the most frequently mentioned is a severe depression of the bone marrow called agranulocytosis.[31] For this reason, dipyrone was taken off the market in Australia in 1965,[32] and it may no longer be sold in the United States as a routine treatment for pain, arthritis, or fever.[33] According to the labeling required by the U.S. government, dipyrone preparations "should be restricted to use for their antipyretic effect in serious or life-threatening situations where salicylates or similar drugs are known to be ineffective or are contraindicated or not tolerated."[34] No other indications for use are approved in the United States. The American Medical Association's *Drug Evaluations* states that "no dosage [of dipyrone] for analgesia is justified"—its "only justifiable use is as a last resort to reduce fever when safer measures have failed."[35]

Sterling Drug does not sell dipyrone in continental United States, but its Winthrop division does sell it in Puerto Rico, under the brand name NOVALDIN.[36] NOVALDIN is also for sale in the Dominican Republic, where ads appeared in two 1974 issues of a professional journal for pediatricians showing a "contented child" and "happy mother" smiling over the "agreeable flavor" of NOVALDIN drops for children. No warnings are given in these advertisements.[37]

But Sterling's Winthrop subsidiary more frequently markets dipyrone in Latin America under the brand name of CONMEL. In Brazil, where CONMEL is widely used, it can be bought in drug stores in individual cellophane packets marked "Analgesic, Antithermic, Antirheumatic."[38] Indications for use written on the packet are "migraine headaches, neuralgia, muscular or articular rheumatism, hepatic and renal colic. Pain and fever which usually accompany grippe, angina, otitis, and sinusitis. Toothaches and pain after dental extractions."[39]

The most recent edition of the Brazilian *Index Terapêutico Moderno,* which is based on information supplied by the manufacturer, recommends CONMEL for the "symptomatic treatment of all diseases characterized by fever and acute pain, including grippe, colds, pneumonia, and other infectious illnesses."[40] To the nation's doctors, to whom the index is distributed, the manufacturer offers the following enthusiastic description of CONMEL's role in medical practice:

> CONMEL is an indispensable supplement in the initial and continuing treatment of the very varied minor ailments which constitute a good portion of medical practice. In daily practice many opportunities to prescribe CONMEL will be found. . . .[41]

In 1972, CONMEL was number 20 on the list of best-selling ethical drugs in Colombia.[42]

In addition to CONMEL, Winthrop markets combination products containing dipyrone in various Latin American countries, under brand names such as BESEROL and DOLOPIRONA.[43]

But again, Winthrop is not alone in this practice. These American companies also market dipyrone in Latin America for the treatment of minor ailments: Endo, a subsidiary of DuPont, markets VALPIRONE;[44] ICN markets GENSERVET;[45] McKesson, a unit of Foremost-McKesson, markets DIPIRONA MK;[46] Merrell, a division of Richardson-Merrell, markets DORFLEX;[47] Schering, a division of Schering-Plough, markets CORICIDIN S/A (not the same CORICIDIN Schering sells in the United States) and CORILIN children's suppositories;[48] Searle markets STEGALGINA;[49] and Upjohn markets ALGINODIA.[50]

None of these multinationals markets dipyrone in the United States.[51]

Long-acting Sulfonamides

While they fight bacterial infections, long-acting sulfonamides can also cause Stevens-Johnson syndrome, an often fatal skin disease.[52] When this danger became apparent around the mid 1960s, governments such as Czechoslovakia, Hungary, Australia, Belgium, and the United States moved to restrict the use of, or even ban, some or all of these drugs.[53]

Between 1957 and 1965, 116 cases of Stevens-Johnson

syndrome occurred in various countries after the use of long-acting sulfonamides. Twenty-nine of these cases were fatal. Seventy-nine of the 116 cases involved children; 20 of these children died.[54]

Short-acting sulfonamides do the same job as long-acting sulfonamides and are potentially safer because they are eliminated from the body so much faster. However, because the long-acting agents are excreted slowly, a smaller dose or less frequent administration can maintain a therapeutic blood level.[55] Long-acting sulfonamides can therefore be more convenient and less expensive to use. These factors may be very important in poorer countries, but in such cases everyone concerned needs to be informed of the serious risks involved.

In Europe and North America, long-acting sulfonamides are rarely considered drugs of choice. The American Medical Association's *Drug Evaluations* states that the long-acting agents "offer no clinical advantages over the short-acting agents," and that "the use of the long-acting agents is justified only under extraordinary circumstances."[56]

Nevertheless, long-acting sulfonamides are often promoted in Latin America for the treatment of all diseases for which sulfonamide therapy is indicated. MADRIBON, a popular product marketed by the Swiss multinational Roche, is recommended in package inserts and drug compendia as this kind of all-purpose sulfonamide. No warnings are given about the possibility of fatal Stevens-Johnson syndrome.[57] MYLOSUL, a Parke-Davis product, is recommended by the manufacturer in the Mexican *Diccionario de Especialidades Farmacéuticas* for the treatment of "acute and chronic infections due to germs sensitive to sulfonamides. . . ."[58] LEDERKYN, marketed by Lederle, is recommended in the Mexican drug compendium for treatment of a long list of infections for which a short-acting agent would be just as effective and far safer.[59]

Long-acting sulfonamides are also marketed in combination with other drugs, sometimes for the treatment of the most minor ailments. In Mexico, for example,

Norwich Farmacal markets VIRUBAC, which contains a long-acting sulfonamide, a virustatic agent, and an antihistamine. VIRUBAC is recommended in the Mexican *Diccionario* as an "auxiliary in the symptomatic treatment of grippe, common cold, and illnesses related to, and bacterial complications of, the same."[60]

Indomethacin

This potentially dangerous drug continues to be broadly indicated outside the United States long after overenthusiastic company promotion has been curtailed here.

Merck Sharp & Dohme introduced indomethacin under the brand name INDOCIN in the United States in 1963. Company promotion originally extended to indications much broader than the four kinds of arthritic disease approved by the FDA. But after this practice was exposed in Senate hearings in 1968, the manufacturer changed its promotion.[61]

INDOCIN causes a high incidence of severe adverse effects: according to the AMA, about 15% of patients experience gastrointestinal disturbances, and effects on the central nervous system are common.*[63] Fatalities have been reported from perforation and hemorrhage of the esophagus, stomach, duodenum, and small intestine and from hepatitis and jaundice.[64] Current FDA-required labeling carries the "IMPORTANT NOTE" that "INDOCIN cannot be considered a simple analgesic and should not be used in conditions other than those recommended under INDICATIONS."[65]

Outside the United States, Merck maintains its high opinion of indomethacin's broad efficacy—and presumably its safety, since the company promotes it for ailments for which safer drugs are available. A package insert for INDOCID (the brand name used in Latin America) obtained in Brazil in 1974 recommends the drug for many conditions

*A critical review done in 1968 of all available published material on indomethacin reported that in 15 studies, 35% of patients experienced at least one undesirable reaction; in 14 studies, 20% of patients could not tolerate the drug.[62]

for which it could not be recommended in the United States, including pain and inflammation after dental procedures, bursitis, and lumbago. The insert even recommends the short-term use of INDOCID to reduce fever while using other drugs to treat the fever's cause.[66]

Similarly, a Venezuelan package insert obtained in 1974 broadly recommends INDOCID for the treatment of "a good number of inflammatory disorders of the locomotive and musculoskeletal systems." Under "side effects," the Venezuelan insert states that headache "can occur at the beginning of INDOCID treatment" and that "gastrointestinal discomfort occurs infrequently.*[67] But *Side Effects of Drugs* (a series of books which report unwanted effects occurring anywhere in the world) claims that gastrointestinal disturbances with indomethacin are "very common," and that headache occurs in 20–60% of patients.[68]

A Question of Time

If a drug has been proven safe and effective for the treatment of certain diseases, that does not necessarily mean that it will be safe and effective for another use developed later. For this reason, the FDA requires manufacturers to prove a drug's safety and efficacy for a

---

*In a seven-page letter dated 11 November 1975 Merck Sharp & Dohme International emphasized that the insert we obtained in Venezuela was a "patient package insert" containing no specific indication, no dosage information and a warning that INDOCID should be used only under strict medical supervision, all of which is literally true. It is difficult, however, to understand why this should make the exaggeration of claims and the minimizing of risks any more acceptable.

"It would take a resolute patient to self-medicate after reading these warnings, and clearly the patient is not provided with sufficient information to use the product without a physician's advice and guidance," says Merck's letter. In fact, the patient needs very little resolution to buy INDOCID over the counter in capsules of 25 or 50 mg. and to self-medicate according to a package circular which begins by saying how effective it is as an anti-inflammatory, analgesic and antipyretic drug and in its third paragraph says, "Initiating treatment with small doses which then increase gradually as is shown to be necessary, and continuing for an adequate period (up to a month is the recommended period), produces the maximum benefit with a minimum of adverse reactions."

new indication before that use can be added to the drug's labeling and advertising in the United States.[69] But a manufacturer does not have to wait for such proof before promoting the drug for the new use in other countries.

DEPO-PROVERA is an Upjohn product, marketed in the United States since 1960. An injectable derivative of the female hormone progesterone, it has been proven effective and safe for use in such conditions as inoperable cancer of the uterus.[70]

In 1963, Upjohn received the FDA's permission to test DEPO-PROVERA in women for use as a contraceptive when injected once every three months. Studies begun in 1965 proved the effectiveness of the drug for birth control, but they also clearly demonstrated that use of the drug could cause prolonged and possibly even permanent infertility.[71]

Other problems, even more serious, were suggested by ongoing animal tests. In 1970, beagles being given the hormone in low and high doses developed benign and malignant breast tumors.[72] Although it was not known whether the drug would therefore cause tumors in women, oral contraceptives which caused similar results in beagles were withdrawn from the U.S. market at about that time.*[73] That decision was made in light of the availability of other oral contraceptives, but there were no other injectable contraceptives on the market. The FDA believed that there was a need for a long-acting injectable contraceptive for the small number of women—such as the mentally deficient—who could not reliably use other methods of birth control. So DEPO-PROVERA tests were allowed to continue.[74]

In October 1973, despite the questions that had been raised about the safety of DEPO-PROVERA, the FDA announced that it would soon approve the drug for limited use as an injectable contraceptive. But because of the risks involved, the FDA stressed that the drug was not for use by women who could use any other method of birth control.[75]

More controversial information about the safety of

---

*C-QUENS, one of these withdrawn oral contraceptives, is discussed more fully on page 44.

DEPO-PROVERA was revealed in April 1974 at hearings held by the House Inter-Governmental Relations Subcommittee. Subcommittee investigators pointed out that Upjohn statistics—presented over a year earlier to FDA advisers—showed that cancer of the cervix occurs in DEPO-PROVERA users at rates several times higher than in women generally. The FDA, after reviewing the cervical cancer statistics, concluded that the increased incidence was probably due to differences in the patient population used in DEPO-PROVERA trials. In an analysis published in the *Federal Register*, the FDA recognized that "clearly there is appropriate concern" about the cancer-causing potential of DEPO-PROVERA, but said that this concern should also be extended to oral contraceptives.[76]

On September 6, 1974, the FDA issued labeling regulations which indicated its intention to approve DEPO-PROVERA as a last-resort contraceptive. A special leaflet, which was to have been given to the patient or her parent or guardian before the first administration of the drug, says:

> "It should be used only if:
> "Other methods of preventing pregnancy have failed *or*
> "You are not able to use other methods of preventing pregnancy such as the 'pill,' an IUD, or a diaphragm, *and*
> "You accept the small possibility of permanent infertility (inability to have children) *and*
> "You understand the risks and drawbacks described below. . . ."[77]

In October 1974, the FDA's pending approval was stayed. Commissioner Alexander Schmidt said he would not approve marketing of the drug "until safety issues were settled."[78]

And yet, despite these significant safety questions raised since 1970 by studies on DEPO-PROVERA, Upjohn has been promoting the drug for birth control in Latin America—and not just for women with no alternatives. Instead, the company advertised the drug in Colombian medical journals as the birth control agent "for the modern woman." It claimed that the drug was "accepted by women of all social classes."[79]

Another Colombian advertisement, which appeared in 1972 and 1973 issues of *El Médico* and *Revista Colombiana de Obstetricia y Ginecología,* proclaims "clinical confirmation" that DEPO-PROVERA is "safe, effective, acceptable." The ad quotes scientific articles published in 1968 and 1969, totally ignoring the disturbing data released since 1970. This ad was being published as recently as October 1973.[80]

Just as manufacturers are often quick to recommend a drug for a new indication, they can be very slow to modify or remove outdated indications from their foreign labeling and promotion.

The rauwolfia alkaloids—introduced here in the early 1950s—were among the first tranquilizers used in the United States.[81] But they were found to frequently induce depression, which was occasionally so serious as to require hospitalization or result in suicide,[82] and their use in the treatment of psychiatric disorders had to be radically curtailed. They were quickly replaced by the phenothiazine derivatives, drugs which were both more effective and easier to control.[83]

Today the rauwolfia compounds are used in the United States mainly to treat hypertension (high blood pressure). They are also indicated for the relief of symptoms of agitated psychotic states, primarily in patients who cannot tolerate the phenothiazines or those who also require antihypertensive medication.[84]

In Latin America, however, rauwolfia compounds are often promoted as tranquilizers with the enthusiasm that faded in the United States 20 years ago. Squibb, for example, markets a rauwolfia product brand-named RAUDIXIN which was obtained in Brazil in 1974. The package insert indicates RAUDIXIN both as an antihypertensive drug and as a sedative. As a sedative, RAUDIXIN is described as the "ideal medicine for the treatment of emotional disturbances such as states of tension and anxiety, and in states characterized by nervousness, irritability, excitability, and insomnia." RAUDIXIN's therapeutic properties and the almost total absence of undesirable side effects, the insert claims, make

RAUDIXIN "the drug of choice in daily practice."[85]

Presented with this package insert, Squibb's public affairs director explained that it was "written about 20 years ago. It accurately reflected the medical and pharmaceutical practice at that time, and conforms with Brazil's drug regulatory requirements."[86] Although Squibb's Brazilian subsidiary claims not to have promoted RAUDIXIN "for emotional disturbances or any similar purpose" for "about 10 years," a revised insert was apparently never issued.

Swiss manufacturer Ciba also broadly recommends its rauwolfia products as tranquilizers. A package insert for SERPASOL, obtained in Brazil in 1974, indicates the drug for nervous agitation, irritability, anxiety, nervous tension.[87]

Contraindications

Indications explain the situations in which a drug should be used. Contraindications tell when it should not be. Both directions can be critical.

Drug labeling and advertising in the United States must include a full statement of all factors which would make taking a given drug too dangerous. Such factors might relate to the patient's age or medical condition, drug allergies or sensitivities, or to some other drug being taken at the same time. For women who are pregnant, nursing, or even menstruating, some drugs may be particularly dangerous. Some drugs can be so harmful to a fetus that they should not be used by any woman of childbearing age in whom pregnancy is a possibility.[88]

Despite the critical importance of warning doctors, pharmacists, and patients about these special dangers, many manufacturers include in a drug's Latin American labeling only incomplete or modified versions of the necessary restrictions. The rationale is that, as with too few indications, too many contraindications will hurt sales volume.

Tetracyclines are a very widely used group of antibiotics. If taken by a pregnant woman, or by a young child during the period of tooth development, tetracyclines can damage the enamel and dentine and permanently stain developing teeth a disfiguring greyish-brown or yellow. Although the exact period of tooth development is not known, *Drug and Therapeutics Bulletin,* published by Consumers' Association of Great Britain, estimates that the risk of tetracycline-induced tooth damage lasts from the fourth month of gestation to seven years of age.[89] Required labeling in the United States is based on a slightly different calculation, recommending that except in unusual circumstances, tetracyclines should not be used by women during the second half of prengancy, nor by infants or children less than eight years old.[90]

In Latin America, however, manufacturers market tetracyclines with only limited warnings. Lederle,[91] Bristol-Myers,[92] and Pfizer,[93] companies which market a variety of tetracycline drugs in the United States and Latin America, all shorten the warning for Latin American users to the last three months of pregnancy, the period immediately after birth, and the period of infancy.* Children under eight and women in mid-pregnancy who take tetracyclines may find out later that the manufacturer's restrictions were too narrow.

Some manufacturers promote drugs in Latin America for the treatment of conditions in which the drug is specifically contraindicated in the United States. FDA-required drug-labeling warns women who are menstruating against using dipyrone, for example, because of the possibility of severe hemorrhage. But an ad for BESEROL 500 (a Winthrop product containing dipyrone plus a muscle relaxant) which appeared in the February 1974 issue of *Ginecología y Obstetricia de Mexico* recommends

---

*In his October 25, 1974, reply to our queries regarding the shortened warning, John E. Jefferis, Vice President and Medical Director of Pfizer International Inc. suggested that we had mistranslated the Spanish and Portuguese word *infancia* to the literal "infancy." "For example," he wrote, "the *Dictionary of the Royal Spanish Academy* defines the word *infancia* as the age of a child from birth until he is seven, and a definition given by another dictionary is the period until the child's first teeth are fully developed." Mr. Jefferis is quite correct about the definition of *infancia*, but the copies of Pfizer tetracycline inserts we sent to him all use the expressions *primeira infancia* (Portuguese) or *primera infancia* (Spanish), which mean, quite clearly, "babyhood."

the product "for menstrual pain," proclaiming 93.5% "excellent results."[94] The source for this statement was a sample of 138 patients, in whom the only factor analyzed was the presence or absence of pain after treatment during three menstrual cycles. (Two women had to suspend treatment because of the severe nausea and vomiting which ensued.)[95]

Adverse Effects

No drug is free of toxic effects. They may be trivial, but on occasion they are serious and may be fatal. Manufacturers are required by the FDA to include in their U.S. drug-labeling and advertising a fully informative statement of the adverse reactions that have been associated with a drug's use.[96]

But products that have caused serious or even fatal adverse reactions are sometimes sold in Latin America as though they were completely safe. The concealment of possible harmful effects is another temptation to which manufacturers often succumb for the sake of sales volume. Who would buy dipyrone for a cold or headache if informed of the risk of a fatal blood disease?

Birth Control Pills

A particularly grievous example of this kind of concealment is represented by some brands of birth control pills. Unusual considerations of risk versus benefit are involved here. As the FDA has stated, oral contraceptives "are used for long periods of time by large numbers of women who, for the most part, are healthy and take them as a matter of choice for prophylaxis against pregnancy, in full knowledge of other means of contraception. . . ."[97]

Because of these special circumstances, the FDA requires that all users be directly warned by manufacturers of the possibility of fatal reactions to birth control pills. Each package of pills must include a statement that begins: "The oral contraceptives are powerful and effective drugs which can cause side effects in some users and should not be used at all by some women. The most serious known side effect is abnormal blood clotting which can be fatal."[98]

Other serious side effects reported in the FDA-approved labeling include mental depression, swelling, rash, and jaundice. Absence of menstrual cycles after stopping the pill is also possible.[99]

About a dozen package inserts and instruction sheets which currently accompany birth control pills sold in Latin America in 1974 were reviewed. Only one insert contained a warning about the possibility of fatal side effects. The other leaflets collected contained either no warnings at all or a wide range of vague or inadequate warnings.

Brands without any serious warnings included OVRAL (Wyeth), purchased in Venezuela;[100] NORDIOL (Wyeth-Vales), purchased in Mexico;[101] NEOGYNON CD (Schering Germany), purchased in Mexico;[102] OVULEN and OVULEN ½ (Searle), both purchased in Colombia.[103]

The label for OVRAL (Wyeth), purchased in the Dominican Republic,[104] contains a section called "secondary effects," but the manufacturer limits those listed to such things as stomach ache, nausea, headache, and weight loss or gain. Labels for NORLESTRIN (Parke-Davis) were gathered from both Colombia and Brazil. The Colombian label was the only one of those collected which contained a warning of possible fatalities.[105] But the NORLESTRIN label obtained in Brazil mentions only minor complaints under "side effects" and states that "there were no thromboembolic manifestations (blood clots) . . . in more than 1,000 patients given NORLESTRIN."[106]

Although Searle's OVULEN labels from Colombia do not contain any warnings, the company does give doctors a question-and-answer booklet to distribute to women using the drug. However, the booklet currently in use in Colombia—a copy of which was provided by Searle to show that the company does warn people about the possible dangers of the pill—gives the following incorrect information: "No significant increase," the booklet states, "has been observed in the incidence of thrombophlebitis, or of any of its complications, in women taking oral contraceptives. . . ."[107] This statement directly contradicts the current required labeling of OVULEN in the United

States, which states that "an increased risk of thromboembolic disease associated with the use of hormonal contraceptives has now been shown. . . ."[108]

Some of these birth control labels may be quite old; the OVULEN label from Colombia, for example, is copyrighted 1965. But they were, nevertheless, the labels accompanying birth control pills purchased in 1974. Companies apparently do not feel compelled to arrange for newer and more informative labels to be included with their products.

Concealment of adverse reactions in Latin American marketing is particularly flagrant in the use of a drug called chlormadinone acetate in gynecological and contraceptive products. Chlormadinone acetate, combined with mestranol, was once sold in the United States as a birth control drug called C-QUENS. After C-QUENS was already on the market, ongoing studies in dogs showed an increased incidence of breast tumors resulting from the chlormadinone acetate component.[109] Although there was no increase in the frequency of breast tumors in women using the drug, the findings raised a safety question. After consultation with the FDA, the manufacturer decided in October 1970 to stop producing the drug.[110] When the FDA decided in March 1972 to withdraw its approval of C-QUENS, Lilly did not object.[111]

But the Mexican subsidiary of Syntex Corporation still sells at least five gynecological and contraceptive products containing the drug: SECUENTEX-21,[112] SECUENTEX-28,[113] DUPLOSYN,[114] LUTORAL,[115] and LUTORAL CON ESTROGENOS.[116] None of the entries for these products in the Mexican *Diccionario de Especialidades Farmacéuticas* contains any mention of the disturbing safety question that led to the withdrawal of chlormadinone acetate in the United States.

Ads for some of Syntex's chlormadinone acetate products appeared in the April 1974 issue of *Ginecología y Obstetricia de México.*[117] One of the drugs advertised, LUTORAL CON ESTROGENOS, contains the same ingredients as C-QUENS, the withdrawn birth control product. LUTORAL CON ESTROGENOS is recommended as a cycle regulator for menstrual disturbances; like a contraceptive, a cycle regulator is often taken for extended periods of time. In fact, the amount of chlormadinone acetate taken in one menstrual cycle of LUTORAL CON ESTROGENOS is over three times higher than that taken in a cycle of C-QUENS.

Nevertheless, under "secondary reactions," the LUTORAL CON ESTROGENOS ad states that "the discomforts caused by this product will be due to intolerance of the estrogen in the formula [which is mestranol, not chlormadinone acetate] and will consist mainly of nausea, vomiting, and migraine headache."[118]

If healthy, long-term users of birth control pills have a special claim to be informed of possible toxic effects, sick people too have a right to know the risks they are taking. Nevertheless, many drugs that have caused serious or even fatal adverse reactions are marketed without adequate warnings.

Cinchophen

This antique drug was introduced in 1902 as treatment for gout. But it frequently caused hepatitis, which often was fatal. The first death from cinchophen was reported in 1925; by 1936, 88 deaths in the United States, England, Germany, and what was then Austria-Hungary had been attributed to cinchophen and neocinchophen, a related drug.[119]

When the FDA polled 266 medical school professors and other experts in 1941, 79% thought that cinchophen could not be administered in therapeutically active doses by physicians or by others with any confidence that "serious deleterious effects" would not result.[120]

The American Medical Association stated in 1965 that, although it was "unfortunately" still being marketed, cinchophen's use "has been abandoned in rational therapeutics."[121] Cinchophen has not been on the market in the United States in recent years.[122]

Marketing in Latin America, however, has continued much longer. Schering sold ATOPHAN (cinchophen) in Brazil for half a century for use "against rheumatism and uric acid" until it was finally dropped from the company's product line some time in 1974.[123] As late as 1972, in that year's edition of the *Index Terapêutico Moderno*, the manufacturer continued to recommend ATOPHAN broadly for rheumatic ailments, gout, and other painful inflammatory diseases, with no mention of the possibility of hepatitis or other liver damage.[124]

Abbott also sells cinchophen, under the brand name CINCOFENO. A bottle of CINCOFENO tablets purchased in Venezuela in July 1974 came without a package insert. The label on the bottle describes the drug as an antirheumatic and analgesic which will "stimulate the elimination of uric acid." A dosage schedule is also printed on the bottle. There are no warnings.[125]

Dr. J. L. R. Barlow, International Medical Director for Abbott, explained that the company does not distribute any warning literature on CINCOFENO "because it is an old drug with a very limited market. It is prescribed primarily by older physicians who have used the drug for many years and have had a great deal of experience with its use and potential side effects." For old drugs like CINCOFENO, "a continual information program by the manufacturer not only is not necessary but would be wasteful."[126]

Chloramphenicol

The ability of this antibiotic to cause a fatal blood disease, aplastic anemia, has been publicized off and on for more than 20 years in both the medical and lay press.[127] Public health authorities and medical experts in several developed countries have warned against irresponsible and indiscriminate use of this antibiotic; the trend in these countries has been to restrict its use to those few infections, such as typhoid fever, for which there are no suitable alternatives.

At the same time, the drug is used widely in many less developed countries, because of its broad antibacterial spectrum, its effectiveness, and its low cost.

Doctors in poor countries often feel justified in prescribing dangerous drugs because of the special medical and economic problems of the people they treat. A missionary working in Bolivia described this situation in a letter written in July 1974:

I spoke to one of the doctors . . . about the common use of [chloramphenicol]. The response was that in the States, because of our better state of general health, we could afford to have the luxury of saving that drug for rare cases. Here, the people's general health is so poor that one must make an all out attack on illness. . . .[128]

But the special circumstances do not make the drugs any less dangerous in poor countries. If anything, they make adequate labeling even more important. In letters published in a 1970 issue of the *New England Journal of Medicine*,[129] two doctors described the incidence of adverse reactions to chloramphenicol in Colombia, where the drug has been widely used since the early 1960s.

Dr. Hernando Sarasti, of the Clínica de Marly in Bogotá, wrote that "our experience in Colombia is that the development of aplastic anemia after the ingestion of chloramphenicol is not rare at all. Dr. C. Mendoza and I were able to document 35 cases during the period 1961–1965. . . . We are sure that the cases we studied represent only a small sample of the total number. Diseases supposedly 'rare' in South America, and common in other countries, usually make their appearance as soon as somebody starts looking for them. Colombians, unfortunately, are not immune to the toxic effects of chloramphenicol. . . ."[130]

Dr. Jacobo Ghitis, Professor of Medicine at the Universidad del Valle Medical School in Cali, commented along similar lines. ". . . It is agreed by all Colombian hematologists that as soon as chloramphenicol became freely available in this country, the expected occurred—that is, aplastic anemia became a dreadfully common disease. In fact, I saw 40 cases during the two years after the introduction of chloramphenicol as an inexpensive ['generic'] drug. . . ."[131]

Dr. Ghitis added that "although chloramphenicol continues to be used freely in Colombia, the incidence of aplastic anemia has decreased sharply. Perhaps we are witnessing a situation of iatrogenic (physician-induced) selection."[132] This selection is explained by Dr. Sarasti's letter: chloramphenicol, he suggests, "is probably acting as a macabre mechanism of selection by eliminating all children sensitive to it. After several generations this may bring about a new chloramphenicol-resistant population. . . ."[133]

Just as the existence of different kinds of medical problems in poor countries does not make chloramphenicol any less dangerous, so it does not excuse manufacturers who fail to warn users in these countries about the risk of aplastic anemia.

The following are examples of such failures:

•AMBRA-SINTO, the chloramphenicol / tetracycline combination marketed by a Dow Chemical subsidiary, carries no warnings about the potential dangers of chloramphenicol in a package insert obtained in Brazil in 1974. Yet warnings about the less serious dangers of tetracyclines are included.[134]

•TETRAFENICOL, a USV-Grossman product containing chloramphenicol and tetracycline, is promoted to doctors in Mexico in a slick brochure. "Secondary reactions" listed in the brochure are "appetite loss, nausea, vomiting, diarrhea, inflammation of the tongue, rash, and tooth discoloration." There is nothing in the brochure about fatal blood disease.[135]

•CLOROMICETINA, one of the many Parke-Davis brand names for chloramphenicol, is broadly promoted in Brazilian medical journals for use in "all infections sensitive to chloramphenicol." In small print, clearly not intended to alarm, ads published in 1974 state: "For more detailed information, including the precautions and adverse reactions that include bone marrow depression, consult the chloramphenicol monograph."[136]

A survey done by the International Organization of Consumers Unions (IOCU) in 1972 revealed a wide variation in the chloramphenicol labels distributed in different countries by Parke-Davis, a company which for many years defeated efforts to limit the use of chloramphenicol in the United States. Parke-Davis told IOCU that it was standardizing its international chloramphenicol labeling;[137] this was confirmed by Parke-Davis' medical director in England in an August 1974 letter to *The Lancet*, a British medical journal.[138] The medical director wrote: "Parke-Davis labelling for 'CHLOROMYCETIN' is now standardised worldwide and contains indications and warnings compatible with good standards of medical practice."

But the mild warning in recent Brazilian ads contrasts sharply with these words required in the United States: "WARNING: Serious and fatal blood dyscrasias . . . are known to occur after the administration of chloramphenicol. . . ."[139]

Pentazocine

This powerful painkiller was introduced by Winthrop Laboratories in August 1967.[140] Although legally classified in the United States as a non-narcotic—which means that it is not subject to the controls of federal narcotic laws—injectable pentazocine has caused instances of psychological and physical dependence.[141]

In most cases—but not all—this dependence has occurred in patients with a history of drug abuse. In September 1970, after an increasing number of reports of abuse, pentazocine was included in Canada's list of controlled drugs.[142] Brazil[143] and Mexico[144] have also taken steps to limit the availability of this drug.

In a letter published in a June 1969 issue of *The Lancet*, three doctors at the drug-abuse clinic of the Texas Research Institute of Mental Sciences described four recent cases of probable pentazocine addiction.[145] All four patients were women, aged 27 to 58, who had begun taking pentazocine (brand-named TALWIN in the United States) for various kinds of pain or chronic sinusitis. Each had been taking injections daily—in slowly increasing doses—for about a year. All four women were "felt to be prone to overusage of drugs." All four had tried to stop taking the drug, but could not do so because of severe withdrawal symptoms.

J. Michael Mungavin, medical director of a Winthrop subsidiary in England, commented on the Texas report in a letter published in *The Lancet* two weeks later.[146] "As the discoverers and manufacturers of pentazocine," Mungavin wrote, Winthrop was "anxious to maintain well-documented information on the use of the product. . . ."[147] The company knew of 57 reported cases of alleged dependence on pentazocine. "We have kept careful records of alleged cases of pentazocine misuse reported to us, as have our associates in the United States; and our medical literature recognizes the possibility of misuse liability."[148]

In Colombia, however, where injectable pentazocine is marketed by Winthrop under the brand name SOSEGON, the drug was purchased with a package insert beginning "powerful analgesic with no risk of addiction." The insert also stated that SOSEGON is a "new analgesic which does not produce physical dependence."[149] When asked to comment, Winthrop executives said that this insert had been issued in 1968, and that there had been three subsequent revisions of the text.[150] But this insert accompanied a SOSEGON package available for purchase in 1974.

Nor does all company advertising "recognize the possibility of misuse liability." In August 1972, an ad in the Mexican edition of *Médico Moderno* told doctors to prescribe SOSIGON (the brand name in Mexico) "for your next patient with pain." The "effectiveness" of the injectable form is mentioned—but not its potential to produce dependence.[151] Dr. Monroe Trout, Vice President for Medical Affairs at Sterling Drug, Winthrop's parent company, called this "reminder advertising."[152]

The May 1973 issue of the same magazine carried a slightly less enthusiastic ad, not quite recommending SOSIGON for everyone in pain. In addition, "secondary reactions" are listed; but these are restricted to the "most common," such as nausea and vomiting. Doctors are not warned about the much less common, but much more serious, possibility of addiction.[153]

Dosage

Small and large distortions in labeling and advertising claims—especially in the areas of indications, contraindications, and adverse effects—can be used to manipulate sales. So can distortions in other areas.

Dosage is just one more example. If a slightly higher dosage is recommended, a larger quantity of a drug will need to be purchased. Unfortunately, the higher dosage may increase the risk of unwanted effects.

Kanamycin, marketed by Bristol (Bristol-Myers) under the brand name KANTREX, is an antibiotic which can cause serious toxic effects, principally deafness and kidney damage. In order to minimize the drug's toxicity, FDA-required labeling sets a maximum daily dosage which should not be exceeded.[154] The Pharmaceutical Society of Great Britain advises an even smaller daily dose "to avoid loss of hearing and kidney damage."*[156]

But KANTREX labeling in Latin America is not so restrictive. Package inserts obtained in Colombia[157] and Venezuela[158] recommend up to double the dose per kilogram of body weight that is recommended in the United States.

In 1972, KANTREX was number 18 on the list of best-selling ethical drugs in Colombia.[159]

* * *

The promotional practices described in this chapter do not occur in a vacuum. The self-medication habit is deeply ingrained in Latin America. It is a fact of life. It is also a source of considerable income for the pharmaceutical industry.

Although drug companies protect themselves by obeying local laws requiring them to print "for sale by prescription only" on drug packages, the companies are well aware that many people in Latin America buy drugs without a doctor's advice. They also know that the package inserts loaded with wide indications but few warnings usually reach people with no medical knowledge against which to evaluate promotional claims.

---

*Because of the increased risk of irreversible hearing loss with prolonged treatment, the British society suggests limiting the course of kanamycin treatment to one week. U. S. labeling similarly warns that "THIS DRUG IS NOT INDICATED IN LONG-TERM THERAPY (e.g. tuberculosis). . . ." But a promotional brochure distributed to doctors in Brazil specifically recommends a dosage schedule for the treatment of tuberculosis.[155]

4/AMBIVALENT HOSTS

Why is it that governments in Latin America exercise so little control over the drug industry?

Generalizations about Latin America and Latin American governments are always dangerous, but there is one fundamental consideration that explains the weakness of regulatory mechanisms not only in Latin America but in other parts of the world as well: Most governments in less developed areas are, rightly or wrongly, anxious to attract foreign investment. And they are in competition with other developing countries for it. Stringent controls are not part of the "favorable business climate" sought by multinational investors.

What drug industry investors look for when considering foreign investment was expressed in a rather cute way by George R. Cain, then Board Chairman and President of Abbott Laboratories, speaking to the Financial Analysts Federation in Philadelphia in 1965:

> The international aspects of the drug manufacturing firms of the United States are complex and many-faceted. So, it's natural to ask, "Why assume the risks of expanding overseas?"
>
> The answer: The total returns from our international operations more than justify the risks.
>
> This statement may be difficult to prove when I now refer to the problems or situations prevailing in one of our major markets which I shall call Country X.
>
> 1. In the past 10 years continuing legislative inquiries have deliberately contributed to adverse press publicity.
> 2. Suggested price controls have been seriously studied and some adopted.
> 3. Legislation designed to remove drug patents has been formally introduced.
> 4. Use of generic name drugs only has been advocated by some teaching universities.

5. Country X proposes tighter controls at the federal and provincial levels.
6. Only certain panel approved drugs would be reimbursable.
7. The politicians of Country X have adroitly used the spectre of drug prices as the cause of rising costs for all medical care.
8. And, finally, legislation has been drafted that would dictate to the physician the types of drugs available for the hospitalized patients.

You, too, might well ask, "Why get into that kind of a mess?" My reply, "Why not? We are already in and operating, for Country X is the United States."

So perhaps one answer as to why we go overseas is to get away from it all! By comparison, some overseas markets are simple.[1]

A government seeking foreign capital to develop a drug industry within its own borders is clearly off to a bad start if it has adopted price controls, has introduced legislation designed to remove drug patents, has allowed legislative inquiries to create adverse publicity, or has tried to control the proliferation of brand names by favoring generic name drugs or drawing up lists of drugs it will reimburse or permit to be prescribed within its social security system.

The remarkable thing is that Latin American governments, including those, such as Colombia and Brazil, which are most favorable to multinational enterprise, have attempted all these things and more, in an effort to resist being totally manipulated by their guests.

This chapter tells of some efforts by governments, or groups within government, to put reins on the multinational pharmaceutical industry. Some have been partially successful, some have failed completely. But, as we shall see, multinational enterprise knows how to lose battles while winning a war.

Prices

Despite industry's avowed preference for a totally free market, a number of Latin American governments impose some form of control on the price charged to the pharmacist and/or the consumer for finished drug products.*[4] This price is generally within the reach of the urban upper and middle classes, if at times only barely, because these classes constitute the political power base of most Latin American governments.

Chronically short of foreign exchange until very recently,[5] many Latin American governments have been faster to react against multinational drug-pricing schemes when they involve a drain on the country's international balance of payments.

As long ago as 1963 a scandal erupted over the pricing of pharmaceutical imports in Brazil. A parliamentary inquiry launched in the early 1960s under the Quadros and Goulart regimes produced a report charging that the Sydney Ross Company was paying its parent firm (Sterling) $595 per kilogram to import phenylephedrine hydrochloride while the international market price was $100, that Parke-Davis was paying $300 for chloramphenicol while it was being sold on the U.S. market for $55, and that Roche was paying $1,140 for its imported LIBRIUM while the same chemical compound could be bought in Italy for $100. The report accused the companies of declaring such inflated prices in order to make illegal remittances of hard currency to their parent firms, and also to inflate their costs so as to minimize their taxable profits.[6]

As a result of the parliamentary findings released in 1963—and the public indignation they caused—President João Goulart created GEIFAR: Executive Group for the Pharmaceutical Industry. GEIFAR's goals were to control prices, supervise imports of raw materials, and strengthen the national drug industry.[7]

On February 21, 1964, GEIFAR issued its first set of regulations: drug prices in all major cities had to be equalized, prices had to be printed on all packages and the

* It seems to be the U.S. consumer who, on the average, pays the highest drug prices in the world.[2] But the difference between the prices charged in Latin America and those charged in the U.S. is slight compared to the difference in per capita incomes; drugs are still not within the financial reach of the majority of Latin Americans.[3]

industry had to be prepared to show a production cost breakdown when asked.[8] Five weeks later, the Goulart regime was overthrown. Led by a right-wing military movement, the coup had the open support of multinational companies as well as most local industrialists.[9] The drug firms were not bothered by GEIFAR thereafter.

The first Latin American drug-pricing scandal which resulted in permanent change took place in Colombia in the middle of 1969, an election year.

For years, Colombian customs and foreign exchange officials had casually noticed striking differences between the prices paid by foreign pharmaceutical concerns for some of their imported raw materials and those paid by local manufacturers for similar products.[10] But no one had ever checked into the matter. Then in mid-1969, through office scuttlebutt, the matter came to the attention of Alonso Lucio, an ambitious young lawyer in the Customs Bureau.

Lucio obtained authorization for a probe from his supervisors in the customs office. He collected the drug import licenses issued to 16 foreign companies in the years 1967–69 and recorded the import prices declared when the licenses were issued. He then wrote to several European firms with the story that he was opening a plant to manufacture drug products and wanted price quotations on certain raw materials for those years to guide him in his own purchases. When he received the quotations from the European firms, he was incredulous.[11]

Some of the price differences Lucio discovered were even more startling than those uncovered in the 1963 parliamentary inquiry in Brazil. He found, for example, that Merck Sharp & Dohme of the United States had been selling dexamethasone to its Colombian subsidiary for $31,900 per kilogram, while the drug cost $7,500 per kilogram on the European market. In another case, eight European laboratories quoted a price of $45 or less per kilogram of diazepam; Roche was paying its parent company $2,500 for the same quantity.[12]

Lucio summoned company executives to his office for

questioning under oath about the price differences. The executives explained that, as subsidiaries of multinationals, they were simply paying the standard prices charged by their parent corporations.[13]

Lucio and his aides checked out this claim with the help of the Chilean government, which at the time maintained fairly strict price controls on drug imports. They also checked the prices paid in a Central American country where import prices were even less regulated than in Colombia. The large difference in prices paid for triamcinolone by Squibb subsidiaries in the three countries indicates the results of the comparison:[14]

Country	*Price paid per kilogram* (US$)
Chile	13,500
Colombia	35,000
Central American country	60,000

"So what was the international price for these raw materials?" Lucio asked. "There was no international price for Squibb or any other multinational drug company with operations in these three countries. The prices were set depending on the price controls a given country had and the needs of the company."[15] The multinationals seemed to be charging whatever they could get away with.

In their sworn declarations, the "trademark" laboratories offered other explanations for the fact that they were charged prices so much higher than the European quotations. They cited their parent companies' high expenses for research and development and quality control. The European firms, the executives claimed, did not do very much research and development, and they produced lower-quality drugs.[16]

Lucio argued that research and development costs could not justify such extreme price differences. He also rejected the quality claim, saying that Colombian Ministry of Health tests on imported raw materials had revealed no substantial differences in quality.[17]

The court eventually decided against the companies. They were fined 22 million pesos—well over a million dollars.[18] Sixteen drug companies were found guilty of paying excessively high prices to their parent firms for imported "raw materials"—drugs in bulk for mixing and packaging locally. Like the Brazilian report, the accusation implied that this kind of overpayment was a disguised form of returning currency to the home office in excess of permitted levels and of concealing real profits in order to evade payment of Colombia's 40% profits tax.[19]

The companies jointly appealed the fine to Colombia's highest administrative court. Their appeal was rejected.[20]

The scandal was on the front pages of Colombia's newspapers for months. At the height of the publicity, *El Tiempo*, Bogotá's leading daily, editorialized:

> The scandalous overpricing of drug imports, proven by the investigations of various official agencies, deserves punishment without mercy. What happened is repulsive. Just when the country needs to administer its foreign exchange more carefully, the pharmaceutical companies have been playing tricks on the customs authorities by presenting them with false invoices and fabricated prices. There is no question that the parent firms were direct accomplices in these immoral maneuvers.
>
> . . . This has been the worst scandal in the history of foreign investment in Colombia. It is a disturbing symptom of the mentality behind many of those moneyed interests involved in our country. Since the days of the former director of Incomex, Dr. Valencia Jaramillo, the foreign commerce authorities were aware of some aspects of this problem. On one occasion they made a polite complaint to the drug firms, asking that they cease practicing what was clearly an abuse. They acted in private, but it was useless.
>
> Apparently there was not sufficient proof of the magnitude of overpricing at that time. Now the evidence leaves no doubt. . . .
>
> *El Tiempo*, February 7, 1970[21]

A Harvard graduate student in economics, Constantine Vaitsos, was in Colombia during the scandal, working in the National Department of Planning.[22] Vaitsos examined Lucio's data and then extended the inquiry into rubber, electronic, and chemical products, using customs declarations from the same period of time. He also gathered additional data on drugs. Though he found overpricing in all these fields, none was as extreme as pharmaceuticals. Vaitsos incorporated his findings into his doctoral thesis and also published a number of articles in economic journals.[23]

The Vaitsos data from Colombia started an international debate involving not only pharmaceutical firms but all multinational corporations. Researchers in Chile, Argentina, and other Latin American countries have done similar studies, and found similar pricing discrepancies.[24] The Vaitsos data is an important element in the wide-ranging critique of multinationals leveled by Richard Barnet and Ronald Müller in their book *Global Reach*.[25]

Not surprisingly, the data itself has been attacked. Friends of industry have criticized Lucio and Vaitsos for quoting prices from Italy, where international patent laws were not respected at the time of the inquiry. Italian drug companies, critics claimed, were "pirating" the patents held by other multinational firms and selling drugs cheaply because they had no research and development costs to recover.[26]

In fact, Lucio and Vaitsos had also obtained price quotations from many countries that do respect the patent laws. While Italian prices averaged somewhat lower, the differences were nothing like the 250%, 3,600% or 5,000% discrepancies between "international" prices and what the multinationals were charging their subsidiaries.[27]

The other common argument used to justify multinationals' high drug prices—their better quality controls—was refuted by Vaitsos in advance. On the basis of pharmacological findings, he eliminated from his research list all drugs in which quality differences would justify a price increase or decrease of more than 10%.[28]

What Lucio and Vaitsos uncovered—the same thing uncovered in Brazil in 1963—was the multinational practice called transfer pricing. Inflated prices are charged for parts, machinery, and technical assistance, in addition to raw materials; this helps the parent company collect the profits it thinks it deserves. But transfer pricing can be a heavy drain on the host country's supply of foreign exchange.[29]

Government action to force down import prices, such as occurred in Colombia after the companies lost their appeal, can reduce the drain on a country's foreign exchange. In addition, such action can force companies to pay local taxes on more of their profits. But retail prices will not necessarily be lowered—which is what happened in Colombia.

And so, four years after the conclusion of his investigation, Alonso Lucio (now an executive of a parking lot chain in Bogotá) is disappointed with its results. "Before our investigation," he recalls, "the country was importing an average of $2.5 million per month in pharmaceutical raw materials. As a result of the investigation, imports dropped to $1 million per month, with no resulting shortages on the drug market."[30] This meant the country had $18 million more in hard currency each year to spend on importing essential goods for the country's development.

"But what was my goal in this investigation?" Lucio continues. "I wanted to benefit the consumer. So I am still complaining about the Lleras and Pastrana governments. Although they levied and collected the fines, they left the matter at that."[31] The Superintendency of Prices, after collecting the fines, did not drop retail prices. Instead, soon after the fines were paid, the drug companies succeeded in pressuring the Superintendency for a general price increase.[32] In the end, the consumer paid the fines.

Inflating the prices charged to subsidiaries is, of course, only one of the bookkeeping mechanisms available to multinational concerns.[33]*

***Back in the U.S.A.**

Shortly after the government of Colombia discovered the inflated prices multinationals were charging their subsidiaries, the U.S. government became aware that it was also being taken. Under a foreign aid program called the Commercial Import Loan program (which is almost entirely phased out now), the U.S. Agency for International Development (AID) had been financing—at very inflated prices—the purchase of millions of dollars of pharmaceuticals. *(continued on overleaf)*

While the industry was forced to cut down on transfer pricing in some countries like Colombia, in general the drug business in Latin America has continued to yield substantial profits.

Patents, Royalties, and Licensing Agreements

A patent creates a temporary monopoly on the sale of a new product. This temporary monopoly—which in the United States usually lasts for 17 years—enables the patent holder to set prices without fear of being undercut by competition. The goal of the patent system is to create the incentive necessary for both invention and investment.[43]

Commercial Import Loans were designed to provide needed foreign exchange to less developed countries, in order to finance the import of commodities and capital goods for general use in the private sector. Under the terms of the program, the U.S. government provided a certain amount of dollar credit to a foreign government. The recipient government then allocated the dollar credits among private companies so that they could import needed products and equipment from any U.S. company. The U.S. government paid the U.S. company for the goods from the foreign government's dollar credit account, and the foreign companies reimbursed the foreign government in the local currency. The recipient government had eventually to repay the United States in dollars, but on very long terms at low interest rates.[34]

As it turned out, the great majority of "foreign" companies were subsidiaries of U.S. multinationals, which took advantage of loopholes in AID regulations to practice transfer pricing at the expense of U.S. tax money, the foreign consumer, and the foreign country's balance of payments.

In 1970 hearings held by the Senate Subcommittee on Small Business, the prices AID was paying to drug companies under this program were compared with competitive prices on the European market. AID payments were found to range from 3 to 113 times the European price for an equivalent product. When questioned about the figures by Senator Gaylord Nelson, the subcommittee chairman, an AID official conceded, "American suppliers are insulated from foreign competition, and the only standard that we hold them to is that their prices in AID sales do not exceed prices in non-AID export sales."[35] However, AID officials admitted that they had found many instances where the

The international patent system is based on the 1883 Treaty of Paris. Anyone who has obtained a patent in one of the countries that signed the treaty has priority rights to register the patent in any or all of the other member countries. The holder is supposed to use the patent, or forfeit the right to it after a specified period; forfeiture can be avoided, however, by "legitimate excuses."[44]

Patents create an incentive for the growth of new technology. But Latin Americans have discovered that, under the system, new technology is developing in the United States and Europe and not in Latin America. In 1969, a study by the European Common Market reported

---

prices charged by the drug companies had exceeded prevailing market prices;[36] in fact, AID had collected about $1 million in refunds for overpricing, and still had claims outstanding for about $2 million. The largest claims were against Wyeth ($218,573), Eli Lilly ($238,281), Abbott Laboratories ($371,903), Merck Sharp & Dohme ($394,067), Roussel Corp. ($699,860), and Gedion-Richter Pharmaceuticals ($802,617).[37]

Senator Nelson pointed out that although high prices for U.S. products in foreign countries benefit the U.S. balance of payments, the foreign consumer does not benefit. "When the poor consumer goes to buy [the drug] after it is processed," he observed, "he must pay 20 to 30 times as much as he would have to pay if it was coming from another country."[38]

The subcommittee's statistics also showed wide variations in the prices a U.S. parent charged its subsidiaries in different countries.[39]

Largely because of the revelations at the Nelson hearings in 1970, AID decided to adopt strict drug-pricing regulations. Effective December 30, 1970, prices paid to U.S. suppliers were carefully keyed to the world market price and the domestic price of generic drugs.[40] As a result of these restrictions, a number of large pharmaceutical manufacturers (including Bristol-Myers, Squibb, Schering, and Abbott), unwilling to limit their profits, dropped out of the program.[41]

In an interview in July 1974, an AID commodity management official responsible for reviewing pharmaceutical purchases said that "as a result of the price regulations, there are very few commercial loan transactions involving pharmaceuticals—and those that are going under AID financing are not going to subsidiaries."[42]

that 49% of the world's best-selling pharmaceuticals introduced since 1950 had been discovered in the United States. The other 51% had been discovered in Europe and Japan.[45]

Over the years, it has become evident tht the patent system helps to strengthen the power of multinational firms because of their large research and development establishments.[46] Many Latin American governments which originally signed the Treaty of Paris have recently moved to weaken the system in various ways.

The Andean Pact* countries—Bolivia, Chile, Colombia, Ecuador, Peru, and Venezuela—began to modify their patent systems by issuing the famous Decision 24 in August 1971. This decision established a commission with the power to "designate production processes, products or groups of products for which patent privileges will not be granted in any of the member countries."[47]

Decision 24 also has other far-reaching provisions that caused consternation among foreign businessmen in Latin America. As codified, it calls for the gradual transformation of almost all foreign-held companies into national companies or mixed enterprises (51% or more local capital). It prohibits, among other things, remittances to foreign shareholders of profits in excess of 14%; acquisition by multinationals of local firms except in cases of imminent collapse; certain restrictive clauses in licensing agreements and purchase contracts; royalty payments by a multinational's subsidiary to its parent firm; and any new foreign investment in certain key public sectors such as energy, communications, and transportation.**[48]

Implementation of Decision 24 has occurred much

---

*This new regional organization, conceived in 1969, has its headquarters in Lima. Its formal title is the *Junta del Acuerdo de Cartagena.*

**In licensing agreements, patent or trademark holders give other companies permission to market the patented product or use a brand name under certain conditions, e.g. at a predetermined price. Royalty payments are made to the holder of the patent or trademark for each article sold under licensing agreement.

faster in some countries than in others. Chile under Allende, for example, enforced similar regulations even before the code was promulgated. Under the present military junta, however, Chile is trying to avoid carrying out certain parts of Decision 24.[49] But in the matter of patents, pharmaceuticals will probably lose their patent privileges in several, if not all, Andean Pact countries.

The patent system for pharmaceuticals also appears to be on its way out in Argentina. An Argentine economist, Jorge Katz, recently investigated how the patent system worked in his country.[50] He found that about 75% of patents obtained during the 1957–67 period were actually for the registration in Argentina of foreign patents held by about 100 multinational corporations. He took a sample of these foreign patents, and found that 45% of the patents in the sample were for products which were neither being manufactured in Argentina nor imported into Argentina. These patents simply served to prevent the development of local technology to compete with multinational products in case the companies decided to sell any of these products in Argentina at a future date.

More than 60% of the foreign-owned patents studied by Katz were held by "chemical" companies, a category which includes pharmaceutical firms. In fact, Katz found that the vast majority of "chemical" patents were for drugs.

In 1970, Argentina was the scene of an important court battle on the issue of patent protection for pharmaceuticals. An Argentine firm, Unifa, had been buying a drug called dimethylchlortetracycline from Italy, where the Paris agreement was not recognized at the time. American Cynamid, which held the patent on this drug but was not marketing it in Argentina, took Unifa to court in Buenos Aires. The court ruled that Unifa could not sell the drug; damages were awarded to Cyanamid. Unifa then appealed to the Supreme Court, which unanimously reversed the lower court's decision. The Supreme Court said, in effect, that not only matters of law but matters of health were at stake, and that Argentine law did not permit anyone to exercise a monopoly in a way that was prejudicial to public health. The court ruled that Unifa could continue to provide the drug to the Argentine people.[51] Half a dozen other cases involving multinational firms in patent litigation with local firms are now in the Argentine courts, but they are not being pressed very hard because of the precedent set in the Unifa case.[52]

In 1974, the Costa Rican legislature began considering bills which would reduce the validity term of patents from 20 years to five years and which would withdraw patent protection for drugs.[53]

Brazil, despite its policy of encouraging multinational investment, has removed pharmaceuticals from the protection of the patent system. In October 1969, during a short period of direct military rule, a group of nationalist army officers slipped through a decree stating that substances, raw materials and compounds used for the making of drugs and food, as well as the processes devised to produce them, would no longer be protected by the privilege of patent.[54] Patents registered prior to October 1969 are considered valid, though none will be honored after 1984. The drug industry, taken by surprise, tried to fight back.[55] But the New Code on Patents and Industrial Property, issued in December 1971, reaffirmed that medicines, along with basic food commodities, could no longer be patented in Brazil.[56]

The breakdown of the patent system in any given country is, however, less a threat to multinational industry if the industry can succeed in controlling the entire market. One way to achieve market domination is simply to buy out the local competition. This seems to have been the reaction in Brazil where, from the beginning of 1972 through March 1975, 11 Brazilian drug companies passed under foreign control—more than half to American companies.[57]

Another way to protect a monopoly, in the absence of patents, is to control the source of raw materials.

Raw Materials and Know-How

Individual governments, if they so choose, can deal with business monopolies inside their own borders. But when the monopoly, or oligopoly, is international, they may be hamstrung.

The ability of multinationals to control the supply of certain raw materials was demonstrated in 1972 in Europe, when the Common Market caught American Cyanamid and Commercial Solvents Corporation in a display of corporate power.[58] The victim in the case was Giorgio Zoja, an Italian company which in 1969 was making most of its money from the sale of an antituberculosis drug called ethambutol. Ethambutol is made from a paraffin nitration by-product produced only by Commercial Solvents.

In 1969, shortly after Zoja refused a merger offer from a pharmaceutical subsidiary of Commercial Solvents, the Italian firm found that it was suddenly unable to buy the chemical substances from which ethambutol is made. American Cyanamid, the largest supplier of these chemicals and also producer of its own ethambutol drug for TB, would not sell to Zoja, and neither would any other supplier. The cooperation from American Cyanamid enabled Commercial Solvents to put the squeeze on Zoja for three years.

The Common Market eventually fined Commercial Solvents and enabled Zoja once again to purchase ingredients for ethambutol. But if there had not been an international court of appeals of this sort, Zoja would presumably have had to cease production of ethambutol—or, perhaps, reconsider the merger offer.

Brazilians learned what multinational control of raw materials meant very recently when there was a sudden crisis among diabetics over a supposed shortage of insulin.

On April 25, 1975, diabetics in Florianópolis, capital city of the State of Santa Catarina, could not find insulin in local drugstores. With the help of some sensationalist coverage in the national press, panic spread to other cities, hoarding began, and within a few days there was a shortage all over Brazil.

It was quickly verified that a subsidiary of Eli Lilly and Company, Eli Lilly do Brasil Ltda., was the sole manufacturer of insulin in the country. The raw material, in the form of insulin "crystals," comes from Lilly's Argentinean plant (the only producers in Latin America), where the crystals are manufactured from the pancreas of cattle and hogs.

The crisis subsided when Lilly obtained a special license to import the finished drug from the United States for a short period of time until the supply situation could be normalized.[59]

But some Brazilians began asking why the country needed to be entirely dependent on a single foreign supplier. Why could Brazil not manufacture its own insulin since it has one of the largest cattle populations in the world? "It's uneconomical," said Henrique Paulo Barros Barreto, medical director of Eli Lilly do Brasil, Ltda., in a press intervew.[60] The age at which livestock are slaughtered in Brazil is apparently different from that of Argentina, where the slaughtering age makes insulin manufacture more profitable.

About two weeks later, however, it came to light that some 400 tons of pancreas were being exported from Brazil every year. The largest known exporter was the Brazilian subsidiary of Farbwerke Hoechst, the multinational pharmaceutical and chemical firm from Germany,[61] which apparently finds some source of profit in the pancreas of Brazilian livestock. It was also learned that insulin had been manufactured in Brazil between 1945 and 1960 by a local firm called Laboterápica. But Laboterápica was bought out by Bristol-Myers in 1957. After becoming Laboterápica Bristol, the company decided that the market for insulin was unsatisfactory and ceased production. Representative Francisco Amaral charged, in June 1975, that this had taken place out of respect for "something called the distribution of areas of influence, or areas of profit."[62]

It may be a matter of pure efficiency or of pure oligopoly, but the effect upon Brazil is the same. The country pays about $11,000 per kilogram[63] to import a product which it already possesses the know-how and the resources to manufacture. In case of a shortage which might affect the lives of many citizens, it is completely at the mercy of a foreign supplier.

Approximately 75% of all raw materials used in the Brazilian pharmaceutical industry are imported. In 1974, these cost Brazil some $224 million in foreign exchange.[64] The situation is similar in other parts of Latin America. A 1971 survey of the drug industry in five Central American countries estimated that 90% of raw materials came from outside the region.[65]

The Sad Story of CEME

There is a nationalist faction within the Brazilian military elite which does not like multinational enterprise's stranglehold upon an industry so vital as pharmaceuticals.

It is probably due to this faction's influence, and the failure of drug companies to conform to the basic export thrust of Brazil's economic policy, that the country decided to exclude pharmaceuticals from the patent system. This same nationalist current, in a regime otherwise so benevolent to multinationals, also explains the existence from 1972 to 1975 of the *Plano Director de Medicamentos* (Master Plan for Pharmaceuticals) which, had it not been emasculated, might have freed the Brazilian drug industry from foreign control and forced it to work harder to meet the health needs of the majority of Brazilian citizens.

The Master Plan was the brainchild of a new government body called the Central de Medicamentos (CEME), an institution whose leaders seemed to care about the welfare of the poor majority in Brazil and who, when they began operations in 1971, were directly responsible to the President of the Republic.

The Master Plan contained a list of 400 basic medicines. These medicines, CEME claimed, could solve most of the country's chemically treatable health problems.[66]

The Master Plan suggested ways to produce the 400 medicines cheaply and efficiently and to distribute them all over the country: to the poor, to government institutions, to the armed forces, to the national social security system, and to minority groups like the Indians and the settlers in the Amazon.[67]

The Master Plan also proposed reviving state-owned laboratories and giving preferential treatment to local companies, with the ultimate goal of having the country produce most of its own pharmaceutical raw materials. Other provisions in the plan included tight controls on the sale and promotion of drugs, regulations on the content of the *bulas* (package inserts), and restrictions on the distribution of free drug samples.[68]

Part of the Master Plan was actually put into effect. Between 1972 and 1975, CEME arranged for 130 basic drugs to be produced in 17 laboratories around the country—in universities, in the army, and in other scientific institutions.[69] Backing the plan was the powerful National Bank for Economic Development, which had already agreed to provide CEME with substantial loans for investment in drug production.[70]

On June 29, 1974, the president of CEME, João Felicio Scardua, dedicated a new laboratory in Porto Alegre. In his dedication speech, he claimed that within five years the bulk of essential raw materials in the pharmaceutical sector would be manufactured in Brazil. "No country can achieve independence in the pharmaceutical sector without its own technology and know-how. . . . For this reason, CEME is pursuing a policy which aims at eliminating the point of strangulation, namely, the lack of research."[71]

The drug industry's public reaction to CEME and its Master Plan was mixed. There were some vague threats of retaliation from certain industry spokesmen,[72] but the cooler heads among the multinationals chose a different strategy. They would favor the distribution of medicines to the poor, offering to sell their own products to the government at cut rates for this purpose. Some would also take advantage of new government incentives to set up more research facilities of their own in Brazil. The real threat to them was the plan to develop an independent Brazilian technology in the laboratories of the army, the universities and the local drug firms as well as the plan to control the proliferation of many varieties of essentially similar drugs.

Cyanamid do Brasil's Director declared: "CEME should limit itself to the task of producing drugs that private industry initiative is not yet producing. . . . We all agree with the principle that the government must only interfere in the production of goods which private initiative cannot produce or has no interest in producing."[73]

Roberto Schneider, president of Pfizer's Brazilian subsidiary, put it this way: "We are prepared to cooperate with CEME, to provide the drugs at a 50% discount—in fact, we have some room for an increase in production—but we are only prepared to do it as long as the government does not distribute the medicines to those who can buy them."[74]

Clearly, there would be a struggle for influence inside the government. Struggle there was (though the role of the multinationals in it is nowhere traceable), and by the middle of 1975 the result was clear. CEME had been effectively shorn of any power that threatened the continued growth and expansion of foreign drug firms.

In March 1974 João Felicio Scardua, President of CEME, brought to the new President of Brazil, General Ernesto Geisel, the draft of a decree transforming CEME into a state-subsidized public corporation. This new status would have enabled CEME to pursue more vigorously the development of an independent Brazilian drug industry. Though itself a public corporation, CEME would have been given powers to regulate foreign investment in the industry.[75]

Such a decree was never issued. Instead CEME suddenly found that it had been removed from the Office of the Presidency and placed within the Ministry of Welfare.[76] Then, in March 1975, the Minister of Welfare sent to the president a draft law containing his own version of what CEME should be: another welfare agency charged with the free distribution of medicines to the poor. All responsibility for research and development was taken away, and there was no mention of regulating foreign investment.[77]

Finally, in April 1975, the President signed a decree transferring all of CEME's research functions to the Ministry of Industry and Commerce while leaving the distribution responsibility under the Welfare Ministry.[78] In July 1975 the Minister of Welfare published a new list of the basic medicines the production of which CEME was supposed to coordinate and encourage.[79] The number of drugs was now reduced to 293. Certain essential drugs were no longer on the list, and, more importantly, the list had been reduced to a mere guideline. CEME, and other government institutions which might distribute drugs to the poor, could substitute for the drugs named on the list any similar drug on the market.

The upshot is likely to be more business for the multinationals, because they can now sell their own versions of the drugs on the list to the government so that the government can in turn distribute them to the poor.

In the end there will be some free medicines for the very poor—at government's expense. For the companies, the only change produced by the Master Plan has been a very slight move toward transferring some of their research and development onto Brazilian soil.

The promise of new fiscal incentives has led eight multinationals to come up with projects for setting up synthesizing and/or fermentation facilities to produce drugs locally: Hoechst, Bristol, Wyeth, Rhodia, Squibb, Wellcome, Roche, and Cyanamid.[80] Cyanamid already has some modest research facilities in Brazil, as does Mauricio Vílella (owned by the British Beecham group). [81] The only significant investment by a multinational in local research up to now has been Johnson & Johnson's $2.5 million plant, built in 1971, which screens compounds developed by the firm's Belgian subsidiary for effectiveness against tropical diseases.[82]

The whole CEME affair may thus have forced multinationals to decentralize their research facilities a little bit. But the original dream, to create an independent Brazilian technology, was thwarted.

* * *

Price manipulation, exploitation of the patent system, control over research and raw materials: these are some of the ways in which multinational industry wields its power. It is clear from each of the cases mentioned in this chapter that industry is far from invulnerable. It may well have lost the battle to maintain the patent system for pharmaceuticals. But the ability of industry to adapt to changing circumstances, and come out on top in the end, is uncanny.

Governments which appear to have the people's interests at heart when they initiate some effort to control corporate activity somehow lose their will along the way.

5/SUGAR REPUBLIC

"An abundance of food is a sweet reward."

—G+W 1973 Annual Report

The 1974 annual stockholders' meeting was convened in mid-December at Lincoln Center in New York City, just a few blocks up Broadway from the sleek new Gulf+Western building which dominates Columbus Circle and looks out over the southwest corner of Central Park.[1] In his letter to shareholders, Charles G. Bluhdorn, Chairman of the Board, took the opportunity not only to highlight the upswing shown in the 1974 figures but also to give a positively glowing prediction for August 1974 through January 1975: "For the first quarter that ended October 31st, Gulf+Western is reporting net earnings of $2.00 per share on a primary base against $1.28 per share in primary earnings last year. I will go on to tell you that we expect, in the first six months ending January 31, 1975, to report primary earnings in the area of $4.00 per share. . . ."[2]

Why the optimism? From what source were these new profits anticipated? G+W is a conglomerate. It is into many things: movies, auto parts, paper, zinc, insurance, cigars. But a look at G+W's annual report for 1974 and subsequent reports suggests that a very big, if not the biggest, reason for the enthusiasm at the annual meeting was not Muriel cigars or Paramount Pictures: It was sugar.

As every U.S. consumer knows, the price of sugar skyrocketed during the last half of 1974. At its November 20 peak, before consumers finally demonstrated their resistance and cut down on sugar-buying, the price was 65½¢ a pound.[3] That was more than double the cost back in July, when the books for G+W's annual report were closed. Even in July, when retail prices were only half their 1974 peak, the biggest earner of all G+W's enterprises was sugar. Although the conglomerate's food and agricultural products division (85% of whose earnings were from sugar and its by-products) accounted for only 6% of all G+W's sales, it was responsible for 26% of the company's operating income, more than any other division.[4]

Who ever heard of Gulf+Western sugar? The U.S. consumer buys sugar marketed by the big refiners like Amstar, SuCrest and Great Western. They, in turn, buy raw sugar from suppliers on the sugar exchange, among them Gulf+Western. Though it maintains domestic operations in Florida, most of the sugar G+W supplies comes from the Dominican Republic.[5]

As a result of the enormous rise in sugar prices in late 1974, the U.S. Justice Department began in January 1975 an investigation into the operations of the major sugar refiners who sell directly to the consumer.[6] Our own small investigation, conducted at the production end, took place in mid 1974. After visiting sugar estates and adjacent contract farms in the Dominican Republic controlled by Gulf+Western, our reporter filed this story.

* * *

A Town Against Sugar

La Otra Banda is a small town near the city of Higuey in the Dominican Republic. It is in the eastern province of Altagracia, a region where much of the country's sugar is produced. The town is little more than a settlement built up along the narrow highway that runs north toward the Atlantic coast. It is a tight-knit community of a few hundred people who live primarily from their subsistence plots of farmland, raising the yucca, beans, fruits, and some rice that are the mainstay of their diet, along with a few animals. Some residents also plant a little coffee, peanuts, or other cash crop to provide a meager source of income, probably close to the national average of about $200 per family a year.

The social indices of infant mortality, disease, and illiteracy attest to the price paid for survival here. But with each generation, survival has become more difficult. For as their numbers have increased, the amount of land available to them for growing food has shrunk—diverted to the sugarcane acreage required to meet the demands of Gulf+Western Industries, Inc., a U.S. multinational that operates the "world's largest single sugar producing mill" in the Dominican Republic.[7] Although some of the younger people of La Otra Banda have tried to escape by moving to nearby Higuey or Santo Domingo or New York City, for the most part the people stay and scratch out an existence.

Suddenly this pattern of resignation was broken in March 1974, when the people of La Otra Banda, joined by thousands of supporters from Higuey and neighboring towns, seized a few hundred acres of land that were about to be planted with sugarcane. Merchants from Higuey provided tractors and seed, and the people planted beans, yucca, and plantains and demanded that the government make good on its pre-election promise to turn over land to the poor.[8]

But the break with tradition was only momentary. Legal title to this tract of land was, it seems, in the name of the Valdez family, a big landowner in the region, and Valdez wanted to plant sugarcane to sell to Gulf+Western's giant Central Romana mill, about 25 miles away.[9] The army was called in to dislodge the peasants from the field. The soldiers plowed the crops under and the land was ready again for cane. But the bitterness and resistance stirred by the expansion of sugarcane in this area may have prompted Valdez and his supporters to take a second look at this particular piece of land. By late May of 1974 the site had not yet been touched. It was a patch of no-man's-land between unbroken fields of cane and the subsistence plots around the houses of La Otra Banda.[10]

Sugar is the Dominican Republic's dominant crop, and Gulf+Western is the country's largest private sugar producer. Gulf+Western's Central Romana mill (a wholly-owned subsidiary) produces more sugar than any other mill in the world and regularly accounts for about 30% of the Dominican Republic's total production of sugar.[11] About 90% of the sugar produced in the Dominican Republic is exported,[12] most of it to the United States,[13] where it is used to make soft drinks, candy, cakes, and cookies. Sugar exports earned $206 million for the Dominican Republic on the world market in 1973.[14] The foreign earnings from sugar are supposed to further the economic development of the Dominican Republic by enabling it to buy the capital goods, raw materials, and foodstuffs that either are not or cannot be produced domestically.

The problem for most of the Dominican people, however, is that those foreign earnings have not been transformed into more food on their plates.

Beginnning in 1960, the food production index, exclusive of sugar and cacao, fell behind the index of population growth. Despite the improved productivity of agriculture in recent years, it still has not caught up.[15] One reason for this has been the steady "sugarization" of the land. The acreage under sugar cane has nearly doubled in the last 20 years.[16] Over the last 70 years it has increased perhaps 20-fold,[17] until now about 25% of all cultivated land in the Dominican Republic is devoted to sugarcane.[18] And the steady "sugarization" of the country continues. Sugar on the world market was over 40¢ a pound at the end of 1974, compared to an average of 2¢ a pound from 1965 to 1968.[19] This boom is applauded by government and company executives, but to the people of La Otra Banda and other undernourished small farmers, subsistence farmers, and landless laborers—who together comprise about 75% of the rural population[20]—the endless vista of cane fields looks like a great green plague slowly destroying their land.

Gulf+Western is one of the largest private landowners in the Dominican Republic. According to its own figures, which many maintain are much too low, the company directly controls more than 8% of all land under cultivation in the country.[21] In the four eastern-most provinces of the country, where La Otra Banda and the Central Romana mill are located, the company controls nearly three quarters of the arable land.[22]

Antecedents

Formed in 1957, Gulf+Western is a pioneer in that most modern form of business enterprise, the conglomerate—a corporation that buys, sells, and manages other companies the way corporations of an earlier era dealt with individual commodities.

Gulf+Western entered the Dominican Republic in 1967 by buying the South Puerto Rico Sugar Company (SPRSC), an enterprise that already had a controversial history.* SPRSC's vast, feudal-like estate had been accumulated for the most part through trickery and violence.[23]

In managing its acquisition, Gulf+Western has certainly been more sophisticated than its predecessor, and more conscious of its image, especially back in the United States. "As a large corporation operating in the Dominican Republic, Gulf+Western is one of the major employers in the country and keenly aware of its corporate responsibilities there," says the 1974 annual report. As evidence of its concern, the company points to a program it has for improving workers' housing, to donations it makes to schools and orphanages, and to the various ways in which export earnings, which Dominican law requires G+W to exchange for pesos, are used: tourism, fruits and vegetables for export, banking, cement, cattle-breeding, and the operation of an Industrial Free Zone.[24] All these things are presented by G+W as corporate contributions to the development of the Dominican nation. But while it is

*A fictionalized account of this history is Ramon Marrero Aristy's *Over*, published in 1939. It is one of the more scathing anti-imperialist novels written by a Latin American in this century. Although the company was not mentioned by name, there is no doubt that the target of Marrero Aristy's attack was the sugar operation now owned by Gulf+Western.

true that some things have changed since G+W took over, some things have not; and among the changes, not all were for the better.

The Colonia System

Alberto Giraldi owns a 1,500-acre farm in the town of Pintado, not far from the Central Romana mill. The thin, energetic, gray-haired Giraldi carries a gun, a big .45, strapped to his thigh, because he believes that two attempts on his life have been made as a result of his uncompromising opposition to certain Gulf+Western policies. His farmhouse was attacked twice in late 1968, the second attack resulting in the death of his foreman. At the time, Giraldi was president of the association of *colonos,* the 400 farmers who sell their sugarcane to Central Romana. In the interests of his constituency, Giraldi was fighting to have introduced into a bill then being discussed a series of measures which would have regulated the company more closely and strengthened the bargaining position of the *colonos* in their dealings with the mill. Very few of those measures were ultimately adopted. "I call this company a state within a state that constitutes an attempt on the life of the nation," Giraldi said. "It is stronger than the government itself, and it continues to expand."[25]

Much of Gulf+Western's sugar expansion has been by means of the *colonia* system. As of October 1973, the company had, in addition to the 109,642 acres of cane planted on company-owned land, another 49,362 acres on the land of *colonos*—some, like Giraldi, owning a lot of land and others very little.[26] Expansion through *colonias* has been necessary because, on the books, government regulations prohibit foreigners from buying land for the purpose of planting cane.[27] Also, the economic feasibility of using land for sugarcane is greatly dependent on the land's relative proximity to the mill and the loading stations.[28] Expansion, therefore, must take place on the land at the perimeter of the company's property, or on small pockets of land belonging to others within the general territory of the company's holdings.

Under the *colonia* system, the company enters into a contract with a farmer in which the farmer typically must agree to plant every available inch of land with cane. In return, the company advances the farmer whatever he needs to convert the land to sugar at the appropriate time, which is determined by the production schedule of the mill. In addition, the farmer is paid a percentage of the value of his crop after it is harvested. Contracts vary with the bargaining power of the farmer, but the effect in all cases is to integrate the individual parcels of land into the company's operations.[29]

"The only thing they let you keep is a dog," said one young man, referring to the frustration of the small farmer who puts his land into sugar.[30]

If larger landowners are receptive to the company's offer, small and subsistence farmers frequently are not. They are unwilling to give up a secure, if meager, source of food for their families in return for an uncertain amount of cash to be determined by company bookkeepers according to methods they do not always understand. Some of these farmers are old enough to remember the wild expansion of cane lands during the First World War in response to soaring world prices. The peasants call this period "The Dance of the Millions." Many small farms became *colonias* of the Central Romana, and then, when prices collapsed following the war, the farms passed into company hands.[31]

But the small farmer who at first refuses to plant cane often changes his mind. Residents of La Otra Banda complained of heavy aerial spraying of herbicides that damage plants and trees on land adjacent to cane fields, fences being mysteriously broken at night, access being denied to certain roads, and the company police force making sure that animals which stray into the cane fields are either destroyed or taken to a distant police station, where the owner must pay a stiff fine to retrieve them.[32]

When large landowners put their property into sugar, small and subsistence farmers are often hurt, too. This is because many of the peasants in the Dominican Republic have lived on the big Dominican estates for generations without holding legal title to their land. They work the land under a variety of economic arrangements. Often the small plot of land the peasant family farms for itself is "tolerated" by the big landowner, who is willing to trade off a small portion of his low-quality land in return for a ready supply of cheap labor to care for his cattle or cash crop.[33]

But when the estate owner rents land to G+W, it is obviously understood that all the land corresponding to the legal title goes into sugarcane.[34] Not only is the peasant's food supply then destroyed but also even the irregular and poorly paid jobs he and his family would perform on the estate are lost, for most of the work done in the cane fields of G+W is done not by Dominicans but by Haitians.

The community of La Otra Banda, for one, is convinced that the expansion of G+W and sugarcane is against its interests. According to various residents, the cane extension has already reduced the amount of food available on the local market.[35] Moreover, no new markets or industries are created by the new work force: the wages of the Haitian workers are so low that they have no discretionary income to spend at the local markets, and their subsistence wages are absorbed by the specially licensed stores within the plantation. Finally, G+W's relative self-sufficiency, from its own cement block factory for new housing to repair shops for vehicles, significantly reduces the degree to which a large corporation ordinarily generates secondary business activity.[36]

The Cane Cutters

"Haitians are used for cutting cane because it is not possible to get enough Dominicans for the difficult work," says a Gulf+Western brochure called *The Sugar Story*.[37] But another of the company's publications, this one aimed at potential investors in G+W's Industrial Free Zone, claims that within a 20-mile radius of La Romana there are 25,000 persons available for work.[38] The apparent contradiction between these two claims, that G+W cannot draw "enough" native labor although 25,000 Dominicans are "available," is rather easily resolved: Dominicans say that they will not work in the cane fields because the wages are impossible to live on.[39]

Cane cutters in mid 1974 were being paid $1.15 per ton.[40] Officials of both Gulf+Western[41] and the State Sugar Corporation[42] have claimed that a worker can earn up to two or three dollars a day, which would require him to cut 1.74 or 2.6 tons, respectively. But an independent study done in 1967 found that the average daily amount of cane cut per worker was only 1.3 tons,[43] which, at the $1.15 per ton rate, would net a worker only $1.50 per day. This corresponds to what the workers themselves were saying in 1974. According to them, their usual pay is no more than $7 or $8 a week.[44]

As one Dominican worker who swears he will never cut cane again said, "The last time I worked in the harvest I spent six months cutting and I couldn't even buy a pair of pants."[45] He now works as a woodcutter, and though he often cannot find more than one day of work a week, the $10 he earns in that one day is more than he would make all week in the cane fields.

Like California fruit growers in the 1950s, the company can keep its wage scale low by employing cheap foreign labor. There are no exact figures, but studies carried out in 1967, the year that G+W took over, suggest that Haitians may make up more than half the labor force on both government and La Romana properties.[46] A visit to the cane fields in 1974 indicates that this situation has not changed very much.

Another reason G+W has been able to keep wages so low is the successful destruction in 1966–67 of the workers' union, which was once part of the national Sindicato Unido. Despite the fact that sugar prices rose more than 1,500% during the intervening decade, Central Romana's cane cutters earned more in 1963 than they were earning in mid 1974.[47] In early 1963, backed by the reform-minded government of Juan Bosch, the union won a dramatic increase in real wages. This gain was significantly reduced after a military coup overthrew Bosch in September 1963.[48]

However, the union was still a force to be reckoned with when G+W was completing negotiations for the takeover of the Central Romana mill.

Negotiations for the acquisition of the South Puerto Rico Sugar Company had gone on for some time. During the year 1966, Charles G. Bluhdorn, Chairman of the Board of Gulf+Western, became a Director of SPRSC.[49] In January of 1967, Bluhdorn announced the deal whereby G+W was to buy SPRSC for $60 million.[50]

But during the transition period between the January announcement of the purchase and the formal takeover some months later, some strange things happened. On January 17, 1967, Guido Gil, a young lawyer who represented the militant Sindicato Unido in La Romana suddenly disappeared and was never heard from again.[51] Union leaders insist that he and another popular leader, Miguel Fortuna, were murdered.[52] They say that at this same time a new spy system was introduced into the mill and fields and their meetings were regularly broken up.[53] In early June of 1967, the union's account with the Royal Bank of Canada in La Romana was frozen.[54]

Effectively barred from organizing the workers, the Sindicato Unido was eventually replaced by another union, more sympathetic to the company, to which the field workers now pay dues.[55]

Working conditions reverted to the past in other ways as well. The title of Marrero Aristy's 1939 novel, *Over,* for instance, refers to a technique used by G+W's predecessor, the SPRSC, to cheat the cane cutters. Company weighers would mark down on cutters' pay tickets an amount less than the real weight they had cut. The weigher always sent more cane into the mill than the worker got paid for; any weigher who did not regularly deliver his "over" to the mill would soon be out of a job. Workers and other people interviewed in 1974 insisted that this practice, with numerous variations, is still very much alive. But it is just as difficult to prove today as it was many years ago, since G+W maintains complete authority over its scales and its books.[56]

Abundance for Export

Faced with mounting criticism over the extension of cane lands, the government in 1972 passed a law that was supposed to restrict this growth. But the law had a very big loophole. It authorized the "amplification of areas of cultivation of sugar cane destined for industrialization as long as the prevailing conditions on the international sugar market, in regard to the price of sugar, remain favorable to the national economy." The principal restriction was that the area to be used should not already be cultivated with "other productive crops, but, to the contrary, should be uncultivated, or at least, that the type of crop cultivated there not be remunerative, or that said land be dedicated only to agriculture of mere subsistence."[57] In effect, the government was telling the State Sugar Corporation, Gulf+Western, and the Vicini Group—the three companies that account for the Dominican Republic's entire sugar production—that they should go ahead and plant as much sugar as they thought they could sell.

The production of sugar for the export market is related to other agricultural trends in the country.

In 1970, the last year for which complete data is available, the Dominican Republic produced $290.3 million in agricultural goods, or about $75 worth per inhabitant. About 64% of that production was exported. The exports were concentrated in a few "traditional" products: sugar, coffee, cacao, and tobacco, which together accounted for about three fourths of all exports, including nonagricultural products. Sugar maintains its historically dominant position with 54.1% of all exports, but the country also exports tomatoes, cucumbers, onions, green peppers, yucca, sweet potatoes, coconuts, plantains, avocados, pineapples, bananas, mangoes, vegetable oils, and beef.[58]

The production and flow of these goods are determined for the most part by market forces at the international level. The goods go wherever there is money to purchase them. Over 75% of this production, consequently, is bought by the United States; another 15% goes to Western Europe and Japan.[59]

One Meal a Day

While the Dominican people have watched nearly two thirds of their agricultural production be exported, food prices in the country have climbed steadily: the rise from 1969 to 1974 was nearly 50%.[60] Most Dominicans do not have the money necessary to eat decently. Although there are no known studies on the subject, firsthand observations suggest that many—perhaps most—Dominicans eat only one meal a day.

Take the Taveras family in the town of La Romana,[61] where G+W's Central Romana mill is located. They live about a mile from the sugar mill and the sprawling company installation that overlooks the Caribbean. The dusty streets of the Taveras's neighborhood are lined with one-story cement houses and a few older wooden homes set back in yards. The roads are paved here, but a few blocks away the terrain is nearly rural, reflecting the disorderly growth of the town as country people gradually gave up the struggle on the land and settled near the town wherever they found space.

Fourteen persons live in the Taveras's four-room dwelling. Presiding over the house is Doña Ana, 52-year-old mother of nine children, one of whom has four children of her own. Arriving around one in the afternoon, a visitor found the family in the midst of a meal consisting of one small bowl of soup per person. The soup was called *bollo* and contained a dumpling made of corn flour, along with some noodles and chicken parts. Asked what they usually ate, Doña Ana replied, "Whatever turns up." "As far as the capital will reach," someone else said. Doña Ana herself was a heavy, slow-moving woman, but all the others looked very lean. Some of the young men were shirtless and the outline of their ribs was clear beneath the tight skin. The six-month-old baby seemed terribly sick, with its runny nose and constant crying.

Of the nine adults in the house, only one had a steady full-time job. She worked in a textile factory in G+W's Industrial Free Zone, where she earned $15 a week. Another woman earned $25 a month at a part-time office job; two others took in washing and ironing, for which they made a dollar or two a day, when there was work. Most of the men did irregular odd jobs around town, usually in some way connected with the mill, for which they made about $6 a day. None of the men had worked in more than a week, even though they had appeared every day at the 3 p.m. lineup in front of the company employment offices. That day Doña Ana had $2.08 to spend for food, the full cost of *bollo* for the family. They had eaten nothing in the morning and would eat nothing in the evening, a pattern which they said was normal.

When there is more money they buy rice, beans, and beef; on some Sundays they have a salad of cucumbers, tomatoes, lettuce; occasionally there is fried fish, which they said was cheaper than meat. The day before they had eaten only *bollo,* with yucca and more water than usual to make it stretch, and the last Sunday "there was nothing; we drew a blank."

This one-meal-a-day pattern was repeated consistently among the cane cutters' families.[62] During the six-month harvest, there are about 100,000 people living in the fields who are directly dependent on the wages paid by Gulf+Western.[63]

Late one morning in June 1974, four boys walked along a road near one of the company *bateyes* (villages). The youngest was 12 and the oldest, 15. Each carried a machete; they were on their way to rest during the hot early afternoon hours. The only thing they had eaten since rising at dawn was sugarcane. The juicy inner core of the cane, from which the industrial process extracts the sucrose that eventually becomes sugar, is also the universal food of the field workers. Throughout the day, whenever there is a break in the work, they slice off the green covering of stalk and chew on the sweet white core. It is a free source of energy, and its liquid eases hunger. Asked about their next meal, the four boys said that they would not eat until six that evening, when they expected to have yucca and *arepas* (fried corncakes). What about meat? they were asked. One boy smiled shyly and said, "That's pretty hard to get."[64]

Sometimes the company kills an old ox and sells the meat for 25¢ a pound, but even that price may be too high for the budgets of these workers. From a dozen other cane cutters in the area that day, the story was the same:[65] sugarcane during the day and a meal at night. Even beans seemed to be somewhat of a delicacy, and one man said he could not remember the last time he had eaten meat—"maybe a year or two ago."[66]

The reporter who was asking these questions had a bushel basket filled with mangoes in the back of his pickup. They cost 50¢ at a highway stand about five miles away. As he prepared to leave, he offered one to the man with whom he had been talking.

Three or four others standing nearby moved in closer and held out their hands. Suddenly there were dozens of men scrambling around the basket; some carried away several mangoes, stuffed into their pockets or held in their ragged shirts, eating as they sprinted into the fields. The basket was empty in 20 seconds. There was no way to stop them.[67]

The incident recalled an earlier statement by a G+W executive when he was asked why he always carried a loaded pistol.

"This is a country where anyone who has three people working under him has to carry a gun," he said.[68]

A survey of the nutritional status of Dominicans made in 1969 by Dr. W. Henry Sebrell of New York's Columbia University (with the help of the Williams-Waterman Foundation and the Pan American Health Organization) showed that of the carefully selected sample of some 5,500 persons, more than half were anemic and revealed a chronic malnutrition since birth. Although the weight of a Dominican baby is approximately normal at birth, the child begins to demonstrate subnormal growth at the end of the first year, with the deficit increasing after each year of life. The average 13-year-old was found to be 22 pounds under normal weight and 12 centimeters (4.72 inches) shorter than normal height.[69]

In analyzing the nutritional value of family diets, the

survey found that average calorie intake was 79% of the amount recommended by INCAP, the Institute of Nutrition of Central America and Panama (a deficit of 452 calories per person per day). The average protein intake was 62% of the amount recommended. These average figures probably understate the degree of malnutrition in large sectors of the population.[70] Analysis of the diets of two poor communities, for example, showed protein consumption among these people to be only 34% of the recommended intake.[71]

Many nutritionists emphasize the importance of education in correcting the deficiencies in people's diets. They point out, for instance, that the traditional plate of rice and beans would satisfy protein and calorie requirements if the rice and beans were consumed in the proper amounts and proportion, which usually requires an increase in the amount of beans. But the economic barriers standing between ordinary Dominicans and a more nutritional diet are formidable. At 25¢ a pound, the price of beans is 30% higher than that of rice.[72] And this price difference is a decisive factor for many families who often do not have enough on their plates to fill their stomachs.

Political Influence

The political opposition has made G+W one of its prime targets for criticism. But the sympathies of the government, headed by Joaquín Balaguer, lie with the company.[73]

A multinational firm's political influence on a government is generally difficult to trace. But many Dominicans believe that G+W had a hand in digging the enormous loopholes in the 1972 law restricting extension of sugar acreage. Many also believe that G+W and other big landowners are using political influence to sabotage the land reform laws. So convinced was he of this influence that Marino Vinicio Castillo, a former member of the Land Reform Commission, resigned his post in protest. He claims that at least 10% of the land G+W utilizes for sugar is choice agricultural soil which is subject to expropriation under existing laws.[74]

The government has, however, imposed some restrictions on G+W. It does require the company to keep about half its earnings in the country. But the result has been such massive reinvestment and diversification that G+W now penetrates many more sectors of the Dominican economy. A newspaper article in August 1973 estimated that "in the Dominican Republic there are at least 89 companies that Gulf+Western possesses, controls, or influences in some form."[75] The company has investments in tourism, cement, cattle-raising and agricultural commodities other than sugar and furfural (a chemical by-product of sugar used in plastics).[76] Moreover, through its former finance company, COFINASA, G+W bought shares in scores of Dominican businesses, from fertilizers to rum to luxuriously appointed medical centers.[77]

But the extent of G+W's grip on the Dominican economy provoked such political opposition[78] that, under pressure, the company formally divested itself of COFINASA—though under an arrangement in which G+W retains a great deal of influence over the finance company's activities. Some $75,000 of COFINASA shares were sold to the Bank of America, and another $75,000 were "donated" to the Fundación Universitaria del Este. One important string attached is that 65% of the income from these shares is to be used for development of sports in the Dominican Republic "and in particular for the maintenance of the magnificent installations of the Juan Pablo Duarte Olympic Center," a new sports complex built for the recent Pan American Games. What COFINASA had in mind for these funds, still administered by the COFINASA board of directors, was indicated two weeks later with the visit of Irving M. Felt, Chairman of the Madison Square Garden Corp., to the Dominican Republic to advise the government on how to use the new sports center.[79] Gulf+Western holds a controlling interest in the Madison Square Garden Corporation.

One of G+W's most significant investments outside of sugar has been in the operation of a tax-exempt Industrial Free Zone which has been used primarily by U.S. plants seeking cheap labor. Under a 30-year contract with the

Dominican government signed in 1969, G+W has been empowered to operate this zone near the city of La Romana. "The unusual characteristic of such a contract is the fact that it places this zone among the very few in the world that are directed by private enterprise with its attendant efficiency," observes a company publication.[80]

Any company chartered outside the Dominican Republic which settles in the free zone receives a 20-year exemption on all taxes—corporate taxes, taxes on profits and dividends declared locally, production or sales taxes, patent taxes, and municipal taxes. The companies are also exempt for 20 years from all duties and excise taxes on imported goods necessary for production, and on goods and products exported to foreign countries.[81]

The theory behind the zone is that the country will benefit from the increased employment created by the new industries. A G+W publication estimates, using 1970 data, that there are 15,355 unemployed workers in the town of La Romana out of an economically active population of 26,856, and that within a twenty-mile radius of the zone there are 25,000 persons "available for work."[82] In its first four years of operation, the zone created about 2,500 jobs.[83]

But wages in the zone are generally very low. In mid 1974 hourly wages in the free zone ranged from a 25¢ minimum to 60¢ for some specialized workers; zone rates were even lower than the national rates in certain industries.[84]

G+W maintains a tight hold over labor policies in the zone. According to a G+W publication, which was designed to attract companies to the zone, "The Central Romana Sugar Mill has a highly experienced personnel department from whose record files the firm can select all the labor force needed for each type of industry. The plant manager will only need to submit his list of requirements and the time-consuming job of careful selection and recruitment in all labor categories will be handled by this department."[85] Union organizers claim that G+W's control over zone labor policies also extends to the firing of workers suspected of being sympathetic to efforts—thus far unsuccessful—to unionize these plants.[86]

Many of the zone's companies come from Puerto Rico, where they had previously moved their U.S.-based operations in order to take advantage of tax breaks and lower wages. Companies in the free zone include: two bra manufacturers, subsidiaries of Maidenform and Warnaco; two cable manufacturers, subsidiaries of Tenna Corp. and Potter Instruments; Romana Industries, a subsidiary of the Pajama Corporation of America; Makress, Inc.; Romana Athletic, a subsidiary of Brooks Shoe; Textiles International; National Components, Inc.; Berkeley International Hairgood, Inc.; and Delta Brush, subsidiary of Binney & Smith, Inc.[87]

The Role of the U.S. Government

In the last 60 years, the United States has twice launched military invasions of the Dominican Republic. The first was mounted in 1916, for the ostensible purpose of straightening out the Dominican Republic's financial obligations to European nations; this invasion was followed by eight years of U.S. military occupation and 30 years of dictatorship under Rafael Trujillo.[88] The second invasion in 1965, for the purpose of "preventing another Cuba,"[89] was followed by 15 months of military occupation and the accession to power of Joaquín Balaguer, former assistant to Trujillo, who in the summer of 1974 was elected for his third four-year term.

It is impossible to separate these invasions from the activities of the multinational corporations in the country. During the first invasion, the South Puerto Rico Sugar Company began operating its Central Romana mill; with the aid of land reform laws written and enforced by the U.S. occupation government, SPRSC acquired its first 144,000 acres.[90] During the second occupation, Gulf+Western began negotiating the acquisition of SPRSC. An intensive U.S. aid program soon followed.[91] Since the 1965 intervention, U.S. aid to the Dominican economy averaged close to $50 million a year.[92]

The U.S. government has provided a good deal of additional assistance to the multinational corporations operating in the Dominican Republic. In November 1972, Gulf+Western Americas Corp. borrowed $765,000 from the Export-Import Bank to finance the purchase of sugar mill equipment. Early in 1974, G+W obtained a $3.5 million loan from the same source for expansion of Central Romana's furfural plant. Eximbank loans carry interest rates well below those charged by commercial banks.[93]

Gulf+Western's molasses production is insured by another U.S. agency, the Overseas Private Investment Corporation (OPIC), in the amount of $4.8 million. Other U.S. food companies in the Dominican Republic are likewise insured by OPIC: Carnation for $7.9 million, Stokely-Van Camp for $1.9 million, and Warner-Lambert (its confectionary products) for $1.15 million.[94] If there were "another Cuba" in the Dominican Republic, it is OPIC—and ultimately the U.S. taxpayers—which would have to make good to the companies for their losses.

The amount of direct U.S. assistance to Dominican agriculture has been cut back drastically in recent years. Today there are only two full-time U.S. Agency for International Development technicians in the agricultural sector. They work with the government in an attempt to develop programs aimed at increasing production of rice, beans, corn, oil crops, fruits, vegetables, dairy products, and meat.[95] But the success of these programs has been mixed. Although there have been significant increases in the production of poultry, pork, rice, and some vegetables in recent years,[96] there is little evidence that the increased production is achieving the intended goal[97] of providing a healthier diet for Dominicans.

The major problem is that with very few exceptions (such as sporadic government bans on the export of rice and beef), much of the increase in production finds its way into the international market on the basis of the same rationale offered by the sugar industry for so long: the need to increase foreign earnings. Today, with the added "developmental" goal of encouraging profit-oriented industry in the Dominican Republic, the government tends not to interfere with companies' marketing plans. "Where the food goes depends on markets," said a USAID official in Santo Domingo.[98]

Officials of the United States, President Gerald R. Ford among them, have insisted on the need to encourage the poor countries of the world to become self-sufficient in food.[99] But while the President laments the failure of countries like the Dominican Republic to feed themselves, the major share of the food produced in that country goes not to the people who live there but into the export market to increase foreign earnings—and profits for Gulf+Western.

6/ONE MAN'S MEAT

Food imperialism, through the marketplace, by the rich over the poor, is one of the most crucial problems confronting man.

Lyle P. Schertz, Deputy Administrator
U.S. Department of Agriculture[1]

There are two basic perspectives from which authorities today tend to view the world food shortage. One emphasizes the need for increasing food production (while holding down population growth). The other emphasizes the need for more equitable distribution of available food and of the income needed to purchase it. The U. S. government and spokesmen for multinational agribusiness talk mostly about production,[2] while some of the world's best-known experts in nutrition are showing an increasing concern over distribution.

No one denies that the world's production of food must increase dramatically if it is to keep pace with the population growth expected in the coming decades, but the experience of the last 20 years has taught nutritionists that dramatic production increases do not automatically result in more food for the really hungry people of this earth. Very much depends upon the kind of food produced, the social and economic conditions under which it is produced, and the ultimate consumer for whom it is produced.

"In the formulation of supply strategies," writes Alan Berg, who currently directs nutrition programs for the World Bank, "the relation between food supply increases and the circumstances of the malnourished is seldom explicitly taken into account. . . . Explicit measures are almost never taken to raise the effective demand of the poor. Nor are agricultural research efforts usually designed with an acknowledged concern for the nutritional content of output—especially of food largely eaten by the poor."[3] Berg points out that in Taiwan, where average per capita income is only $270 per year, the malnutrition problem is not as great as in Mexico, where the average annual income of $530 is more unevenly distributed.[4] Indeed, Mexico has a serious malnutrition problem despite the fact that the new miracle wheat and corn varieties were developed there and Mexico is now an exporter of grains.[5]

Dr. Moises Behar, Director of the Institute of Nutrition of Central America and Panama (INCAP), was reported recently by *The New York Times* as telling the Pacific Science Congress that the ordering of social structures is of far greater importance in combating world hunger than economic development or the Green Revolution. Malnutrition, said Behar, "is primarily a manifestation of social injustice." Behar praised "the extraordinary and well-intentioned achievements in agricultural technology" that followed the introduction of improved crop strains, but he added, according to the *Times,* that most of those living on subsistence agriculture could not benefit from this new technology.[6]

Multinational enterprise, especially that portion of it called "agribusiness," plays a key role in the solution of the world food problem. Its interest in, and contribution to, increased food production is undeniable. But its role in improving distribution is another matter. We have seen what little benefit Gulf+Western's sugar operations in the Dominican Republic have been to the subsistence farmers and landless laborers of that country. We now look at another case, this one from Colombia, in which a multinational's leadership in improving production of one type of food has displaced land from production of another—resulting in a net loss in the amount of protein available to the poor.

Pulses and Poultry in Colombia

Pulses are the edible seeds of various vegetable crops such as peas, beans, lentils, chickpeas, pigeon peas, and broad beans. Pulses are 18–25% protein—and protein of a very high quality. In addition, says Alan Berg, "Pulses are one of the best sources of iron: an average serving of beans, for example, provides six to twelve times the iron of a slice of unenriched bread. Their riboflavin content is five times greater than most cereals, their thiamine content ten times greater. For these reasons, pulses are frequently called 'the poor man's meat'."[7]

In certain parts of Colombia, including the departments of Cauca and Valle, pulses—mostly in the form of "dry beans"—are the basic food of the majority of the population.[8] But Colombian production of pulses has been steadily declining since the mid 1950s, and the chief reason for the decline has been the loss of area in Valle and Cauca to other crops.[9] In 1958 about 51,000 acres were planted with pulses in the Cauca valley; during the period from 1970 through 1974 the average was 7,178 acres.[10]

No sorghum was planted in Cauca in 1958, but from 1970 through 1974 it was planted on an average of 61,446 acres.[11] During this same period, soybean acreage increased from about 15,000 to an average of 141,674.[12] Like pulses, soybeans have a very high protein content, but in Colombia people do not eat them. Both soybeans and sorghum are grown for animal feed.

The impetus for this shift of land away from pulses for human consumption to soybeans and sorghum for animal feed came with the arrival of the Ralston Purina Company in Colombia in the early 1950s.

Poultry and Purina

Ralston Purina's Colombian subsidiary, Purina Colombiana, is essentially a feed company. The growth of a feed company obviously depends upon the growth of an industry to consume that feed. And so Purina, wherever it goes, promotes just such growth, typically by developing a local poultry industry.

The effectiveness of this strategy is well illustrated by the fact that in countries like Mexico and Colombia, where the poultry and concentrated feed industries have grown rapidly in tandem over the last two decades, the poultry industry absorbs more than 70% of the production of the feed industry.[13] For other reasons, too, poultry production has been traditionally favored by the U.S. feed companies that, like Purina, have been moving into underdeveloped areas at a rapid rate since World War II. The poultry business requires less initial capital and land than the cattle feed-lot business. Moreover, poultry feeds are among the most profitable for the feed industry. Most important, though, the poultry business guarantees a steady demand for the feed industry's products: once a flock of chickens has been purchased, a farmer has no choice but to continue buying concentrated feed. Chickens cannot be turned out to pasture like cattle or hogs.

The concentrated feed industry began in Colombia in the early 1950s with the introduction of Purina products into the country.[14] In 1957, Purina established its first local factory in Cartagena, on the Caribbean coast.*[15] The arrival of Purina stimulated the development of several local feed companies,[16] which now sell between 60% and 65% of all the concentrated feed in Colombia.[17] But Purina's 35% to 45% share still makes it the dominant force within the industry.[18] Purina's sales (and profits) have risen steadily over the years; in 1973, 240,000 metric tons of feed, costing about $12 million, were sold in Colombia.[19]

In its early years there, Purina worked hard to expand the local market for its poultry feed. A farmer who bought Purina's feed could also buy baby chicks from the company. Furthermore, he could obtain from Purina the technical assistance and credit necessary to get himself started as a chicken farmer.[20]

In order to meet the demands of this expanding market, Purina found it necessary to guarantee the continuing availability of essential feed ingredients such as sorghum and soybeans. The company began financing the

*In 1958 Purina's construction was helped along by a modest loan of $83,000 from the U.S. government under the Cooley Loan provision of Public Law 480. In Mexico, Peru, and Chile, Purina obtained over $2 million worth of these loans. These loans are made in non-convertible local currencies.

production of these crops by paying farmers in advance for them. Purina itself also offered credit and in addition encouraged both government and private credit institutions to lend money for these crops.[21] The drive to expand the production of feed crops was very successful. Feed crop acreage, as we have seen, grew dramatically.

So did the production of poultry and eggs. In 1957, when Purina built its first factory in Colombia, the country was importing eggs.[22] By 1961, egg imports had stopped and poultry production had begun to rise sharply.[23] From 1966 to 1971, annual broiler production doubled, from 11 million to 22 million birds.[24] From 1970 to 1973, annual egg production increased from 1.1 to 2.0 billion.[25] The commercialization of poultry production had now made chicken cheaper than red meat for the first time in Colombia's history.

Poultry, Eggs, and Purchasing Power

In other circumstances this breakthrough in poultry and egg production might have meant a significant improvement in the national diet. Most non-vegetarian peoples would add eggs and meat to their diets if they could afford it. But the poorest and most malnourished sector of the Colombian population still cannot afford to eat chicken and eggs very often, despite their greater availability. For Colombia has one of the worst income distributions in the world.

Per capita income in Colombia was $335 in 1969,[26] but 27% of the population earned less than $75 a year.[27] In 1970 the average price of a kilogram* of chicken in Bogotá was 84¢ and the average price of a dozen grade B eggs was 40¢.[28] This means that for about a quarter of the population, a dozen eggs and a kilogram of chicken cost the equivalent of a week's earnings or more.

According to industry figures, per capita egg consumption has been growing in Colombia since 1963.[29] But the way income is distributed in Colombia, these per capita figures do not mean that the lower-income

*A kilogram is a metric unit equal to 2.2046 lbs.

population has been eating more eggs. They simply mean that the middle and upper classes are eating more eggs, either directly or in the form of processed foods.[30]

The Protein Deficit

The displacement of cropland from pulses to feed crops did not simply replace a cheap source of protein with an expensive one. It also reduced the total availability of protein in the country, because animal sources of protein are less efficient to produce than are vegetable sources. It takes about 6 grams of vegetable protein to produce 1 gram of protein in the form of chicken compared to only 2.6 grams to produce it in the form of eggs, according to estimates made at the Universidad del Valle.[31] The land used to grow pulses can satisfy the protein requirements of more people than land used for animal feed crops.

The following chart, based on actual growing conditions in the Valle region of Colombia, shows the number of people who can obtain their minimum protein requirement for one day from a hectare* of land according to how the land is used.[32]

Land used to grow:	*For humans to eat:*	*Supplies one day's protein** requirement for:*	*At (1972) cost to consumer of:*
Feed crops	as chicken	1,430 people	200 pesos/kg
Feed crops	as eggs	3,900 people	140 pesos/kg
Beans (*frijol*)	directly	4,300 people	75 pesos/kg
Soybeans	directly	22,700 people	12 pesos/kg

If its hungry masses had taken a sudden liking to soybeans, then clearly the shift in production from pulses to soybeans would have been good for Colombia. But, in

* A hectare is a metric unit equal to about 2.47 acres.

** These figures take into account the biological value of the protein in each case.

order to remain cheap, soybeans have to be eaten directly, as pulses are. Efforts in Colombia to process soybeans in a form that is both palatable and inexpensive have, as we shall see in the following chapter, been unsuccessful.

Purina did not come to Colombia to promote soybeans for human consumption. Its aim was simply to promote the feed industry from which it derives its profits. In a context different from Colombia's, this effort might have contributed to the struggle against malnutrition, had it stimulated, as a by-product, the production of more chickens, more eggs—*more protein*—for a protein-poor population. Unfortunately, and not only indirectly, the precise opposite has occurred. As more and more productive land has been diverted from the cultivation of pulses to feed crops, Colombia's domestic production of protein has fallen increasingly short of the needs of its people.

In 1960, when the country's population was 15.4 million, domestic protein production in Colombia fell short of the nation's protein requirements by 40,000 metric tons. By 1970, the population had increased about one third (to 21.1 million), but the protein deficit had almost tripled, to 115,000 metric tons. At present, population is estimated at 23 million, and the protein deficit somewhere between 130,000 and 150,000 metric tons.[33]

Ralston Purina's Director of Latin American Operations says that "the contribution of our company worldwide is definitely positive. . . . I think we have been pioneers in developing more food for the people of the countries where we are."[34] In the case of Colombia, this may indeed have been Purina's intention, but the effect of the company's presence there has been something quite different: more food for a minority and less for the majority.

7/THE PROTEIN BUSINESS

In the decade of the 1960s, U. S. multinationals in the food industry tried to develop, produce, and market protein-rich processed foods as a means of combating malnutrition in underdeveloped countries. Using various combinations of natural (especially vegetable) sources of protein, companies such as Quaker Oats, CPC International, Coca-Cola, General Foods, General Mills, and Monsanto manufactured pre-cooked flours, grain-oilseed mixes, and even soft drinks, in an attempt to show that private enterprise could make a significant contribution to the fight against malnutrition in these countries.[1] Some of these companies embarked on such ventures at their own initiative.[2] But many were persuaded to enter the field by U.S. government officials who were convinced that the research and development expertise, marketing skills, management ability, and investment capability of the U.S. food industry could be harnessed into producing low-cost highly nutritious foods to help solve the problem of malnutrition.[3]

The reasons U.S. companies undertook these experiments were varied. According to Alan Berg, now head of nutrition for the World Bank, the main motives were the corporations' desire to improve relations with governments in foreign countries and with U.S. government agencies involved in financing development; general public relations considerations; the fear of being left behind by competitors should the field become more commercially important; and an altruistic concern with social good. But the most important motive, Berg says, was "corporate image."[4]

One of the earliest commercial ventures in protein-rich

foods involving a U.S. multinational in an underdeveloped country was initiated in the 1950s, when General Mills and a Mexican firm set up a joint venture to introduce PROTEA—a protein-rich Multi-Purpose Food (MPF)—into Mexico.[5] (The basic formula for MPF had been developed by Dr. Henry Borsook of California Institute of Technology in 1944.[6])

Many more ventures were begun in the middle 1960s, especially after the U.S. government in 1964 established the Commercial Studies High-Protein Food Program, which was designed to induce food companies to experiment in this field. Under this program, initiated by the Agency for International Development, U.S. corporations were given grants of up to $60,000 to explore the feasibility of developing and marketing high-protein foods for low-income markets.[7] But this program, as well as a successor program, the Nutrition and Agribusiness Group, which made grants to local companies in the underdeveloped countries themselves, produced only limited and disappointing results. Both were allowed to lapse at the end of their statutory lives. The Commercial Studies program awarded its last grants in 1970, and the second program was being phased out in mid 1974.[8]

In fact, the outstanding characteristic of nearly all the attempts by private companies to market protein-rich foods to the poor has been their lack of success. The major reason for this is that most companies found it impossible to market protein-rich products at a price that was both low enough for people to afford and high enough for the company to make a profit.[9] As soon as companies realized that the foods could not be profitable, they abandoned the projects. The only successful commercial ventures were those in which the food attracted a middle-income market.* But in almost no case was a commercially sold protein-rich food successful in reaching the people who really need it—the poor.

---

*VITASOY, for example; see discussion of high-protein beverages beginning on page 108.

Quaker and Incaparina

The most important protein-rich product produced in Latin America is Incaparina, a pre-cooked flour mixture developed by the Institute of Nutrition of Central America and Panama (INCAP). Supported by the Pan American Health Organization and the World Health Organization, INCAP has worked to provide low-cost high-protein foods to the poor in many Latin American countries. Incaparina, in various formulations, has been marketed in El Salvador, Guatemala, Nicaragua, Panama, Brazil, Colombia, and Venezuela, sometimes by local firms and sometimes by multinationals.[10]

The case of Incaparina in Colombia illustrates many of the problems inherent in the attempt to solve protein-calorie deficits in underdeveloped areas through private enterprise.

Productos Quáker, S.A., the wholly-owned Colombian subsidiary of Quaker Oats Co., undertook in 1961–62 to adapt to the Colombian market the protein-rich Incaparina formula developed by INCAP. In order to obtain a license to use the INCAP formula—and to obtain the benefit of the world-wide publicity which Incaparina had received—Quaker had to meet the nutritional specifications laid down by INCAP and receive its approval for the price charged. But Quaker could, and did, modify the original formula. The company partially substituted soy and corn flour to match the original Incaparina's protein content of 27.5%.[11]

The initial sales campaign pushed INCAPARINA as a low-cost nutritional beverage for poor people.[12] The beverage form held more promise than the cereal or porridge form tried in some other countries, because the Colombian consumer was used to the traditional *colada,* a beverage based on grain or other flours. And the initial sales were indeed promising. By 1967, INCAPARINA sales had reached 2,000 metric tons a year—the annual capacity of Quaker's Cali plant.[13] But due to a combination of factors, including taste- and eye-appeal problems, a price-cost squeeze, and the introduction of more attractive competing products, INCAPARINA began losing sales and money in 1967. By 1969, sales had plummeted to 1,200 metric tons,[14] and the product was withdrawn from the market at the end of 1973.[15]

Because INCAPARINA's total sales figure in Colombia was one of the higher in the Latin American protein-rich food experience, nutritionists from the Food and Agricultural Organization of the United Nations (FAO), the World Food Program, and other international agencies tend to regard INCAPARINA as a success in Colombia, according to Alan Davis, president of Productos Quáker, S.A.[16] But Productos Quáker "never considered INCAPARINA a market success . . . sales were a drop in the bucket compared with our oat products."[17] Of 200 million pesos ($8 million) in Quaker-Colombian sales in 1973, only 4 million pesos, or 2% of sales, were in INCAPARINA. Davis continues, "We were always either losing money or at best breaking even on INCAPARINA. . . . In 1973 we lost a million pesos, and had we continued production this year we would have lost at least that much—that's $40,000."[18]

From the beginning the Colombian government had imposed price controls to keep INCAPARINA accessible to the poor. Thus Quaker, like most companies involved in protein-rich food schemes, found itself in a constantly tightening cost-price squeeze. The cost of INCAPARINA's basic ingredient rose sharply with worldwide oilseed prices in 1973, the last year of production. To cover the cost increases and still clear the 20–25% profit that Quaker considers "minimally needed to survive" in the Colombian market would have required a 100% price increase, putting the product clearly out of reach of the target population.[19]

There were other reasons, of course, for the failure of the product and the ultimate decision to withdraw it. One was the lack of any backing for INCAPARINA by extensive promotional campaigns. "We never put money behind it because of price controls," Davis admitted.[20] Furthermore, in the advertising that was done, errors of social psychology may have contributed to consumer rejection of INCAPARINA. Davis says, "It was almost turned into a medicinal product."[21] A Colombian home economist and dietician suggested that it was rejected because it was seen by many as "poor people's food" and therefore of a lower quality.[22] Dr. Teresa de Buckle, a Colombian nutritionist, put it a different way: "People, as malnourished as they may be, have taste."[23]

Some of INCAPARINA's troubles may also have been due to the problem of product acceptability, related to eye and taste appeal. Until 1969, Quaker's INCAPARINA had an unappetizing greenish hue, caused by the cottonseed flour ingredient.[24] It was only after the relative success of POCHITO and COLOMBIHARINA, competing "white" products launched by local processors in 1967,[25] that Quaker began offering an alternative. In 1969 it introduced INCAPARINA BLANCA, made from rice and soy flour, and began packaging both products in more functional plastic bags instead of paper wrapping.[26] None of these changes, however, improved sales significantly.[27] Davis himself blames INCAPARINA's low consumer acceptance on the soybean taste. But Productos Quáker made no attempt to process the soy flour to improve its flavor. Even though such processing might make sense in a large market like Brazil or the United States, said Davis, it is too expensive for the limited Colombian market.[28]

The problem of consumer acceptance was apparently not overcome even though INCAPARINA was at first widely distributed throughout Colombia. Once in the stores, it simply "didn't move much."[29] Consequently, smaller stores in poor urban neighborhoods would no longer occupy their limited shelf space with the product, thereby further reducing its accessibility.

The strength of INCAPARINA's competitors also influenced Quaker's decision to pull the product off the market. "Since COLOMBIHARINA and [beginning in 1969] DURYEA* were available," and unlike INCAPARINA, not subject to price controls, "we didn't feel too bad about

---

* A product of CPC International. See further discussion beginning at page 105.

pulling out," Davis said.[30] The company claims to have written its customers suggesting COLOMBIHARINA and the more expensive DURYEA as substitutes.[31] Soon after INCAPARINA's withdrawal, however, Molinos Santa Rita, a Colombian firm, also withdrew COLOMBIHARINA, and the ability of poor people to afford DURYEA is highly questionable.

But Davis insists that the withdrawal of INCAPARINA did not indicate the company's lack of concern about nutrition. Oats, which account for 50% of the subsidiary's annual sales and reach a broad spectrum of consumers, are a highly nutritional product, according to Davis.

"The parent corporation was disappointed when we decided to drop the product," Davis states. The subsidiary's marketing department recently considered repackaging INCAPARINA AS CAPITÁN KOOL, with a publicity campaign appealing strongly to children. But the idea was quickly dropped. The marketing manager said, "Let's save CAPITÁN KOOL for a good product. Let's not waste any more time on INCAPARINA."[32]

Other Quaker subsidiaries in Latin America have also participated in protein-rich food ventures:

•*In Venezuela*, Quáker-Venezuela introduced an Incaparina product in 1965 in a poorly promoted trial market in one provincial city. Although several factors contributed to the product's commercial failure, one of the most important was the lack of a Venezuelan tradition of grain-based drinks (an important difference from the Colombian case). The high costs of labor and packaging, the lack of local government support, competition from USAID-donated powdered milk in the institutional market, and the product's high cost in comparison with corn meal (the staple grain) combined to kill the company's interest in finding a more adequate protein-rich food vehicle.[33]

•*In Nicaragua*, Quáker de Centroamérica test-marketed NUTREMAS, also based on the Incaparina formula, in 1968–69. "Unfavorable consumer reaction" led the subsidiary to drop this experiment, which was to have served Costa Rica as well.[34]

•*In Guyana*, a Quaker subsidiary successfully manufactures and distributes the soy-based soft drink PUMA. (See page 109.)

•*In Colombia*, Productos Quáker, in another effort there, test-marketed a protein-enriched version of its AREPARINA-brand cornflour, to be used in making the traditional *arepa* cornbread, but the effort was unsuccessful.[35]

CPC International: A Tale of Two Coladas

Beginning in 1969, one of INCAPARINA's competitors in the protein-rich grain-based beverage market in Colombia was DURYEA, a product of CPC International, one of the largest multinational food manufacturers in the United States. A 28%-protein mixture containing cornstarch, high-lysine corn flour, and soy flour, DURYEA was the fruit of years of research conducted by CPC, Massachusetts Institute of Technology, and the Universidad del Valle in Colombia.[36] One of CPC's competitors, however, has suggested that DURYEA was also the fruit of CPC's desire to pick up a corporate image dragged down by another of its products—MAIZENA, a cornstarch so widely used in Latin America that its brand name has become the popular word there for cornstarch.[37]

CPC, formerly known as Corn Products Company, entered Latin America in 1928 and began operations in Colombia in 1933.[38] In 1959, it obtained a loan of $600,000 from the U.S. government for the expansion of its MAIZENA production in Colombia. In 1964, it received an additional loan of $210,000 for further expansion. Made in non-convertible local currency, both these loans were part of the U.S. Food for Peace program (P.L. 480) known as "Cooley loans."[39]

MAIZENA, like other cornstarches, has several culinary uses, but in Latin America it is very commonly used among the urban poor as a weaning food for infants. In Colombia, for example, MAIZENA is mixed with water and raw sugar to make a *colada*.[40] In Brazil, it is combined with milk and sugar to make a baby porridge.[41] CPC's promotion reinforced this practice and the idea that MAIZENA was an excellent infant food by showing pictures of fat, healthy babies in MAIZENA advertising material.[42]

But as early as 1946, Dr. Renato Woisky, head pediatrician at Santa Casa charity hospital in São Paulo, had begun fighting this concept and the image that MAIZENA had already acquired in the poorest sections of that community.[43] His belief that infants filled up with cornstarch are prevented from obtaining other needed nutrients was endorsed by other nutritionists who attacked CPC promotion designed to convince the poor to buy a product that made babies fat but not healthy. Several years ago, in response to complaints from such eminent authorities as Moises Behar, head of INCAP,[44] and Max Milner, former secretary of the U.N. Protein Advisory Group,[45] CPC did agree to stop advertising MAIZENA as a weaning food. But eating habits entrenched among the poor by decades of promotion have not been disrupted by this latter-day change in tactics. MAIZENA continues to be extremely popular as a baby food; it is one of the few processed food products sold in small stores in poor neighborhoods throughout Latin America.

CPC executives in Colombia deny that MAIZENA's bad image was a factor in their decision to introduce protein-rich DURYEA, also a *colada*-type product for babies. But Alan Davis of Productos Quáker, a competitor of CPC, believes that CPC's need "to improve an image hurt by MAIZENA" was the driving force behind DURYEA.[46]

In formulating DURYEA, CPC tried to avoid some of the errors that had contributed to INCAPARINA's downfall. According to Wolfgang Klein, Assistant Manager of CPC's Colombian operations, "In our mind, you cannot sell nutrition. . . . We took a critical look at what others did wrong, and learned from their mistakes. INCAPARINA was not approached from a marketing standpoint."[47]

DURYEA was introduced to the market with great fanfare. Maizena, S.A., CPC's corn products division, hired a new advertising firm to handle the account.[48] The product was promoted not as a poor people's food but as a weaning food for babies, with a box reminiscent of baby cereals sold in the United States. Although the use of soy flour, as in INCAPARINA, gave the *colada* a somewhat heavy taste, DURYEA was formulated with a greater concern for flavor and eye appeal.[49]

After five years on the market, however, DURYEA sales had not reached INCAPARINA's 1967 peak of 2,000 metric tons per year. Monthly DURYEA sales in mid 1974 stood at about 150–160 metric tons.[50] Nor did all of these sales go to the nutritionally needy: unlike INCAPARINA, which was promoted as a poor people's food, DURYEA is also purchased by high-income families.[51]

Although the company claims that DURYEA is "going where it should be"[52]—to the malnourished—the product's price (twice that of INCAPARINA, because DURYEA is not subject to government price controls) may have effectively removed it from its target population.[53] Colombian nutritionist Dr. de Buckle believes that DURYEA may only be reaching as far down as the lower middle class.[54] Spot checks of small stores and government-run supermarkets in poor neighborhoods indicate that while CPC's distribution system gets DURYEA into the larger enterprises, the small stores with limited shelf space prefer to carry the faster-moving MAIZENA, which outsells DURYEA nearly everywhere.[55]

J.B. Cordaro, Food Assessment Coordinator for the U.S. Office of Technology Assessment, suggests that the failure of such products to reach the poor is almost inevitable. "While U.S. industry can develop a [high-nutrition] product, it has yet to develop a system to get the product into the target stomach or to sell more food to low- and no-income groups." The industry expectation that foods of this type, once accepted by the upper and middle classes, will "trickle down" into the poorer sectors of the population has not been borne out in practice. While the trickle-down principle has often worked in the United States, "to expect [it] to work in the developing countries is to ignore the non-existence of discretionary income by the consumer."[56]

Even with its higher price, and freedom from price controls, however, DURYEA's profit performance is not much better than INCAPARINA's. Rising costs of corn and soybeans have pinched potential profits.[57] Assistant Manager Klein admits that while "DURYEA is selling well, it is not making money. We are not losing on it any longer, but we are not making money either. The sales figures are beautiful, but the bottom line is zero."[58]

According to Dr. de Buckle, Maizena, S.A., made a commitment to keep DURYEA on the market for five years, a period which would have elapsed some time in 1974.[59] Maizena has, however, apparently extended that commitment and is continuing to market DURYEA (as of late 1975).[60] But there is still no indication that the product is having any significant impact on that portion of the population which is seriously malnourished.

High-Protein Beverages

In the generally dismal book of high-protein low-cost experiments, an international survey suggests that the only thing close to a commercial success story is a soft drink: VITASOY. Manufactured in Hong Kong since 1940 by the Hong Kong Soya Bean Products Co., VITASOY has capitalized on the popularity of soy products in the Far East to become a solid commercial success.[61] Other high-protein beverages have been developed by U.S. multinationals in Latin America and elsewhere—most notably by Monsanto, Quaker Oats, Coca-Cola, and the Yoo-Hoo Chocolate Beverage Corp. of New Jersey (which sells its YOO-HOO chocolate-flavored beverage in Iran and is attempting to reformulate its product to use processed animal and vegetable protein in countries which prohibit importation of the nonfat dry milk on which it is now based[62]).

Most of these experiments, however, have been shortlived or, to date, have enjoyed only limited success. In Latin America, even in the case of the only enduring commercial success—a reformulation of VITASOY called PUMA—it remains doubtful whether the product really meets the challenge of delivering low-cost protein to the nutritionally needy.

Coca-Cola began its efforts in 1968–69, when its Brazilian subsidiary test-marketed a high-protein soft drink called SACI; like PUMA, it was based on a refined soy product, in this case soya bean milk.[63] SACI was soon withdrawn from the market and later replaced by TAI, a similar product with a different flavor, which was marketed for about three years before it was withdrawn at the end of 1973.[64] Coca-Cola, in 1974, claimed that it was evaluating these not-very-profitable experiences before deciding how to proceed.[65]

In 1966, Monsanto Research Corp. purchased from Hong Kong Soya Bean Products Co. the right to market VITASOY outside that company's Asian territory.[66] With financial help from USAID's Commercial Studies High-Protein Food Program, Monsanto adapted VITASOY and began trying, in 1967, to test its appeal in Brazil.[67] Unable to obtain soy flour properly processed for beverage production, however, Monsanto dropped the Brazilian experiment.[68] Switching to Guyana, the company in 1969 began testing the commercial feasibility of the adapted product, which it now called PUMA.[69] A local franchise company already engaged in the soft-drink business produced the beverage, and Monsanto promoted it extensively with publicity designed to associate PUMA with an image of vigor. Early in the Guyana experiment, PUMA sold 29 million bottles a year, far exceeding the original target.[70] Then in October 1971, Monsanto sold all production rights to Quaker.[71] Asked why Monsanto gave up on PUMA, an executive of the company said simply, "We decided we did not want to be in the soft drink business."[72] Quaker recalled the product for reformulation before resuming its profitable marketing.[73]

In the case of both Coca-Cola's experiments in Brazil and Monsanto's PUMA experiment in Guyana, the question remains whether such soft drink products are really adequate vehicles for getting protein to the malnourished.

First, as a food researcher for one of the companies in

this field suggested, the protein content of VITASOY and similar drinks is not very high—3% compared to the 30% in milk.[74] He claimed that a beverage sufficiently light and thirst-quenching to qualify as a soft drink simply could not carry a large percentage of protein.[75]

Secondly, as research by the companies themselves suggests, the drinks are not reaching the most protein-needy. In Guyana, Monsanto found that the strongest market for PUMA was in the 15–29 age group, not among younger children or infants for whom a protein supplement would be crucial.[76] In addition, most soft drinks were bought only on a weekly basis to be consumed on special occasions such as the Sunday meal.[77] Although Monsanto discovered that economically marginal persons usually bought two or three soft drinks per week, this intake was not considered sufficient to make the dietary protein increase significant.[78]

The SACI-TAI market test, according to Stul Beckman, a Coca-Cola executive in Rio de Janeiro, revealed that these products were well-accepted by the working-class population but did not reach poor people suffering from malnutrition.[79] As in the DURYEA case in Colombia, the people most in need of protein supplements in their diet were also least able to pay the extra costs of industrial food processing.

Thus, although they appear to offer the only potential for commercial successes in the low-cost nutritious food field, soft drinks have very limited possibilities for delivering protein to the poor. The real irony is that these limited achievements are so dwarfed by the bonanzas that are PEPSI and COKE.

8/I'D LIKE TO BUY THE WORLD A COKE

SACI, TAI, INCAPARINA, NUTREMAS, AREPARINA—dead or dying all of them, abortive efforts by multinationals to deliver protein-rich foods to poor people at prices they can afford.

Yet U.S. food companies have been very successful at marketing some kinds of products to poor people, even very poor people, in Latin America. Unfortunately, like CPC's MAIZENA, these successful products are generally foods with little or no nutritional value. The leaders in this field are undoubtedly COKE and PEPSI.

"Poor people always find enough money for a COKE," according to Quaker's Alan Davis.[1] While this claim may exaggerate reality, it accurately states Coca-Cola's hopes. The Latin American marketing strategies of the soft drink companies reach down to almost all income levels. Unlike the protein-enriched soft drinks, the ordinary variety costs so little to make that a large part of what a person pays to drink them can be reinvested in advertising to get him to drink more.

This lesson was learned years ago in the United States, where the soft drink industry has consistently been one of the most profitable industries.[2] Years of experience there had also taught the companies that the key to successful advertising was associating their products with youth and the good life, so that soft drinks would be purchased even by people who cannot afford to waste money on empty calories.

Translating this success into another language is so much easier for a multinational firm than developing new products to meet specific local needs. Nutritionally worthless foods often have more taste and eye appeal than products developed with a concern for nutritional content. And junk food comes to Latin America with the aura of Yanqui affluence—the opposite of "poor people's food" especially developed for the Latin American market.

But whatever the reasons, the principal contribution of the U.S. food industry to the diets of Latin Americans has been and continues to be the empty calories of COKE and PEPSI. The degrees of market penetration differ: Mexico, for example, is in an advanced state of COKE and PEPSI penetration, while Brazil is still on the way.

Ain't No Mountain High Enough: Mexico

In recent years, per capita soft drink consumption in Mexico has been about 220 bottles a year, or more than four bottles a week.[3] And total consumption continues to grow: more than 10 billion bottles were sold in 1972, and 1974 sales are expected to exceed 12 billion bottles.[4]

In their continuing efforts to penetrate the Mexican market, U.S. companies have devised some ingenious advertising techniques adapted to the local scene. In the center of the bullfight ring in Mexico City, for example, a giant COCA-COLA bottle "dances" around to entertain the audiences before the fights begin. In Oaxaca, at the annual summer folklore festival, tourists pay to enter the stadium while local people picnic on the hillside above and watch the festival from there. Coca-Cola sellers in bright uniforms, carrying portable vending machines on their backs, move among the picnickers on the hillside hawking their wares.

While magazines and television carry the message effectively in large cities, the radio assures that not even the remotest mountain villages are immune from the soft drink invasion. Father Crisoforo Florencio, a full-blooded Mexican Indian, is a priest working in the mountains of Guerrero. In a letter written in June 1974, Father Florencio described how advertising has made soft drinks part of everyday life in his region:

"It seems that soft drinks are a very important factor in the development of villages. I have heard some people say they can't live one day without drinking a soft drink. Other people, in order to display social status, must have soft drinks with every meal, especially if there are guests. . . .

"Near the larger towns where daily salaries are a little higher, soft drinks are cheaper. But in the very remote villages where people earn much less, and where soft drinks have to be transported in by animals, soft drinks cost in many places up to twice as much: Zumpango, Temalacacingo, Tepetlafingo, Metlatonoc, Xixila, and others. In the first three villages people earn about 5 pesos a day (approximately 40¢). Metlatonoc has almost no sources of income. Its economy is very poor in comparison with all the villages of Guerrero. Its goats and lambs—just sufficient to provide food and clothing—are carried to the slaughterhouse and sold. The typical family in Metlatonoc can't earn more than 1,200 to 2,000 pesos a year. But even the little they receive each year they spend drinking soft drinks. In the richest village in this area, Olinala, where the majority of people are artisans and earn from 25 to 70 pesos a day ($2.00 to $5.60), about 4,000 bottles of soft drinks are consumed each day. Olinala has 6,000 inhabitants.

"The great majority of people are convinced that soft drinks must be consumed every day. This is mainly due to extensive advertising, especially on the radio which is so widespread in the mountains. . . . In the meantime, in these same villages, natural products such as fruit are consumed less—in some families just once a week. Other families sell their own natural products in order to buy soft drinks. . . ."[5]

The U.S. soft drink companies have not only succeeded, through advertising, in increasing per capita consumption of soda in Mexico, but have also, in the process, displaced local beverage companies. Twenty years ago, the Mexican soft drink market was divided equally between Mexican and foreign brands. Today, foreign brands control three quarters of the market. Coca-Cola Export Co. alone controls over 42% of all Mexican soft drink sales, marketing the brands COCA-COLA, DELAWARE PUNCH, FANTA, MISTER Q, PREMIO, SQUEEZE, SPRITE, and TEEM. Even the fruit-flavored soft drink market, the traditional bastion of local bottlers, is now dominated by Coca-Cola's FANTA.[6]

Roberto Guajardo Suarez, attorney for the National Association of Bottlers of Mexican Soft Drinks, believes that Mexican brands will disappear from the market before 1980 unless measures are taken to halt the "monopolistic invasion by American bottlers."[7]

Land of the Guaraná: Brazil

The soft drink market in Mexico may be reaching the saturation point for U.S. companies. But not so in Brazil, which has double the population of Mexico and a much lower per capita consumption of soft drinks.[8] According to industry sources, Coca-Cola and Pepsi-Cola and their subcontractors have captured 40% of the Brazilian market,[9] and the growth potential is enormous. The only obstacle is a local industry, stronger than Mexico's, which produces a popular soft drink from the guaraná fruit, a natural resource of the underdeveloped Amazon region.

Though its efforts at marketing a high-protein soft drink in Brazil have foundered, Coca-Cola is enjoying great success with its whole line of nutritionally worthless products. Especially ironic is the case of Coca-Cola's FANTA ORANGE. Brazil is one of the world's largest exporters of orange juice.[10] It sells 97.5% of its crop to foreign customers. Among them is Coca-Cola, which owns SNOW CROP and MINUTE MAID.[11] But an independent analysis done in 1971 found that FANTA ORANGE contained no orange juice.[12] Meanwhile, many Brazilians suffer from a vitamin C deficiency in their diets.[13]

Entering through the Back Door

Coca-Cola entered Brazil just as Brazil was entering World War II on the side of the United States. Brazil's support of the Allies had been uncertain: the sympathies of its current dictator, Getulio Vargas, were with the fascists, but Brazil was already more economically dependent on the United States.[14]

For reasons of his own, Vargas welcomed Coca-Cola to Brazil with amended legislation and unprecedented economic incentives. In a decree issued October 31, 1939, the law covering chemical compounds in soft drinks was changed in order to allow the use of phosphoric acid. COCA-COLA, unlike most soft drinks, cannot be produced without phosphoric acid; alternative substances would make the drink precipitate and become muddy.

Later that year, Vargas also manipulated the consumption tax regulations. He reduced the minimum size of a soft drink bottle from 333 to 178 cc's, the equivalent of COKE's 6-ounce bottle, by placing a much lower tax on the smaller bottle: 0.05 cruzeiros, or 44% less than the 0.09 cruzeiros which would have been proportionate to the tax on larger bottles. This was a direct incentive to Coca-Cola.[15]

When representatives of the local soft drink industry protested, the Brazilian government appealed to their patriotism, suggesting that failure to give commercial advantages to Coca-Cola would upset the conduct of its foreign policy in a time of world conflagration.[16]

In1941, American military bases were established in the Northeast of Brazil. In 1942, the first bottles of COCA-COLA were being sold in Rio de Janeiro.[17]

Why Brazilians Never Needed Coca-Cola

When Coca-Cola came to Brazil, the country already had a popular soft drink with stimulant properties—guaraná. Like COCA-COLA, guaraná derives its stimulant properties from caffeine; unlike COCA-COLA, the caffeine in guaraná is a natural ingredient, extracted from the seeds of the guaraná tree from which the beverage is prepared.

The long-lived guaraná tree grows in the Amazon basin, where it is an important economic factor for the settlers of remote areas. Present production of guaraná in the Amazon is close to 400 tons per year.[18]

Brahma and Antartica, the two largest Brazilian beverage producers, both manufacture popular soft drinks from the fruit of the guaraná. Since these companies were originally beer producers, accustomed to the technique of pasteurization, they are able to avoid the use of such compounds as phosporic acid, brominated vegetable oil,* and artificial coloring (which have been used in products of the Coca-Cola and Pepsi-Cola companies).Although we were unable to obtain independent scientific proof that the pasteurized guaraná drinks are entirely free of additives, it appears that the Antartica GUARANÁ, at least, shows very few traces of chemical doctoring. Moreover, its caffeine content, though less stable, averages about one third that of COCA-COLA.[20]

Besides Brahma and Antartica, a dozen other companies produced high-quality guaraná in Brazil. But hundreds of small family factories also produced imitations, sold under the same GUARANÁ name.[21] In most cases, these imitations were made with inadequately treated water and a lot of additives. As modern roads reached into remote areas, these small factories often disappeared, their products replaced by the higher-quality guaraná which now accounts for the lion's share of the guaraná market. Although its popularity has been eroded by the new artificial beverages, the guaraná flavor still holds about 35% of the soft drink market in Brazil.[22]

Resistance

When Brazil's tax regulations on soft drinks were revised again in 1945, Coca-Cola got further preferential treatment: Increasing the 44% break it had allowed in 1939, the Brazilian government now taxed Coca-Cola at less than half the rate levied on guaraná drinks.[23]

---

* This stabilizer for flavoring oils has been used in the manufacture of artificial "fruit-flavored" soft drinks such as Coca-Cola's FANTA ORANGE and orange-flavored CRUSH. BVO is still used in the United States, but its use here is controversial. In 1970, it was removed by the Food and Drug Administration from the list of additives "generally recognized as safe," and was made the subject of an interim regulation which permits it to be used in limited amounts "pending the outcome of additional toxicological studies." These studies are being conducted by the Flavor and Extract Manufacturers Association under FDA supervision, with no date set for their completion.[19]

In 1948, under strong pressure from the São Paulo Association of the Soft Drink and Beer Industries, Representative Café Filho investigated Coca-Cola's favored treatment. The company was forced to issue public explanations and disclose its sales figures: On the 240 million bottles sold in the three years between 1945 and 1948, the lower tax rate had saved Coca-Cola and its franchises 24 million cruzeiros—over a million dollars.[24]

Local guaraná producers also tried to fight Coca-Cola by means of legislation. A food and beverage regulation issued by the government of São Paulo in February 1946 banned the use in food and drink of "phosphoric acid and its compounds." But the article banning phosphoric acid was removed from the law without much notice, in an amendment passed December 14, 1952.[25]

In 1955, the governor of São Paulo, Janio Quadros, had the Coca-Cola bottling plant in his State closed down for a time by the police for infringement of the 1946 food and beverage law. Arguing on the basis of the 1952 amendment, Coca-Cola won the case in preliminary hearings.[26] It is the last known case of direct interference by the authorities in the production of COCA-COLA in Brazil.

Years of Consolidation

Local soft drink producers soon realized that it was easier to join Coca-Cola than to resist it. And it was good business besides. Brazil's urban population—people who could be reached by advertising—was growing fast in the late 1940s and early 1950s. And no brand name was more effective than the magic COCA-COLA.

For the businessman, COCA-COLA was a complete system: easy to produce, easy to sell. "I would guess that to produce guaraná would cost much more than to produce COCA-COLA," says one of Coca-Cola's chief chemists. He explains: "The pasteurization equipment needed to produce guaraná costs over $200,000—not the kind of money available to just anyone"[27] (which explains why only large companies produce high-quality guaraná and why Antartica and Brahma slowly got hold of the big markets). Antartica's marketing manager in São Paulo, Charles Rais, calculates the total production cost of COCA-COLA at 30% below that of guaraná. "Since the retail prices are usually equalized, there is a greater margin for profits or promotion. In fact, since COCA-COLA is produced by just adding water and sugar to the syrup provided by the Coca-Cola factory, any bottler can shift to COCA-COLA or PEPSI; while to produce guaraná, it is almost necessary to build a factory for this specific purpose. This is also why Coca-Cola and Pepsi can spend more money on advertising."[28]

Previously independent bottlers, unwilling or unable to invest in equipment for pasteurization, began to line up for Coca-Cola franchises. "COCA-COLA is the first soft drink any bottler wishes to produce; we provide complete advertising and promotion support; we also provide complete technical assistance. It is all included in the price of the syrup," according to Stul Beckman, a Coca-Cola official in Rio.[29]

But Coca-Cola would not accept just any bottler: "We prefer leading members of the local community, people with competence, not necessarily people already engaged in soft drinks," said Beckman.[30]

Ralph Cruz, another Coca-Cola official in Rio, calls this policy "one of the keys to our success . . . the fact that most high officials of Coca-Cola are Brazilian citizens . . . and that bottlers of Coca-Cola are also members of the local community."[31]

The rationale for this policy was suggested by Coca-Cola Co. Chairman J. Paul Austin in a 1973 *Business Week* article which explained why Coca-Cola considers itself relatively immune from the danger of expropriation. "It's a franchise business. If they nationalize the assets, they're nationalizing their own people." The only substantial assets the company has outside the United States, according to *Business Week,* are a few company-owned bottling units and 28 plants that produce its concentrate.[32]

Coca-Cola's expansion through franchising began in earnest in the 1950s.[33] Although the position of guaraná was already being slowly eroded, this was not yet measurable since population and the standard of living of the upper classes were both rising dramatically. The real casualties were plain water and mineral water; once a common sight on the tables of bars and restaurants, particularly in Rio, mineral water became more and more a beverage of the very old or the sick.

Enter Pepsi

In 1952, Pepsi-Cola entered the Brazilian market via the southern border with Argentina, Pepsi's South American stronghold. It started in Rio Grande do Sul, then moved into São Paulo in 1962 and Rio in 1967.[34]

Pepsi-Cola's arrival and expansion in the Brazilian market, together with the presence of Crush and Seven-Up, resulted in a fierce competition among the main soft drink companies, including the producers of guaraná and other local beverages.

COKE still outsells PEPSI by a wide margin, but Pepsi-Cola has greatly influenced the overall soft drink market. As long as Coca-Cola was alone in the cola market and the entire soft drink market was expanding naturally, pressures on local and traditional beverages were minimal. When Pepsi-Cola entered the Brazilian market in 1952, its strategy was, first, to establish strength in a limited geographical area and then to begin biting into Coca-Cola's weakest areas. "To be able to grow, we had to be strong vis-à-vis Coca-Cola, while Coca-Cola had to fight against guaraná and lemon soda," said Pepsi-Cola's marketing director, Julio Pimentel.[35]

The need for continuous growth was the reason Pepsi entered the Brazilian market. "In terms of global strategy, Pepsi needed the Brazilian market because its Argentinian market became stagnant," Pimentel explained,[36] but in order to compete, Pepsi had to diversify.

As happens in the United States, most of the giant

beverage producers in Brazil try to establish exclusive rights at the point of sale—bars, restaurants, canteens—by offering a complete line of beverages as well as back-up equipment such as refrigerators. If he wants to sell COKE, for instance, the retailer is encouraged to carry Coca-Cola's complete line of beverages, and not to sell any other company's products.

Pepsi's solution was to offer an orange-flavored soft drink of its own. It made an agreement with Crush International, which has been operating in Brazil since 1947, and almost every PEPSI bottler began to bottle CRUSH, too.[37]

In 1968, Pepsi founded a holding company to strengthen its point-of-sale monopolies by offering good credit terms to bar and restaurant owners in exchange for exclusivity. A government agency investigated this holding company in 1972, but no action has been taken against it.[38]

New plants, including a Pepsi/Crush plant in Rio which is the largest soft drink factory in the world, continue to be built all over Brazil. In 1971, there were 26 Coca-Cola and 15 Pepsi-Cola bottlers in the country. Today there are 31 independent Coca-Cola bottlers, plus Coca-Cola's own bottling plant in Rio, and about 20 Pepsi-Cola bottlers.[39]

The Monopoly Game

It is not as though exclusivity was unknown in Brazil before COKE and PEPSI came along. Even before their arrival, an alert visitor to Brazil would have noticed stores selling Antartica's more popular GUARANÁ also carrying other Antartica products. And bars selling Brahma's beer tended to stock Brahma's GUARANÁ as well.

But with the arrival of these new competitors, the pressures increased. The breweries began to buy out small producers of local beverages all over the country. Some of these companies, like Fratelli Vita Indústria e Comércio, which operates in Salvador and Recife and was bought by Brahma in 1972, produced high-quality beverages from local fruits.[40] One local producer under siege, Vontobel in Rio Grande do Sul, was already a Coca-Cola bottler; he resisted the breweries by making a special agreement with Coca-Cola which will enable him to expand production with Coca-Cola backing.[41]

The monopoly game has other effects as well. In 1972, in order to obtain greater exclusivity at the point of sale, Coca-Cola began to produce its own guaraná: GUARANÁ FANTA.[42] Unlike most Brazilian guaraná, however, it is not a pasteurized product; it is made from a syrup. This artificially flavored GUARANÁ is now being produced by 14 Coca-Cola bottlers.[43]

Around the same time, Coca-Cola introduced the soda fountain system, to compete with the hand-squeezed method used to serve natural juice in most snack bars of Rio. The company also introduced on-the-spot mixing by vending machines to be installed in canteens at airports, factories, and clubs. In both cases, the concentrate is provided by Coca-Cola in sealed containers and is mixed with water supplied locally. Although each system has a filter, Coca-Cola's Director in Brazil, Gerald Shaw, admits that the water treatment is not as reliable as the purification provided in bottling plants.[44]

Thus, as the on-the-spot mixing system spreads, COCA-COLA will lose one of its few public health advantages—the fact that it is bottled with pure, treated water, while small local soft drink factories are more careless about water quality. A Coca-Cola high official commented: "In any case, it is the responsibility of the local municipality in each city to see that the water supplied is of good quality."[45]

An interesting by-product of the soft drink competition was the drive to export guaraná. This was the solution found by Alterosa de Cervejas, a Minas Gerais company which had rejected many merger bids from the industry giants. When the company's products had been virtually banned in its home market, Belo Horizonte, due to point-of-sale monopolies by the big companies, Alterosa made a formal complaint to the government, accusing Brahma and Antartica of "monopolistic practices." A subsequent government inquiry was shelved.[46] In 1971,

Alterosa began exporting large quantities of bottled guaraná concentrate; since 1972, the company has been working under franchise agreements. GUARANÁ TROP is now being sold in the United States, Denmark, Germany, Venezuela, England, Kuwait, and Japan.[47]

How to Seduce Children and Their Parents

José Roberto Orsi is a successful young advertising executive, in charge of the million-dollar Pepsi-Cola account in Brazil. He works at the Mauro Salles advertising agency, Brazil's sixth largest, with 1973 billings of $14.29 million.[48] Orsi earns in one day what the average Brazilian worker earns in a month.

Orsi's job is to create and sustain the image of PEPSI-COLA. He has carefully studied the soft drink market in Brazil, a market which he believes has "one of the world's biggest rates of growth. I think that for a market of this importance, a country with 100 million inhabitants, there is no similar growth-rate. You see, the age structure of this country is very peculiar; over 65% of the population is under 25 years old. A man 60 years old today doesn't like PEPSI OR COKE, but the young, they will start drinking now and will never stop, to the end of their lives."[49]

The "Pepsi Generation" advertising campaign was easily adapted to the Brazilian market, but with a local touch: in Brazil, it is "The Pepsi Revolution." Orsi explains: "In this country the youth don't have protest channels; the present generation didn't receive any political or social education. So we provide them with a mechanism for protest. It is protest through consumption; the teenager changes from the old-fashioned COCA-COLA and adopts PEPSI, the PEPSI with a young and new image, and he is happy, because he is young and young people drink PEPSI."[50]

The cola companies have clearly made children and teenagers their top-priority targets in Brazil. Both Coca-Cola and Pepsi-Cola (and, to a lesser extent, Antartica and Brahma) fight to establish points of sale in schools. The companies provide or finance refrigerators and other appliances, in return for permission to sell their products.[51] They also provide free soft drinks for school festivities.[52]

Although soft drinks have not yet permeated everyday life in all classes of Brazil as they have in Mexico, sales are impressive. From figures provided by various industry sources, it is estimated that Brazilians buy 900,000 bottles of PEPSI and CRUSH and 4.5 million bottles of COKE and FANTA daily.[53]

In 1973, the Instituto de Nutrição Anne Dias in Rio de Janeiro did a limited survey of the soft drink habits and preferences of rich, middle-class, and poor schoolchildren from six to fourteen years old. Fifty children from each economic group were asked how many bottles of soft drinks they consumed each day, and which brand they preferred. The rich children all said they drank soft drinks every day, an average of two bottles a day during the summer (summer in Rio lasts nine months) and one during the winter. The preferred brands were: COCA-COLA, 28; PEPSI-COLA, 10; FANTA ORANGE, 5; FANTA GRAPE, 5; GUARANÁ, 2. All the middle-class children also consumed soft drinks, but they averaged only one bottle a day in summer and none during the winter. They preferred: COCA-COLA, 30; PEPSI-COLA, 8; FANTA ORANGE, 4; FANTA GRAPE, 5; GUARANÁ, 3. Among very poor children, whose parents earned no more than $80 a month, soft drinks were consumed only occasionally, even during the summer, with COCA-COLA and FANTA the favorite brands.

The nutrition institute survey also found vitamin deficiencies, even in the diets of the children from rich families. Children from middle-class families showed symptoms of protein malnutrition. Children from poor families were obviously suffering from protein-calorie malnutrition. In all groups, milk-drinking was minimal.[54]

Although very poor children have so far been protected from soft drinks by their lack of money, the soft drink industry now seems to be trying to duplicate its success in Mexico by reaching the less-affluent sections of the population. As Coca-Cola Director Shaw explains: "Now, each company tries to catch what it can. High-income people are accustomed to soft drinks already and their preferences are well defined. But the overall rate of consumption is still very low in this country and, to the extent that lower income categories raise their standard of living, we win more consumers. This is why we keep prices down."[55]

Attitude of the Public Servant

Brazilian physicians and public health specialists have tried to resist the soft drink invasion. Government officials responsible for food and beverage standards, for example, have sought to limit the use of controversial additives in soft drinks. But these public servants have been no match for the big soft drink companies.

As early as 1949, the Technical Studies Committee of the Public Food Service (Serviço de Alimentação Pública: SAPS) made exhaustive analyses of various soft drinks. The committee found that some drinks contained forbidden additives and that almost all of them constituted health hazards in various degrees. In the published findings, SAPS director Armando Peregrino stressed the high caffeine content of COCA-COLA, which his analysis found to average over five times higher than soft drinks of the guaraná type and twice as high as maté tea. Peregrino warned that COCA-COLA, "if consumed to excess, may be damaging, particularly to those with a sensitive organism, like children and teenagers, and even some adults."

The government food official also complained that several soft drink products contained forbidden additives. CRUSH, he said, contained a high percentage of a compound derived from benzoic acid; other drinks used forbidden dyes. "It is necessary," Peregrino concluded, "to regulate the consumption of soft drinks . . . or even to restrict their intake by children and other groups. . . . Furthermore, if [the manufacturers] go so far as to disobey our food regulations and offer to the ignorant consumer products which are direct health hazards, the problem goes beyond the authority of the scientist and becomes a police case."[56]

The SAPS study was published in 1950. But, despite its warnings, soft drinks, like cigarettes, have over the years become an accepted part of daily life.

The Juice Law

The nutritionists and public health officials were not able to hold back the soft drink invasion. But since the late 1960s, they have been joined by a self-interested group—citrus growers and juice producers—in a battle to make at least fruit-flavored soft drinks more nutritious.

FANTA-UVA, Coca-Cola's grape-flavored drink, did not contain any grape juice. But there is a chronic surplus of grapes in the grape-producing areas of southern Brazil. The 1970–71 harvest produced a surplus of 200,000 metric tons, forcing the government of Rio Grande do Sul to take steps towards the formation of a government grape-processing factory.[57]

FANTA ORANGE and CRUSH call themselves "orange drinks," but their orange juice content was minimal or nonexistent.[58] Although Brazil is one of the larger exporters of orange juice in the world, its domestic consumption is low. A labor union study done in 1969–70 of the diets of working-class families in São Paulo found that families with monthly incomes under 500 cruzeiros (about $110) had serious vitamin C deficiencies in their diets. These people obtained only 56.3% of the required daily amount of vitamin C as determined by the Institute of Nutrition of Central America and Panama.

The study also found a vitamin C deficiency in middle-level working-class families, whose monthly incomes ranged between 501 and 1000 cruzeiros ($110–220). These people obtained 79.1% of the required daily amount of vitamin C.

Only in the "high-income" working-class families, with monthly incomes over 1000 cruzeiros, did the study find adequate vitamin C intake.[59]

The result of the citrus growers' interest in soft drinks was a law requiring that specific amounts of locally available natural juices be used in soft drinks claiming to contain fruit juices or even having the image of a fruit-juice drink. This law, called the "Juice Law," was passed in 1972 after a long parliamentary struggle.[60] The Ministry of Agriculture, charged with applying the law, began to force compliance only toward the end of 1974 when it started to announce the standards to which each type of soft drink must conform.[61]

In all likelihood, only drinks like FANTA ORANGE, FANTA-UVA, and CRUSH will be affected. These products must now contain 10% natural juice. The change is not very significant. It means that the soft drink industry will now absorb about 5% of Brazil's total orange juice production. And for the consumer it means a bit more vitamin C. "Try mixing a bottle of water with a cup of orange juice," explained a technician at the Ministry of Agriculture. "You still have a bottle of water. The 10% of juice isn't able to give the taste, the smell, or the color of the present artificial drink. The companies will still use the same chemical additives they always used."[62]

Small producers of artificially flavored soft drinks in Brazil will be hurt most by the new law. Unable to make the changeover, an estimated 80% of them, mostly in the more remote areas of the country, will be driven out of business.[63] The large companies will be, at most, inconvenienced. During the long period of intra-governmental maneuvering over the proposed law, these companies fought for, and won, a 50% reduction (from 24% to 12%) in the Industrialized Products Tax (successor to the Consumption Tax which was so kind to Coca-Cola in its early days) to make up for the extra cost of adding some natural juice to their products.[64]

COCA-COLA and PEPSI-COLA have so far been entirely unaffected by the law. Their producers are arguing that the law does not apply to COKE and PEPSI because they are "artificial products."[65]

Their argument is not without irony.

Although we could not trace the historical record, there are government officials in Brazil today who recall that back in 1944, Getulio Vargas wanted COCA-COLA to be labelled "artificial product." But the company insisted that, because it was made with water and sugar, their beverage was not artificial. Finally, a compromise was reached: COCA-COLA would be called *nome de fantasia*—"a fantasy name."

9/FORMULA FOR MALNUTRITION

Among the affluent, the choice between breast feeding and bottle feeding may be based on personal convenience or life style. Both methods will probably yield satisfactory results.[1]

But among the poor, especially in developing countries, the decision has a different meaning. Breast feeding, even if the mother herself is malnourished, will probably provide the child with adequate nourishment for the first four to six months of life.[2] Bottle feeding, because of the high cost of formula and the hygienic facilities necessary for its preparation, will probably provide the child with overdiluted, contaminated formula in bacteria-laden bottles.[3] The choice between breast and bottle will very often be a choice between health and disease. It may be a choice between life and death. And yet women all over the developing world are choosing bottle feeding with greater frequency,[4] and infant milk companies are aggravating the problem by encouraging poor women to make that choice.

Starving for Profits

U.S. baby milk companies, like their big brothers, the adult food manufacturers, have gone looking for business in developing countries because of disappointing population trends at home.

The low population growth in the United States in the 1960s has limited the sales growth of food processing companies in general. In fact, a business survey published in 1973 stated that U.S. food processing companies had reported the lowest annual rate of domestic sales growth

(5%) of any of the industry groups in the survey.[5] And a 1973 article in *Business Week* explained that food processors, "starving for profits," are looking both at overseas food markets and at nonfood products and services at home, seeking "renewed opportunities for profitable business."[6]

Baby-related industries have been even harder hit by population trends in the United States, for although the population is still growing—albeit at a slower rate—the birth rate itself is in a substantial decline. From a 1957 peak of more than 4.3 million births, the annual number of births had by 1974 declined to about 3.1 million.[7] The 1973 birth rate in the United States was the lowest in American history,[8] a fact reflected in business publication headlines like "The Baby Bust"[9] and "The Bad News in Babyland."[10] The decline in the U.S. birth rate—what *Dun's Review* called "too few mouths to feed"[11]—appears to varying degrees throughout the affluent world.[12]

Searching for opportunities to increase profits, then, some baby companies have diversified into new lines.[13] Others, including the milk companies, have tried to expand markets for their traditional products in that area of the world where population is still increasing rapidly: the third world.[14] For example:

•*Abbott Laboratories,*[15] the pharmaceutical multinational whose Ross Laboratories division manufactures SIMILAC and ISOMIL formulas for infant feeding, is expanding rapidly overseas, with the pediatric market a major focus. The overseas portion of Abbott's pediatric sales (including formula products and drugs) rose from 14.3% in 1969 (overseas pediatric sales of $12.5 million) to 22.2% in 1973 ($31.3 million). From 1972 to 1973, Ross expanded domestic sales for the formula products it markets by 9% but foreign sales by 32%. In Abbott's 1973 annual report, marketing plans for the company's International Division were confirmed: "In essence, our strategy for 1974 remains unchanged: Maintain consistent growth in the pharmaceutical area, but exert the major thrust at the newer, more dynamic hospital and pediatric markets."

•*American Home Products,*[16] parent company of Wyeth, the pharmaceutical firm which produces SMA, S-26, and NURSOY infant formulas, is also profiting from the overseas expansion of its line. SMA and S-26 showed substantial international sales increases during 1973, the company reports. Expansion of infant formula manufacturing facilities is planned or under way in Mexico, Ireland, the Philippines, and South Africa.

•*Bristol-Myers,*[17] whose Mead Johnson division manufactures ENFAMIL, OLAC, and PROSOBEE, includes among its problems over the last five years "the sudden decline in the birth rate which affected ENFAMIL and other pediatric products." Bristol-Myers' international division, with sales up from just over $100 million in 1968 to $400 million in 1974,[18] is the fastest-growing part of the company. Infant formulas constitute an important segment of the division, according to the 1973 annual report, particularly in Latin America and the Pacific.

Infant milk companies from other affluent, baby-poor countries also operate in Latin America and the Caribbean. Nestlé, the Swiss multinational giant, dominates the market in Central and South America.[19] The British firms Cow & Gate and Glaxo are also active, mainly in the English-speaking countries of the Caribbean.[20]

The Baby Killer

In a statement released in late 1973 by the U.N.'s Protein Advisory Group,[21] pediatricians and food industry executives agreed that "infants of more affluent socioeconomic groups in industrialized and developing countries, in the absence of breast feeding, suffer no nutritional disadvantage when fed properly constituted and hygienically prepared processed commercial formulas. . . ."

"However," the advisory group recognized, "the early abandonment of breast feeding by mothers among lower socioeconomic groups can be disastrous to infants, particularly when this occurs without adequate financial resources to purchase sufficient formula and without knowledge of and facilities to follow hygienic practices necessary to feed infants adequately and safely with breast milk replacements."

This "disastrous" trend has led the British charity War on Want to identify infant milk formula as a "baby killer" in the developing world.[22] The recently completed Inter-American Investigation of Mortality in Childhood, checking the causes of approximately 35,000 childhood deaths, found that nutritional deficiency was the most important contributor to excessive mortality in the first year of life,[23] and that nutritional deficiency as an underlying or associated cause of death was—in every community studied—"less frequent in infants breast fed and never weaned than in infants who were breast fed not at all or for only limited periods."[24]

That breast fed babies have a better chance for survival has been principally attributed to the problems associated with artificial feeding among the poor in developing countries.

First, commercial formula products are prohibitively expensive, "totally beyond the economic range of the group to whom they are supplied," according to pediatric nutritionist D.B. Jelliffe.[25] A study based on June 1970 retail prices in Jamaica, West Indies, for example, found that it would cost about $73 to feed an infant processed foods (milk-based infant food, cereal-based infant food, and babies' vitamin drops) for the first six months of life, or about $2.75 a week.[26] Of those Jamaicans lucky enough to have jobs in 1972, 40% were earning $11 a week or less.[27]

As a result, the formula is frequently "stretched"—over-diluted by women to make it last longer. A 1969 survey in Barbados investigated how long one-pound cans of powdered milk were being used to feed two- or three-month-old babies who were solely bottle fed. Of the survey's 222 respondents, 18% indicated that a one-pound can lasted four days or less (roughly the correct duration).

But 82% answered that the can lasted between five days and three weeks. "It is clear," the survey concluded, "that milk is being administered in greater dilutions than is desirable."[28]

The other major problem associated with artificial feeding in developing countries is caused by the general lack of hygienic facilities. Jelliffe has written that "the possibility of producing an uncontaminated feed is almost nil, when a mother may have only one feeding bottle and nipple, no storage space (let alone electricity or a refrigerator), water from a near-by pond or stream, and because of minimal education, difficulty in following advice on preparing feeds properly."[29]

In these circumstances, the bottle and milk themselves become transmitters of disease. The infant is subject to repeated infections, often taking the form of diarrhea, during which periods the child's body cannot utilize even the nutrients it receives.[30]

When breast feeding was widespread among the poor, severe malnutrition was usually held off until the second year of a child's life. But the rapid decline of breast feeding over the past two decades has caused the average age of children suffering from severe forms of malnutrition to drop from 18 to 8 months in some parts of the world.[31] A 1972 survey in Trinidad indicated that 70% of cases of severe malnutrition in Port-of-Spain were children under one year of age.[32] Furthermore, according to information collected by the Inter-American Investigation of Mortality in Childhood, deaths from malnutrition now statistically peak as early as the third and fourth months of life.[33] This age drop in the onset of malnutrition is critical, because of its effects in the first year of life on intellectual development. "All the evidence that is accumulating," according to an expert in child health, "points to the fact that the earlier in life there is nutritional insult, and the longer this persists, the more likely it is that intellectual development is going to be impaired."[34]

The infant milk companies are quick to point out that poor women are abandoning breast feeding for many and complex reasons. Women are going out to work in increasing numbers, leaving their babies at home; poor women are imitating the rich who have switched to artificial feeding; they are adopting urban ways as they migrate to the cities; they are adopting the western view of the breast as a sexual object rather than a source of food; they may favor artificial feeding because it demands less intimacy with (sometimes) unwanted children. For example, O. Ballarin, director of Nestlé in Brazil, claims that women are abandoning breast feeding for reasons that have nothing to do with company promotional activities, and that the industry is filling a need by making commercial substitutes available. "*But the fact remains that for some years already many newborns are not* (even if some could be) breast fed, and therefore something must be done," Ballarin stresses.[35]

Certainly nutritionists have recognized that there is legitimate need in developing countries for substitutes for human milk. Some women (less than 5%) cannot breast feed for physiological reasons.[36] Others cannot breast feed because they work away from home. (However, the percentage of women in the work force is generally low in Latin America,[37] and the percentage of employed women whose jobs prevent them from breast feeding is even lower.[38])

But the statistics of malnutrition and death among bottle fed infants indicate that the industry's method of filling this need is dangerous. In 1971, experts of the U.N.'s Protein Advisory Group recommended that instead of expensive, easily contaminated formula products, developing countries need something cheap, minimally advertised (if at all), and capable of being reconstituted easily and with least chance of contamination.[39] Other nutritionists have designed nourishing artificial feeding regimes for homes with low income, no refrigeration, and limited cooking facilities.[40] One such plan, based on skim milk powder, vegetable oil, semi-refined sugar, and vitamin drops, would cost about a fourth as much as feeding with commercial formula products.[41]

Industry leaders such as David O. Cox, president of Ross Laboratories, are more willing than Ballarin to recognize the effects of company promotion. Cox claims, however, that responsible firms are promoting just to the rich—people with "discretionary funds"—and that promotion reaches the poor only "coincidentally . . . , producing some motivation to acquire status by use of such products." Cox has stated that "any formula manufacturer who promoted his product for sale to [people without discretionary funds] would be properly suspect of having lost his reason. He would be laying himself open to continual hazard of product failure, in his dependence on the scanty capability of such persons to understand and implement directions for preparing formula and for maintaining sanitation. The result would most often be dilute and contaminated feeding deleterious to the baby's health."[42]

But sane or insane, the companies are not just promoting their products to people with discretionary funds who can afford to use them properly. This class is too small in developing countries, with their skewed income distributions,[43] to provide a big enough market for infant milk formulas. Companies are trying to expand sales down the income ladder in order to obtain the profits necessary for their growth: they are working to create a need for their products among women who might otherwise use breast milk as the sole source of food for their children for the first four to six months of life. Often, company promotion is specifically directed to the poor.

Promoting to the Poor

For years, infant milk company promotional efforts urged women throughout the developing world to feed their babies artificially. Glaxo ads used in the Caribbean in the 1960s, for example, touted OSTERMILK as "the best replacement for mother's milk."[44] Both OSTERMILK and FAREX, Glaxo's cereal product for infants, were recommended "right from the start—the foods you can trust."[45]

But as the harmful effects of artificial feeding among the poor became widely recognized, nutritionists began to scream. In 1970, Jelliffe, then head of the Caribbean Food & Nutrition Institute, described these effects as "starvation and diarrhea, too often leading to death. . . . It is harsh, but correct, to consider some of these children as suffering from 'commerciogenic malnutrition'—that is caused by the thoughtless promotion of these milks and infant foods."[46]

Concerned about damage to its benign public image, the infant milk industry sent high-level representatives to a series of meetings with nutritionists and pediatricians. These meetings, several of which were sponsored by the U.N.'s Protein Advisory Group, produced general agreement by company executives and pediatricians that "breast milk is the preferred food for infants . . ." and that "breast feeding should be maintained if it is at all possible to do so."[47]

Either as a result of these meetings or for other reasons, many infant milk companies have recently modified their promotional strategies directed at the poor. The new goal seems to be "mixed" feeding—bottle and breast—with formula promoted as a supplement to breast milk. OSTERMILK, formerly advertised as "the best replacement for mother's milk," is now "the next best thing to mother's milk," for cases in which "you find you need a substitute or a supplement to breast milk. . . ."[48]

Promotional literature published by other companies stresses the same theme. A pamphlet published by Mead Johnson Jamaica Ltd. emphasizes that "more babies have thrived on Mead Johnson Formula Products than on any other form of supplementary feeding."[49] Cow & Gate's *Babycare Booklet* suggests that the company's milk "can be used as a substitute for breast feeding, or as a supplement."[50] Nestlé's *Your Baby and You* emphasizes the health advantages of a breast fed baby, "even if only partially so nourished." The booklet recommends mixed feeding—"an occasional bottle-feed"—"if you cannot breast-feed Baby entirely yourself."[51] *A Life Begins,* another Nestlé publication, suggests that "It may happen that you do not have enough milk to feed your baby. In this case the meal must be supplemented by bottle feeding."[52]

The mixed-feeding concept has several important promotional advantages. By openly recommending breast feeding, the companies can earn their public relations credits. At the same time, the companies can undermine breast feeding by implying repeatedly that a mother may not have enough milk and may need supplementary bottles of formula. Dr. Spock has called "the combination of a mother lacking confidence in her ability to breast-feed and the availability of bottles of formula" the "most efficient method of discouraging breast feeding."[53]

Mixed feeding may also encourage breast feeding failure for physiological reasons. La Leche League International, an organization devoted to helping women breast feed successfully, explains that "the supplementary formula is one of the greatest deterrents to establishing a good milk supply, and frequent nursing is one of the greatest helps. You see, the milk supply is regulated by what the baby takes. The more he nurses, the more milk there will be. If he's given a bottle as well, he'll gradually take less and less from the breast and the supply will diminish."[54]

Dr. Spock similarly warns that "in many cases of mixed feedings, the breast-milk supply gradually decreases. Also, the baby may come to prefer the bottle and reject the breast altogether."[55]

In addition to contributing to lactation failure, supplementary bottles used in mixed feeding can introduce the same vicious cycle of malnutrition and infection as can an all-bottle routine.

The health of company profits, however, can be improved by mixed feeding. Although each woman may purchase only a few tins of supplementary formula, the number of women who can be convinced to divert scarce resources in this way is extremely large.

The large market for supplementary formula can be

seen in recent studies of infant feeding patterns in various countries. In May 1969 the National Food and Nutrition Survey of Barbados interviewed 311 persons who were directly responsible for the overall care of a child. The survey found that 257 of the 311 children involved (82%) had received mixed bottle and breast feeding. All but seven of the other children in the survey were entirely bottle fed. Nestlé's LACTOGEN was the most widely used formula; other popular multinational brands included COW & GATE, OSTERMILK, SMA (Wyeth), and OLAC (Mead Johnson).[56]

A similar pattern of mixed feeding was discovered in a 1972 survey of the tiny town of La Poterie, Grenada. In 48 low-income households surveyed, each of which had at least one child under the age of five, 50% of the babies were being given a supplementary food in their first month of life. Three quarters were having breast and bottle together before the age of three months. This early supplementation, the survey found, was "overwhelmingly of a cow's milk product, nearly half from one multinational commercial firm" (Nestlé). Of the mothers surveyed, 40% started milk from a bottle because they felt that their breast milk was insufficient for their baby.[57]

The following description of mixed feeding was given by Dr. J. M. Gurney of the Caribbean Food & Nutrition Institute in a 1972 seminar on Food and Economic Planning in Trinidad and Tobago: "Most babies in Trinidad and Tobago start life on their mothers' milk, but cows' milk alternatives are given to at least half the babies far too early. These usually take the form of 'infant formulas.' Such substitutes are often given too dilute, for mainly economic reasons, and therefore cannot provide adequate energy and nutrients. They also contribute both to a failure of lactation on the mother's part and to the introduction of infections."[58]

The dangerous message of mixed feeding, hidden behind sanctimonious praise of breast milk, is being carried to the poor with the enthusiasm and ingenuity of an industry desperate for mouths to feed. The methods used to transmit the message are varied.

Milk Nurses[59]

In various countries of the developing world, infant milk companies employ nurses (sometimes fully trained, sometimes only partially) to make contact with new mothers of all income levels and promote the companies' formula products.

A study of the use of these "milk nurses" in Jamaica was conducted in late 1974 by the Caribbean Food & Nutrition Institute (CFNI). According to information collected for that study, milk nurses were employed by the following companies in Jamaica: Mead Johnson of the United States; Jamaica Milk Products, a Nestlé subsidiary; Hopwood and Co., distributor for the British firm Glaxo Laboratories; Kong's Commercial, distributor for the U.S. firm Ross Laboratories; and Levy Brothers, distributor for the British firm Cow & Gate. Mead Johnson employed 12 nurses: 10 worked in Kingston and its suburbs, one in Mandeville and environs, and one in Montego Bay.

In Jamaica, milk nurses are fully trained nurses who also undergo training by the infant milk companies. A company training program may last six weeks; part of the material covered is "product knowledge." Milk nurses are paid fixed salaries plus travel allowances. Some companies reportedly give bonuses based on overall company profits.

The nurses do not appear to concentrate on mothers of any particular income group: they visit or try to visit all the new mothers whose names they are given. The mothers visited often do not have adequate income to feed their children artificially, but, in general, milk nurses do not tell mothers about the costs involved in artificial feeding.*

The Jamaica Milk Products nurse, who sells Nestlé products, is allowed to enter maternity wards in public hospitals in rural areas in order to talk to mothers directly. This nurse does not make home visits. Nurses for other companies do, however, visit mothers in their homes. They obtain names and addresses of new mothers from both

---

*However, cost was mentioned in one visit by one nurse observed by a CFNI staff member.

government and private hospitals (except for one private hospital in Kingston and the University Hospital of the West Indies). It is not known how or by whom the names and addresses are given.

The nurses usually introduce themselves to the mothers as, for example, "Nurse ____, the Cow & Gate nurse." In addition to product promotion, the nurses give mothers moral support and child-care information. However, among 21 mothers in urban and suburban areas who had been visited by milk nurses and were interviewed by a CFNI researcher, most felt that the nurses had offered very little information unrelated to the company's products. Unless it was specifically requested, no information was given about the mother's health.

Although it is not technically part of their function, nurses from various companies indicated that they often make milk formula deliveries in order to keep their customers. This is especially true in isolated areas and in areas where the neighborhood shop is too small to carry all brands of infant milk.

Mead Johnson nurses do not have to make deliveries: the company has zoned delivery service in which delivery is free if mothers order three or more tins of formula. Milk delivered through this system is usually a few cents cheaper. Nurses employed by Mead Johnson tell mothers which day their zone is serviced.

Milk Banks

These are sales outlets for commercial formula products set up in hospitals and clinics that serve the poor. The banks sell infant milk (sometimes imported tax-free[60]) at discount prices to mothers of limited economic resources. From information collected in 1974 on milk bank operations in Guatemala City and Santo Domingo, the banks seem to be a marketing device—generally introduced by the Swiss firm Nestlé—aimed at expanding the practice of artificial feeding among the poor without interfering with the normal commercial market.

Even at discount prices, commercial substitutes for

breast milk are too expensive for the people milk banks are designed to reach. At Robert Reid Cabral hospital in Santo Domingo, the major public institution specializing in infant care in the Dominican Republic, the milk bank sells Nestlé's NAN, NIDO, and PELARGON. Prices for a one-pound tin range from 90¢ for NIDO (a 40% discount off the commercial price of $1.50) to $1.35 for NAN (33% off the $2 retail price). But very few mothers who go to the bank purchase enough formula each month to feed an infant adequately.[61]

Most of the women who go to the Robert Reid Cabral bank buy a tin of milk "when they can"—often only once every two or three weeks. (A one-pound tin, diluted in the proper strength, will last only a few days. If a mother is bottle-feeding her child regularly at proper strength, she should be buying about 10 pounds a month.) When the tin of formula is used up, if the women have no money and their breast milk has dried up, they give the babies "something else"—usually tea or chocolate drink made with water.[62]

Among the many poor women eligible to buy at milk banks are some—working women and others—who genuinely need a substitute for breast milk. But these women also cannot afford even the industry's "discount" price. In Guatemala City there is a milk bank at the Association for the Protection of Childhood, a welfare organization providing medical and dental services to children as well as day care to children of working mothers. Nestlé products sell for $1 per tin at this bank, compared to retail prices of $1.80 to $2. The women buying milk here are generally working mothers—mostly servants or salesclerks earning between $15 and $45 a month. More than half of them have more than two children and no husband to help them support their families. Fifty mothers at this bank were asked if they could afford to buy a tin of formula every few days; the most common response was that they simply did not buy it that frequently, that instead they "prepared the bottles with less milk and more water and that in this way the milk lasted longer."[63]

In order not to compete with the commercial market for Nestlé products, milk banks exclude women who could afford to pay the current retail price for commercial formula. At Robert Reid Cabral Hospital, the bank is open only to women of limited economic resources with children under one year of age.[64] At the Association for the Protection of Childhood in Guatemala City, milk purchases require a prescription from the Association's own doctors or from a public hospital or clinic. The bank does not sell to mothers with economic resources "because that would be disloyal competition for commercial establishments."[65]

Promotion in Health Institutions

In countries throughout Latin America and the Caribbean, hospitals, clinics, and doctors' offices serving the poor are teeming with materials and people promoting the sale of infant formula products.

Because the promotion takes place within health institutions, it carries with it the persuasive implication of medical endorsement.

•*Salespeople with access to hospitals*: Like the Nestlé milk nurses in Jamaica, company salespeople are sometimes given access to maternity wards of public hospitals. Alberto Martinez, an employee of Nestlé's dietetics division, spends three or four days a week in Hospital de Maternidad Nuestra Señora de la Altagracia, a public maternity hospital in Santo Domingo. His job is to promote NAN, for which the hospital gives him "all the facilities," he said.[66]

In other countries, company representatives enter the hospitals to give presents to new mothers. Reports of this practice have been received from Guyana[67] and Brazil.[68]

•*Promotion by health professionals*: Lic. Patria Rivas, a social worker in Nuestra Señora de la Altagracia in Santo Domingo, helps mothers learn the hygienic procedures necessary to care for themselves and their babies. She is an employee of the hospital, but she considers it part of her job to promote Nestlé products because "they are the best." In this role, she distributes films, pamphlets, magazines, free samples, and "educational" material published by Nestlé.[69]

In Jamaica, too, free samples of formula products are often distributed by a member of the hospital's nursing staff.[70]

•*Printed formula slips*: Mead Johnson, Nestlé, and other companies provide hospitals and clinics with printed prescription slips for doctors to use when prescribing that company's brand of infant formula.[71] Each company supplies its own printed slips, designed to look like hospital stationery, with the name of the hospital or clinic usually printed at the top. Below are listed the company's products and instructions for use so that the doctor can simply check off the name of the product being prescribed.

•*Posters*: With the exception of a few hospitals where these are banned (such as the University Hospital of the West Indies),[72] promotional posters are abundant in health institutions throughout Latin America and the Caribbean.[73] Some posters push particular products; others just display a company's name. In the waiting room of San Juan de Dios General Hospital in Guatemala City, a poster bearing the name Nestlé has a series of photographs demonstrating the preparation of a baby's formula.[74] Roosevelt Hospital in Guatemala City displays this same poster. In addition, signs near the hospital's pediatrics emergency entrance advertise NAN and SIMILAC for sale at the hospital drugstore.[75]

• *"Baby care" booklets*: Infant milk companies publish a lot of promotional literature under the guise of information booklets. These booklets reach the poor through distribution in maternity wards of public hospitals, clinics, milk banks, and doctors' offices;[76] in countries where milk nurses are used, the nurses usually give booklets to the mothers they visit.[77] Some of the pamphlets are directed at the semi-literate; for example, pictures illustrating improper procedures are partially obliterated with slashes.[78]

Most of the pamphlets contain information about prenatal as well as postnatal infant care; clearly, they are intended to reach expectant mothers before they give birth.

In this context, the effort to implant doubts in women's minds about their ability to breast feed takes on a special significance. Since the supply of breast milk is not fully established until the third or fourth day after a child is born[79] (a fact which some of the pamphlets fail to mention[80]), the companies may be trying to get infants started on supplementary formula before breast milk is given a chance.

Moreover, many of the doubts implanted are based on incorrect or outdated information. Nestlé's *A Life Begins*, for example, tells mothers that bottle feeding "must" replace breast feeding "should you fall ill (ask doctor's advice), if you do not have milk or if it is of poor quality or if your nipples develop cracks or become infected."[81] None of these caveats seems justified, however. Medical and maternal experts on breast feeding indicate that ordinary illnesses or breast infections usually do not interfere with nursing, and that, though it is likely to be painful, nursing may even be continued if the nipples crack.[82] Women who "do not have milk" are relatively few, although lactation does stop in cases of prolonged famine.[83] As for the question of "poor quality" milk, except in cases of *severe* maternal malnutrition, breast milk by itself is usually adequate to sustain growth and excellent nutrition in the infant for four to six months.[84] It is true that if maternal nutrition is poor, the production of breast milk may weaken the mother.[85] But as many nutritionists point out, the solution to this problem is not bottle feeding for the infant, but rather an adequate diet for the mother during pregnancy and lactation.

In addition to instilling false doubts in mothers and expectant mothers, most baby-care pamphlets prepared by the infant milk companies also undermine breast feeding by recommending the early introduction of solid foods. La Leche League warns that "the more solids the baby takes, the less milk he will want; the less he takes from the breasts, the less milk there will be." The League suggests not introducing solids until they are nutritionally necessary, at about four to six months of age.[86]

Nevertheless, Nestlé's *A Life Begins* suggests

introducing strained vegetables in the second month of life.[87] Cow & Gate recommends its own brand of cereals for use from two to three months, "when it's time for more than milk."[88] *The Ostermilk Mother and Baby Book* suggests introducing solid foods at "a few weeks of age, or even sooner if your doctor advises it."[89]

These are subtle kinds of promotion, but at least one company does not even bother with such subtleties. *Caring for Your Baby* is published by Ross Laboratories, maker of the SIMILAC line of infant formula. It stresses the use of formula products from birth: "SIMILAC WITH IRON infant formula—the iron-fortified formula providing recommended nutrition when fed from birth. . . ." Breast feeding is not discussed.[90] Another Ross publication, *Your Baby is Coming Soon!*, gives information about labor and delivery to the expectant mother. "Before you go into labor," the booklet urges, "you should know how you are going to feed your baby."[91] Breast feeding is nowhere mentioned as an option. The last page of the pamphlet offers a solution to this important problem: SIMILAC WITH IRON, because "your baby needs *iron* for his whole first year of life." Infant feeding with SIMILAC WITH IRON "gives him the iron he needs at no extra cost. . . ."

• *Vaccination cards*:[92] These four-page cards, containing recommended vaccination schedules and other baby-care information, are given to women in the hospital after they give birth. Two different versions were obtained in Brazil, neither stating the name of the publisher but both recommending Nestlé products. The cards offer the mother "our congratulations on the birth of your baby and our wishes that he may grow up handsome and healthy."

Like the baby-care booklets, the vaccination cards recommend breast feeding but give instructions which tend to undermine its success. For example, the cards tell mothers to give babies between-feed bottles of boiled water or tea sweetened with NIDEX, Nestlé's brand of baby sugar. This practice will decrease a baby's appetite for breast milk and thus reduce the mother's supply.

The cards also discourage breast feeding by suggesting

that the mother's milk supply may be inadequate: "In the case of total or partial lack of breast milk, NANON, the most modern and perfect 'humanized' milk, will offer the baby nutrition similar to that provided by breast milk."

• *Use of formula in hospitals*: The use of commercial formula products in hospital maternity and pediatric wards suggests a powerful endorsement of the practice of artificial feeding.

Many hospitals around the world feed all newborn infants commercial formula products, even if the infant's mother plans to breast feed when she goes home. This is convenient for the hospital staff and encouraged by companies' donations of milk for this purpose. In many Jamaican hospitals, when a baby is taken to its mother a bottle is taken along, usually of Mead Johnson's ENFAMIL or OLAC; Mead Johnson supplies special plastic bottles of its formula for hospital use.[93] According to a Nestlé employee in Santo Domingo, the firm gives Hospital de Maternidad Nuestra Señora de la Altagracia 80 cases of milk per month. Hospitals in the interior of the Dominican Republic also receive free milk from Nestlé: Barahona receives 10 cases per month; San Juan de la Maguana, 25; Azua, 15; and San Cristobal, 20.[94]

Promotion by Assistance to the Medical Profession

Sixteen women at a public maternity hospital in Santo Domingo were interviewed in May 1974. All 16 stated that they preferred breast feeding and that their doctors had recommended breast feeding as healthful. Nevertheless, all 16 had received doctors' prescriptions to buy artificial milk—Nestlé's NAN.[95]

Nestlé has worked hard for decades to get the medical profession's endorsement of its products. All over Latin America the company sponsors courses and seminars on various aspects of maternal and infant care.[96] Nestlé also publishes professional journals such as the twice-yearly *Anais Nestlé* in Brazil, each issue of which is devoted to a different medical topic of interest to pediatricians.[97]

The company also provides direct assistance to

pediatric associations. For the Brazilian Society of Pediatrics, for example, Nestlé prints the organization's *Information Bulletin* and mails it to members. (The Nestlé slogan, "more than 100 years of service to pediatrics," is scattered throughout the four-page bulletin.)[98] In addition, Nestlé publishes the Society's *Proceedings*, prints eye charts, and provides the Society with courtesy services such as a car to meet visiting doctors at the airport.[99]

"In general," a correspondent in Brazil wrote in late 1974, "the medical profession in this country is convinced that Nestlé is the best thing that ever happened to nutrition or pediatrics in Brazil."[100]

* * *

Clearly, the medical profession and government health authorities share much of the blame for the rise in bottle feeding among low-income mothers. Commercial promotion could not be as successful as it is without the complicity of so many health professionals. It is small wonder that so much of company advertising is directed toward them.

The companies portray themselves as instruments of service to good health and nutrition. But where the need for growth in earnings conflicts with the welfare of millions of newborn babies, multinational business seems to put its own health first.

10/THE U.S. GOVERNMENT'S HELPING HAND

The belief that expansion of American business abroad is good for us and good for the world has been a cornerstone of U.S. foreign policy for generations. This conviction has led to a number of programs and policies that encourage American companies to invest abroad, especially in the less developed countries of the world.

Tax Breaks

The biggest boons to U.S. companies engaged in exports or foreign investments have been special tax provisions—"loopholes." Since all tax returns are secret, it is impossible to determine how much these tax breaks have actually reduced any company's taxes. But it is widely acknowledged that the savings are considerable. After allocating deductions so as to take maximum advantage of the foreign tax credit, and after taking advantage of tax deferrals, less developed country (LDC) incentives, Domestic International Sales Corporations, Western Hemisphere Trade Corporations and favorable tax treatment for operations in U.S. possessions, many corporations pay well below the 48% statutory rate. Their executives living abroad escape certain personal income taxes as well.

Tax Deferral

U.S. multinational corporations are permitted to defer taxes on most foreign-earned income (income earned by a U.S.-controlled subsidiary—not a branch—abroad), as long as that income remains overseas. They must, however, pay corporate income taxes to the host government. In certain Latin American countries, the tax rate is lower than the U.S. rate of 48%; in "tax havens" like Panama and the Bahamas, it may be extremely low.[1] To avoid the higher U.S. rate, a multinational may try to maximize its foreign earnings, reinvest them abroad, and defer taxes on this income indefinitely. As G.D. Searle explained to its stockholders recently: "In general it is assumed that earnings of foreign subsidiaries which have not been remitted within three years have been permanently reinvested."[2] An expanding multinational can take advantage of this deferral to provide itself with more investment capital and reduce its need to borrow. The Tax Reduction Act of 1975 partially limited the advantages of this system. It is estimated that this recent legislation reduced the total annual benefit of deferral from around $620 million to about $400 million.[3]

Allocation of Deductions

U.S. corporations must pay U.S. taxes on the income earned by their foreign subsidiaries once that income is returned to the United States. The host government also requires the U.S. company to pay taxes on that income. To avoid double taxation, Congress established in 1918 a foreign tax credit. It works as follows:

When the parent company repatriates foreign-earned income, it is allowed to subtract from the U.S. tax on that income the dollar equivalent of the amount of taxes on the same earnings already paid to the foreign government. Thus, if a company earns $100 abroad, and the host country imposes a tax of $40, the company could subtract from the $48 tax charged by the United States the $40 it had already paid and pay the U.S. government only the $8 difference.

However, there is a ceiling on the foreign tax credit a multinational corporation can take against its U.S. taxes. The ceiling is determined by the foreign tax credit limitation formula. The Treasury first calculates what a company's U.S. tax would be if there were no foreign tax credit. Then it takes a ratio of the company's foreign income (after deductions) over its worldwide income (after deductions) and multiplies that ratio by the full U.S. tax liability. The result is the foreign tax credit, which the company can apply against its U.S. taxes. In effect, this means that the larger the taxable foreign income, the larger the foreign tax credit allowed by the IRS.

In order to maintain as high a ceiling as possible on foreign tax credits, multinational companies often seek to maximize their taxable foreign earnings. One way to do so is to allocate deductible expenses in such a way that as many expenses as possible are deducted from U.S. earnings.

The Treasury Department has reportedly found that U.S. multinationals have been overstating their foreign net income to get the maximum tax credit.[4] It has recently proposed changes in the regulations that would attribute more expenses incurred in the United States (including research and development) to foreign-source income. Since foreign governments often do not allow such deductions, the multinational company would continue to pay the same foreign tax but (applying the limitation formula) would be permitted a smaller foreign tax credit by the United States.

Not surprisingly, drug companies have strongly attacked the proposed regulation changes. According to James Byrne of Tax Analysts and Advocates, "These companies are investing incredible amounts [in legal fees] to fight the changes."[5] One has to infer, Byrne says, that the present regulations represent major savings for the drug companies. In fact, *Business Week* reported that "with their highly centralized research and management and with large royalty charges abroad," drug companies would be hardest hit by the change. "Bear, Stearns (a New York investment banking house) reckons they face a 6% to 8% cut in net income."[6]

Less Developed Country Incentives

When Congress in 1962 revised the tax laws on foreign investment it left some loopholes favorable to subsidiaries operating in less developed countries. The law on this is so complex, it is said, that only the larger multinationals can afford to hire the lawyers who understand it well enough to apply it to their tax returns.[7] There are two tax advantages in this category, just one of which—called the "exclusion of gross-up on dividends"—costs the U.S. Treasury an estimated $55 million a year. In a discussion before the House Ways and Means Committee in 1973, five of the six tax experts convened for a panel appeared to concur in the opinion expressed by one of them as follows: "By and large, these LDC exceptions constitute tax expenditures to our largest corporations without any demonstration of benefits to the economies of the less developed countries involved."[8]

Domestic International Sales Corporations

In 1971, in a desire to stimulate exports and improve the U.S. balance of payments, Congress extended to exporters the same right to defer taxes on income earned abroad as already existed for corporations investing abroad. Under this legislation, a corporation can establish a domestic international sales corporation (DISC) to handle its overseas sales. If 95% of the DISC's gross earnings are foreign and 95% of its assets are export-related, the DISC can defer paying taxes on 50% of its income; the DISC's shareholders—usually the parent company—must pay taxes on the remaining 50%. In reality, most DISCs are paper corporations established by multinational firms solely for tax benefits.[9]

It is not required that companies disclose DISCs in their annual reports unless a DISC reduces a company's statutory tax rate by 2.4% or more. Of 19 drug companies whose reports on 1973 taxes to the Securities and Exchange Commission were analyzed by Tax Analysts and Advocates, just two reported specific figures for tax savings from DISCs. Merck reported 2.2% and American Hospital Supply 1.3%. In addition Pfizer mentioned that it had formed a DISC.[10]

The corporate tax revenue lost as a result of DISCs has been higher than Congress estimated when it passed the legislation in 1971. Senator Edmund S. Muskie predicted in June 1974 that the losses for 1974 and 1975 would be $740 million and $920 million, respectively. But when the tax expenditure figures were published with the fiscal 1976 budget in February 1975, Treasury had upped the estimate to $870 million for 1974; $1.07 billion for 1975; and $1.32 billion for 1976.*[12]

Western Hemisphere Trade Corporations

In 1942, U.S. corporations investing in Latin America complained of financial difficulties exacerbated by rising wartime taxes. In response, Congress passed legislation allowing U.S. corporations to conduct business in Latin America through Western Hemisphere Trade Corporations (WHTCs), the earnings of which would be taxed at a rate of 34% instead of at the usual 48% corporate rate. Similar to a DISC, a WHTC must earn 95% of its gross income outside the United States and 90% of that must be from trade or business. While no physical operation in Latin America is actually required, goods must be sold outside the United States.

WHTCs were originally expected to encourage capital investment in Latin America, but they have largely become wholesalers selling U.S. products abroad. Tax authority Thomas E. Jenks claimed in February 1973 that 400 out of an approximate total of 600 WHTCs fell into this category.[13]

In *The Rape of the Taxpayer*, Philip Stern reports that Eli Lilly sold drugs so cheaply to its WHTC, the Eli Lilly Pan American Corp. (which in turn sold drugs at higher prices to Latin American buyers), that the latter, with tax rates lower than the parent company's, received between 93% and 97% of Lilly's profits on drug sales in the Western Hemisphere.[14]

---

* Though drug company gains are not likely to be affected, these figures may be revised downward (by as much as $30 million in 1975 and more thereafter) as a result of a provision in the Tax Reduction Act of 1975 denying DISC benefits for export of natural resources and energy products.[11]

Possessions Tax

Section 931 of the Internal Revenue Code permits wholly-owned subsidiaries established in U.S. possessions, such as Puerto Rico, to defer all taxes indefinitely. At the same time, the Puerto Rican government grants tax "holidays" of between 10 and 18 years. Profits made in Puerto Rico are thus entirely tax-free during this period.

According to *Washington Research Associates,* an industry newsletter, "If section 931 were eliminated, the industry with the most exposure would appear to be drugs. A change in the tax code in this regard would, unquestionably, have a substantial impact on the overall tax rate and profitability of drug companies with significant operations in Puerto Rico or other possessions covered under the section."[15]

Drug companies with major operations in Puerto Rico include Abbott, Eli Lilly, Merck, G.D. Searle, Schering-Plough, SmithKline, and Squibb. As a result of the tax preference granted operations in Puerto Rico, these multinationals reduced their statutory tax rate in 1973 by figures ranging from 2.2% (Merck) to 24.3% (G.D. Searle).[16]

In addition, branches of U.S. companies receive tax deductions for start-up costs in Puerto Rico. Once a branch operation becomes profitable, it can be transformed into a subsidiary, at which point U.S. taxes are indefinitely deferred and Puerto Rican taxes are suspended for years. Once the Puerto Rican exemption expires, the parent can liquidate the Puerto Rican subsidiary—again, tax-free.[17]

Individual Tax Exemptions

Multinational executives, like other U.S. citizens living abroad, can exclude from taxable income $25,000 if they reside abroad for three consecutive years, or $20,000 if they live abroad for at least 17 out of every 18 months.[18]

* * *

Putting It All Together

For 12 major drug companies, a combination of tax benefits

offered by Puerto Rican operations, unrepatriated dividends, DISCs, WHTCs and other credits resulted in reductions of their tax rates from a statutory rate of 48% to an actual rate, in 1973, of between 7.3% (Pfizer) and 32.5% (Bristol-Myers).[19]

Each tax benefit for multinationals reduces revenue to the U.S. Treasury. The Office of Management and Budget has estimated that these benefits will cost the Treasury the following amounts in 1975:[20]

	Millions of Dollars	
Exclusion of certain income earned abroad by U.S. citizens	95	
Exclusion of individual income earned in U.S. possessions	5	
Exclusion of corporate income earned in U.S. possessions	350	
Exclusion of gross-up on dividends of LDC corporations	55	
Western Hemisphere Trade Corporations (WHTCs)	50	
Deferral of income of Domestic International Sales Corporations (DISCs)	1070	(-30)*
TOTAL	1625	(1595)*

This total does not include the benefits to corporations and individuals from tax deferral, which the Joint Committee on Internal Revenue Taxation estimates will amount to $620 million in 1975. After the Tax Reduction Act of 1975 this figure could, however, be reduced by approximately one third.[21]

Overseas Private Investment Corporation (OPIC)

U.S. multinationals investing abroad have also received significant—though controversial—assistance from the Overseas Private Investment Corporation. OPIC is an

*See note at bottom of page 150.

outgrowth of a guarantee program begun 25 years ago to encourage U.S. business investment in postwar Europe. Under AID, the program evolved into an effort to assist economic development in less developed countries. OPIC, which was organized in 1971, took over this guarantee program with a mandate from Congress "to mobilize and facilitate the participation of United States private capital and skills in the economic and social progress of less developed friendly countries."[22]

OPIC provides assistance primarily in the form of political risk insurance for U.S. company investments abroad. It also makes some direct loans to U.S. companies for development projects abroad and, on a much smaller scale, provides guarantees on development loans made by commercial banks.

There are three types of OPIC political risk insurance: (1) inconvertibility insurance, in case local currency cannot be converted into U.S. dollars; (2) war damage insurance; and (3) expropriation insurance. Inconvertibility insurance and war damage insurance have been profit-making operations.

Expropriation insurance, on the other hand, has been a problem for OPIC. The agency has collected $85 million in premiums, but it is faced with claims of over $397 million. (Of these, $28 million have been paid while $369 million are still under adjudication.)[23]

By providing these three types of insurance, OPIC effectively assumes for multinational corporations major political risks they face by investing in less developed countries. OPIC's rates are low (an average of 1½%) and terms are long (up to 20 years). Political risk insurance offered by private companies is for shorter terms at higher rates.[24]

In addition, OPIC insurance may offer the U.S. investor unofficial political protection by the U.S. government; because the Treasury is ultimately liable for any claim, the government may gear its policies to avoid the danger of expropriation. This was allegedly the case in Chile when the CIA intervened in the presidential elections. Edward Korry, former U.S. Ambassador to Chile, testified before the Senate Subcommittee on Multinational Corporations that in warning Washington of the perils of an Allende government, he noted the potential cost to the Treasury of covering investment guarantees in case of expropriation.[25]

Many multinationals have taken advantage of OPIC's political risk insurance program. Often, a single food or drug company has had several different investments insured by OPIC. Some of these multiple users are Ralston Purina, Schering, Squibb, Pfizer, United Fruit, Gulf+Western, and Stokely-Van Camp. In addition, a few agribusinesses have received large direct loans. Of 18 direct investments active as of June 30, 1973, one of the largest was a loan to Cargill's Brazilian subsidiary for soybean processing facilities.[26]

U.S. Embassy Representation Abroad

A friendly helping hand from the local U.S. embassy is another important service provided by the U.S. government to American companies operating abroad. Embassies, of course, have always helped to promote sales of U.S. products abroad. But in recent years, they have also become increasingly involved in assisting U.S. companies that have direct investments overseas. Though the subsidiaries of these companies claim to be "good corporate citizens" of host nations, they turn to Uncle Sam for help when necessary.

U.S. businessmen abroad usually seek assistance from the embassy in one of two situations: first, in expropriation matters; second, and far more frequently, in instances where the policies of host governments are seen as discriminating against or making special demands on foreign investors.[27]

One example of the kind of assistance embassies provide is contained in the following unclassified cable:

From: SECSTATE WASH DC
To: AMEMBASSY SAN JOSE [COSTA RICA] PRIORITY
Subject: PATENT LEGISLATION: VISIT OF JACK HAGAN. . . .

1. Jack Hagan, patent counsel for American Cyanamid, plans to visit San Jose February 6 and 7 [1973].
2. American Cyanamid has learned through commercial channels that the Costa Rican legislature is scheduled to commence discussion on February 11 of proposed legislation which would reduce the validity term of patents from 20 years to 5 years and which would withdraw patent protection for drugs.

Hagan plans to discuss the proposed legislation with the Minister of Commerce and Industry, the Director of Social Security and, if appropriate, the Minister of Justice. . . .

In view of importance of proposed legislation to U.S. proprietary interests, embassy officer may accompany Hagan on his visits to government officials.[28]

In addition to lending the prestige of the U.S. government to a corporate representative as in the American Cyanamid case, embassies also intervene directly at times.

The disputes that cause the greatest problems, according to a State Department official with responsibility for commercial and business affairs, are those in which the interests of the U.S. company directly conflict with the interests of the host country. U.S. embassies usually try to resolve these conflicts by what the official characterized as "diplomacy"—the embassy will negotiate and negotiate, stalling as long as possible in the hope that the problem will solve itself. But, he said, if the U.S. company believes that its interests are vitally affected—and if that company is big and powerful enough—it will take its case to the State Department. Then, "the bigger the company, the higher the level it can reach—the higher the level, the greater the chances its interests will prevail."[29]

P.L. 480: Food for Peace

The U.S. food aid program—better known as Food for Peace—was established in 1954 under Public Law 480. Food for Peace represents a major part of total U.S. foreign aid efforts, accounting over the years for one third of all American development assistance.[30] Food aid under P.L. 480 takes one of two forms.[31]

Under Title I, the U.S. government gives long-term

low-interest loans to foreign countries so that the countries can buy agricultural commodities from the private U.S. companies of their choice. These "concessional sales" are made when a foreign country requires help in meeting its food needs because of its inadequate domestic agricultural production and inability to buy imported commodities on normal commercial terms.

Under Title II, the U.S. government donates agricultural commodities to foreign countries either by giving the food directly to the foreign governments or channeling it through U.S. private voluntary agencies (such as CARE), international organizations (such as UNICEF), or the multilateral World Food Program. These donations are made to feed needy people, to combat malnutrition, and to meet emergency situations such as famines or natural disasters.

Although Title II has received more public attention than Title I, it is actually the smaller part of the program. Title II accounts for little more than a quarter of the food shipped under P.L. 480. The bulk of U.S. food aid—about 75% or $16 billion worth from 1955 through 1973—has been provided through Title I concessional sales.[32]

Among the principal beneficiaries of U.S. food aid have been the large multinational food and agribusiness corporations that handle, transport, and sell agricultural exports. It is from these companies that the U.S. or foreign government buys most P.L. 480 commodities, and it is therefore to these companies that the profits from those sales go.*[34] On an average, P.L. 480 has meant nearly $1 billion in business for food and agribusiness corporations each year.[35]

Most of that business, according to U.S. Department

---

* According to USDA regulations, the price paid to the U.S. supplier by the foreign government must not exceed the prevailing world price range, which until 1973 was much lower than U.S. domestic farm prices. The U.S. government's Commodity Credit Corporation would then pay the U.S. company the difference between world and U.S. prices. In today's market, however, domestic and world prices are the same, and U.S. companies' P.L. 480 sales are no longer subsidized.[33]

of Agriculture (USDA) officials, goes to "ten companies or less." P.L. 480 is such a "technical field," they explain, that only the biggest companies have the "know-how and sales volume" to participate.[36]

In fact, about half the business generated by P.L. 480 has gone to five companies—the world's five largest grain handlers.* Grain accounts for about two thirds of all commodities shipped under P.L. 480,[38] and the latest statistics compiled by USDA show that from 1954 through 1969 over two thirds of foreign currency sales of grain went to four of those five companies.[39] A conservative extrapolation from available data would put the business generated by P.L. 480 for the big five grain handlers at more than $1 billion apiece over the last 20 years.[40]

In some cases, U.S. agribusiness multinationals have reaped double benefits from P.L. 480. The U.S. parent sells the commodities and then its foreign subsidiary buys them—with local currency—from the foreign government.[41] In several cases, P.L. 480 has enabled U.S. companies operating abroad to obtain both loans and commodities that local shortages of credit and foreign exchange would have prohibited them from buying otherwise.[42]

As a result of the world food crisis, public attention is being drawn once again to P.L. 480 and how it works. Many commentators both inside and outside of Congress are arguing about the size of the U.S. food program and whether humanitarian or "foreign policy" objectives should predominate in its administration. But very little attention has been given to the role of the giant grain and agribusiness corporations in P.L. 480. We were able to learn only enough about their involvement to know that this aspect of the program deserves much closer scrutiny.

---

* Cargill, Inc., Continental Grain Co., and Cook Industries, all of the U.S.; Argentinean-owned Bunge Corp.; and French-owned Louis Dreyfus Corp. Together, these five firms handle 90% of the world's grain shipments.[37]

11/CONCLUSION

Considering food and drugs together from the viewpoint of consumer safety, as the U.S. Food and Drug Administration mainly does, leaves many facets of the drug industry and most activities of the food industry out of focus.

In the earlier chapters of this book we found many safety problems associated with the multinational drug industry in Latin America, but we have tried not to isolate these problems from other aspects of the pharmaceutical industry's impact on people. And in the later chapters we looked at some multinational food companies, not so much from the viewpoint of how safe their products are as from a concern for how appropriate they are to the needs of Latin America's hungry people.

The purpose of this approach was to avoid suggesting that all would be well if (1) each country had an agency similar to the U.S. Food and Drug Administration; (2) there were some kind of international superagency to handle the problems which arise from drugs in international commerce; and (3) executives of certain industries exercised a greater degree of corporate responsibility.

All three of these are desirable goals, but they are insufficient. Moreover, it is unlikely that they can be achieved without a broader kind of regulation affecting the whole relationship of multinational enterprise with developing countries.

To understand why these goals are insufficient and why action on a broader front is necessary, it is helpful to consider the failure of some recent attempts to improve the international flow of information on drugs.

Since the early 1960s, the World Health Organization (WHO) has been concerned with the quality and safety of drugs in international commerce. Between 1963 and 1974, the World Health Assembly and the WHO Executive Board passed 17 resolutions on the subject.[1] During this time, at the urging of the United States (and with its initial funding), a WHO pilot program for monitoring adverse reactions to drugs led to the establishment in 1971 of the Research Center for Monitoring Adverse Reactions to Drugs in Geneva. But the Center was structured in such a way that it has been useful only to some 20 relatively wealthy participating states—Japan and countries of Western Europe and North America. The developing countries, lacking the internal mechanisms to generate contributions to the system, do not receive most of the Center's data and reports. Consequently, their representatives in WHO have shown little interest in the Center. The monitoring system has reportedly been all but eliminated from WHO's 1976-77 budget.[2]

In 1971 and 1972, WHO urged the creation of an International System of Information on Drugs, a storage and retrieval system designed to facilitate the sharing of information generated by national registration and evaluation systems. The intention was to expand the dissemination system represented by the *Drug Information* circulars (referred to in several parts of Chapter 3) which, up to now, have notified WHO members of only a small percentage of national regulatory actions. In 1973, the World Health Assembly authorized a three-year feasibility study to assess the problems such a system is likely to face. The most serious of these problems became readily apparent: of the 25 countries from which basic data is to be collected, only 10 had, by the end of 1974, actually forwarded any information to WHO on newly registered drugs.[3]

Unfortunately, the representatives of many developed nations within WHO are influenced by large pharmaceutical firms headquartered in their respective countries. As such they display a great deal of inertia in response to the most elementary proposals for international exchange of information.

Industry's own resistance to information-sharing was

highlighted when a "Group of Eminent Persons" assembled by the United Nations in 1972 to study the role of multinational corporations recommended, in its June 1974 report, that "host countries should require the affiliates of multinational corporations to reveal to them any sales prohibitions and restrictions in manufacturing imposed by home or other host countries with respect to the health and safety of consumers."[4] Commenting on this recommendation, the USA-Business and Industry Advisory Committee, representing American multinationals, said that the Group's recommendation "implies international health and safety standards" and that, "considering discrepancies in per capita GNP and general conditions," it was "very unrealistic to apply universally. Significant safety and health problems should be handled and policed by national governments."[5]

This comment sidesteps the real issue raised by the Group, which is one of disclosure, not universal standards. A nation with a per capita GNP of $100 and an average life expectancy of 45 years may very well decide that potential benefits of a certain drug for its people far outweigh the risks. But in order to reach such a decision, that nation has a right to know precisely what the risks are and how they have been evaluated in other parts of the world. (And that nation's people have a similar right.) To deny access to such information is to frustrate the formulation of any nation's own health and safety standards.

If there were greater public concern and greater public pressure within the member nations of WHO, their representatives could surely find a way to preserve the monitoring system on adverse reactions and make it useful to developing countries; they would also find a way to strengthen and expand the International System of Information on Drugs. Both of these systems are necessary to assure the quality and safety of drugs moving in international commerce. But multinational enterprise obviously perceives even the most elementary form of information-sharing as a threat.

Even if such systems were fully supported and fully

funded, however, they would solve only one of the problems raised in the initial chapters of this book. In a report to the 1975 World Health Assembly, the Director General of WHO indicated his awareness that the multinational pharmaceutical industry poses many problems beyond those of safety and quality control:

"Many countries are under pressure to increase the number of available drugs to include many duplicate products marketed under different brand names and also products of questionable efficacy that have little or no beneficial public health impact. Experience suggests that the lists of essential drugs required for the great majority of preventable and treatable illnesses are not large and these lists can be regularly updated by replacing older drugs with new ones when they have proven and definite advantages."

"From the commercial point of view, narrow profit margins may discourage manufacturers from producing essential drugs in sufficient quantities to meet health needs, while the prices of certain essential patented drugs may be high because of the lack of real price competition."

"There is an urgent need to ensure that the most essential drugs are available at a reasonable price and to stimulate research and development to produce new drugs adapted to the real health requirements of developing countries."[6]

How is all this to be accomplished? WHO urges individual countries to develop national health policies with priorities structured to meet the needs mentioned. We have already seen how lack of access to crucial information stymies such efforts.

But a more basic obstacle is, as we saw in Chapter 4, that an individual nation's pursuit of such goals is often inimical to the maintenance of the kind of "business climate" that is attractive to private foreign investment. Most efforts within developing nations to limit the number of drugs available, to bring down their prices, and to stimulate local research have been hamstrung for the very good reason that they are a threat to profits. International business does not mind accepting subsidies from a government to try some additional research. It will agree to use excess plant capacity to make drugs it can sell to the government for distribution to the poor. But it will resist—it is bound to resist—policies which mean a reduction of profits.

In this respect, the pharmaceutical industry is no different from any other. For while there are special technical problems posed by industries which deal in inherently dangerous products, the basic obstacles to regulation are not technical ones; they are endemic to the system of multinational enterprise and its ability to play one developing country off against another.

It is competition among developing countries to create a climate favorable to investment by multinational companies that constitutes the basic obstacle to the changes called for by WHO's Director General. International regulation of the pharmaceutical industry is not likely to be effective unless it is related to international regulation of all multinational industry.

To isolate a single industry like the drug industry for regulation is not only difficult but also potentially counterproductive. The multinational pharmaceutical industry must compete with other industries for investment capital. Any meaningful international controls on the pharmaceutical industry are likely to have an adverse effect on overall industry profits. If profits decline, investors tend to shift their money elsewhere to obtain a higher yield. The industry would probably then have less money to spend on research, not more. And there is no guarantee that the know-how presently monopolized by multinational firms would be transferred to local industry; it might simply be diverted to more lucrative kinds of research in other fields.

In this book we have juxtaposed the activities of the multinational pharmaceutical industry in Latin America with those of multinational food and agribusiness companies. In Chapters 5 through 9, we have outlined problems which are just as serious as those associated with pharmaceuticals but much more complex: diversions of agricultural production from subsistence crops to more lucrative cash crops, resulting in poorer diets instead of better ones for the hungriest people; failure to reach the poor with commercial high-protein food ventures, contrasted with extraordinary success in selling protein-less beverages to people who do not need and cannot afford them; persistent efforts to sell inappropriate milk products to mothers who can neither afford nor use them properly.

What these cases illustrate, in common with those encountered in the drug industry, is a set of conflicts between multinational enterprise's pursuit of profit and the best interests of the low-income masses of people in Latin America.

These conflicts are basic. Technical solutions such as those proposed within WHO and a higher degree of corporate ethics or "corporate responsibility" might alleviate some of the conflicts and eliminate specific cases of harm to individuals, but they cannot eliminate the basic conflict. Corporations have to pursue profit. The officers and directors of any business corporation are legally bound to work toward making profit for their stockholders. When the interest of profit conflicts with the needs of poor people for a better life, a corporate executive who chooses the latter at the expense of the former runs the risk of losing his job.

We do not mean to imply that present-day governments in Latin America represent the best interests of the low-income masses. More often than not, they represent the interests of a privileged minority. But within every nation there are forces seeking to improve the situation of the lowest-income population. These forces are weakened by the competition among the governments of developing nations to attract multinational investments, because the very conditions which are attractive to foreign investment give low priority to social equity.

An "investment climate" attractive to multinational enterprise has far-reaching ramifications. It not only dictates a minimum of government interference in matters like product safety and quality, it also means guaranteeing large pools of cheap labor—preferably not unionized or at least not militant; it means tax incentives, freedom to compete with (and/or buy out) local industries, and a limit to price controls; and, above all, it means giving the corporations the freedom to produce and sell not necessarily what is most needed in the country, but what is most economically efficient from the standpoint of profits.

If developing countries do not get together to eliminate or control the competition among themselves for foreign capital investment, cases like those recounted in this book will continue to occur.

* * *

As for the government of the United States, it continues to be the chief defender and least critical friend of multinational enterprise. In his August 1975 address to the Seventh Special Session of the UN General Assembly, the U.S. Secretary of State called the very controversy over the role and conduct of multinational corporations "itself an obstacle to development."[7]

The citizens of the United States should at least be aware that they are such good friends of international business. We help to support multinational corporations by absolving them of the obligation to pay some $2 billion in taxes every year, by guaranteeing that we will bail them out if they are nationalized, and by sanctioning the friendly assistance offered by our commercial and diplomatic representatives abroad. Even our "give away" foreign aid programs are sometimes as much a give away to multinationals as to hungry people in developing countries.

All of this may be in the self-interest of the U.S. public. Perhaps the continued industrial growth and the financial returns to U.S. stockholders which result from multinational expansion are beneficial to this nation as a whole. If they are, then we should not pretend that we are interested in anybody's development other than our own. If not, then these subsidies and other forms of assistance should be thoroughly reconsidered.

Hungry for Profits

Source Notes

Indexes

Biographical Sketches

Publisher's Note

SOURCES

Preface *(text pp. xi–xiii)*

1. Philip H. Dougherty, "How ITT Improved Its Image," *The New York Times*, 18 April 1975.

1/Overview *(text pp. 1–5)*

1. "Directorio de las Mayores Compañías de America Latina," *Progreso*, January-February 1974, pp. 30–48.
2. Richard J. Barnet and Ronald E. Müller, *Global Reach: The Power of the Multinational Corporations* (New York: Simon and Schuster, 1974), p. 157.
3. Ibid., p. 147.
4. For Brazil: Philippe Guédon, President of ABIF, *Ciencia e Tecnologia na Indústria Farmacêutica* (Statement delivered before the Special Committee on Science and Technology of the Brazilian Chamber of Deputies, 7 November 1972), p. 2. For Venezuela: "Venezuelan Drug Bill to Limit Foreign Equity," *Business Latin America*, 24 February 1972, p. 64.
5. Unpublished monograph presented by the Colombian Departmento Nacional de Planeación at a meeting of the Andean Common Market, February 1971.
6. "Directorio," as in note 1. Also: "Mergers, Acquisitions and Market Extensions Reveal Patterns for Growth," *Food Engineering*, January 1974, foldout chart attached to p. 59.
7. "Who's Who in the Brazilian Economy: The 1,000 Largest Corporations in Brazil," *Brazil Report 1974* (São Paulo: Visão Editorial), p. 82.
8. *Inversión Nacional y Extranjera en la Industria Alimenticia: Empresas Principales por Ramas*. List obtained from Programa Nacional de Alimentación, Consejo Nacional de Ciencia y Tecnologia, Mexico City, 1974.
9. U.S. Department of Commerce, Bureau of Economic Analysis, "U.S. Direct Investment Abroad in 1972," *Survey of Current Business*, September 1973, table 8B.
10. See Chapter 10.

2/Pushtherapy in Brazil *(text pp. 6–24)*

1. U.S. Department of Commerce, Bureau of Economic Analysis, "U.S. Direct Investment Abroad in 1972," *Survey of Current Business,* September 1973, p. 28. At the time of the survey, the book value of U.S. direct investment in Venezuela, due mostly to oil investments, was higher than in Brazil, but with nationalization of the oil industry imminent, the value of U.S. investment in Venezuela is certain to be much lower in 1975. Cf. "Property, Plant and Equipment Expenditures by Majority-Owned Foreign Affiliates of U.S. Companies: Projections for 1974 and 1975," *Survey of Current Business,* September 1974, pp. 23–34.
2. *Why Invest in Brazil?* (Official publication of the Brazilian Export Fair held in Brussels, November 1973), p. 6.
3. *Business Round-Up* (Bulletin of the Brazilian-American Chamber of Commerce), December 1974, shows sales in the pharmaceutical industry from January through October 1974 as totalling $744 million. Assuming this volume was maintained, sales for the year would have been roughly $900 million. Foreign companies, according to the government, are responsible for 72% of total industry sales. See Presidência da Republica, Central de Medicamentos (CEME), *O Empreendimento CEME: Resumo Analitico Julho 1974,* p. 3.
4. Mario Victor de Assis Pacheco, *Indústria Farmacêutica e Segurança Nacional* (Rio de Janeiro: Civilizaçáo Brasileira, 1968), p. 15.
5. Richard B. Sellers, statement in *Why Invest in Brazil?,* as in note 2, p. 42.
6. Verified at plant, 1 April 1974.
7. Philippe Guédon, President of ABIF, *Ciencia e Tecnologia na Indústria Farmacêutica* (Statement delivered before the Special Committee on Science and Technology of the Brazilian Chamber of Deputies, 7 November 1972), p. 2.
8. The ranking of these firms is according to net assets as reported in "As 200 maiores," *Visão,* August 1973, pp. 139–160, 270, 306. The positions of several firms are approximate: Parke-Davis, Merck Sharp & Dohme and Lederle, because these firms are not public corporations in Brazil; Johnson & Johnson, Hoechst and Rhone Poulenc, because these firms are major producers of other products besides drugs.
9. "Productos Farmacêuticos, Medicinais e Veterinários," *Visão,* August 1973, p. 190. The source for these figures is the Fundação Getulio Vargas in Rio de Janeiro.
10. Ibid.
11. "Cheap Medicines for Brazilians," *Latin America Economic Report/Andean Times,* 19 July 1974, p. 111. Statistics compiled for 1969 and reported in *Planejamento & Desenvolvimento,* as in note 38 below, give a figure of $2.18 million.
12. *Anuario Estatístico IBGE* (Instituto Brasileiro de Geografia e Estatística), 1973.
13. *Visão,* as in note 9.

14. *Business Round-Up,* as in note 3.
15. This conversation is filmed in a BBC-TV documentary, "The Claiming of the Amazon." The interview was conducted in May 1973 by Bernardo Kucinski.
16. Ibid.
17. Unpublished material from the archives of the newsmagazine *Veja* in Recife.
18. "Entre 100 Pessoas no Paío 72 não Chegam aos 50 Anos," *Jornal do Brasil,* 29 June 1974. This article cites *O Documento Básico sobre a Saúde Brasileira,* a report by the Ministry of Health, based on 1970 figures.
19. Ibid. Cf. "Metade das Mortes em São Paulo Ainda é por Doenças Evitáveis," *Jornal do Brasil,* 13 April 1974.
20. *Relatório das Atividades do Ministério da Saúde* (mimeo, 1972), p. 102.
21. Ibid., p. 101.
22. "Programa Completo dentro de 5 Anos," *O Estado de São Paulo,* 31 March 1974.
23. Senator Benedito Ferreira, *Diario do Congresso Nacional,* 3 July 1971, p. 2844. Cost calculated on basis of 1971 average exchange rate of 5.287 cruzeiros to the dollar.
24. Re São Paulo average: Departamento Intersindical de Estatística e Estudos Sócio-econômicos, *Familia Assalariada: Padrão e Custo de Vida,* Estudos Sócio-econômicos no. 2, January 1974, p. 25. Re 20% and $75 figures: Hollis Chenery et al., *Redistribution With Growth*: A Joint Study by the World Bank's Development Research Center and the Institute of Development Studies at the University of Sussex (London: Oxford University Press, 1974), p. 12.
25. *Jornal do Brasil,* as in note 18.
26. Dr. Geraldo Chaia, testimony before Science and Technology Commission of the Brazilian Chamber of Deputies, *Diario do Congresso Nacional,* 25 August 1973, p. 4839.
27. Ibid.
28. "São Paulo: Crianças à Morte," *Veja,* 1 May 1974, p. 74.
29. Figures for 1960–1970 from Walter Leser, "Crescimento da Populaçao da Cidade de São Paulo, entre 1950 e 1970, e seu Reflexo nas Condições de Saúde Pública," *Ciencia e Cultura,* no. 22 (March 1975), pp. 244–256. Figure for 1973 as in previous note.
30. Pacheco, as in note 4, p. 38.
31. Personal interview with Roberto Schneider at Pfizer plant on São Paulo-Rio highway, 1 April 1974.
32. Personal interview with Dr. Claudio Daffré, São Paulo, 29 March 1974.
33. Ibid.
34. Ibid.
35. Ibid.
36. Ibid. Also, personal interview with Dr. Pedro Ayres Netto, Supervisor at Santa Casa Hospital in São Paulo, 21 March 1974.
37. Ibid.
38. Ibid. Cf. "A Saúde do Povo uma Nova Prioridade," *Planejamento &*

Desenvolvimento (Organ of the Ministry of Planning), December 1973, p. 45.
39. Senator Benedito Ferreira, *A Revolução nos Medicamentos* (Separate printing of speech), Brasília, 1971.
40. Re concentration of drugstores in Copacabana: Juarez Bahia, "Lançar Productos, a Febre dos Laboratórios," *Jornal do Brasil,* 11 June 1974. Re salaries of Brazilian executives: "The Samba Gives Way to the Computer," *Business Week,* 2 November 1974, p. 14A.
41. Personal witness by the reporter.
42. Ferreira, as in note 23.
43. *Familia Assalariada,* as in note 24, p. 13.
44. Personal interview with Dr. Herval Ribeiro, São Paulo, 22 March 1974.
45. Meeting with officials of Sterling Drug Co., New York, 27 September 1974.
46. Letter of 17 September 1974 from Dr. J. L. R. Barlow to the author.
47. Personal interview with Dr. Nelson Moraes, Director of the Health Secretariat at the Ministry of Health, Rio de Janeiro, 7 March 1974.
48. *Relatório das Atividades,* as in note 20, p. 217.
49. *Seminar on Drug Control in the Americas* (Maracay, Venezuela, 15-20 November 1970), Pan American Health Organization Scientific Publication no. 225 (Washington, D.C.: 1971), p. 146.
50. Personal interview with confidential source, 9 April 1974.
51. Diretor do Serviço Nacional de Fiscalização de Medicina e Farmácia, *Portaria No. 18,* 28 September 1973.
52. "Multi compram orgãos com brindes," *Diario do Comércio,* Belo Horizonte, 3 May 1975.
53. "E Falho o controle de remedios," *O Estado de São Paulo,* 3 August 1975.
54. Ibid.
55. Telephone interview with Dr. Uriel Zanon, formerly an official at SNFMF, 7 April 1974.
56. Personal inquiry at Drogamec, São Paulo drugstore, March 1974.
57. Bahia, as in note 40, says that there are more than 20,000 products and 60,000 if different presentations are counted separately. Daffré, as in note 32, says that there are over 30,000 brand names. In São Paulo's *Jornal da Tarde,* 12 March 1974, p. 13, the associate director of a pharmaceutical distribution house is quoted as saying that there are about 20,000 pharmaceutical products. But the most conservative estimate is followed here, that of CEME, the government's agency for producing medicines for low-income people, which counts 10,200 products, according to Representative Jaison Barreto, in a telephone interview, 2 April 1974.
58. Confidential source. Cf. Bahia, as in note 40, quoting the president of the Association of Pharmacy Owners and Officials as saying that there is a "fever" to launch new products.
59. Daffré, as in note 32.
60. Cf. *Compêndio Médico,* 15th ed. (São Paulo: Andrei, 1974), passim.
61. Bahia, as in note 40.

62. Package leaflet obtained in Brazil, March–April 1974.
63. *Compêndio Médico,* as in note 60, p. 475f.
64. Sales position of TETREX: "Fabricantes de Remédios Definem suas Posições," *Jornal do Brasil*, 9 June 1974. Forms: *Compêndio Médico,* as in note 60, p. 549ff.
65. Nildo Aguilar et al., *A Infecção Hospitalar e o Emprego de Antibióticos: Resultados de Pesquisas no Hospital de Ipanema* (mimeo), 1974.
66. Telephone interview with Representative Jaison Barreto, 2 April 1974.
67. Johnson & Johnson, Divisão Farmacêutica, *Boletim de Propaganda e Vendas,* nos. 75–82 (São Paulo, June 1965).
68. Personal interview with confidential source, São Paulo, 27 March 1974.
69. Ibid.
70. Ferreira, as in note 23.
71. Johnson & Johnson *Boletim,* as in note 67.
72. Ibid.
73. NOVULON was on the list of the 50 best-selling drugs in 1968 published in "Problemas da Indústria Farmacêutica no Brasil," *Boletim Informativo da Academia Brasileira de Medicina Militar,* vol. 7, no. 9 (September 1969), p. 19.
74. Personal interview with João Carlos, buyer at the Droga Romano, São Paulo, 1 April 1974.
75. Witnessed personally by the reporter, March 1974.
76. Ferreira, as in note 23, p. 2846.
77. Netto, as in note 36.
78. Cf. "Problemas da Indústria. . . ," as in note 73, p. 13.
79. Jorge M. Katz, *La Industria Farmacéutica Argentina: Estructura y Comportamiento* (Buenos Aires: Instituto Torcuato di Tella, 1973), p. 22.
80. Cf. "Problemas da Indústria. . . ," as in note 73, p. 13.
81. Ibid.
82. Pacheco, as in note 4.
83. *O Empreendimento CEME,* as in note 3, p. 4.
84. Ferreira, as in note 23, p. 2846.
85. Katz, as in note 79, p. 17.
86. Ribeiro, as in note 44.
87. Personal interview with Dr. Mario Migliano, São Paulo, 27 March 1974.

3/Promoting Health *(text pp. 25–51)*

1. "Advertising and Promotion of Drugs," Part IV of *Study of Administered Prices in the Drug Industry* (Report by the Senate Subcommittee on Antitrust and Monopoly, 1961), reprinted in entirety in Morton Mintz, *The Therapeutic Nightmare* (Boston: Houghton Mifflin, 1965), p. 458.
2. *Requirements of the United States Food, Drug, and Cosmetic Act,* FDA 72-1013/revised February 1972 (Washington, D.C.: HEW, 1972).
3. *The Medical Letter: A Non-Profit Publication on Drugs and Therapeutics* (published by The Medical Letter, Inc., 56 Harrison Street, New

Rochelle, N.Y. 10801), vol. 15, no. 6 (16 March 1973), p. 28.

4. Current package insert as approved by the FDA. (*Note:* Unless otherwise indicated, the source for all references to "package insert" is the 1974 edition of the *Physicians' Desk Reference.)*
5. Ibid.
6. *Medical Letter,* as in note 3.
7. Current package insert as approved by the FDA.
8. *AMA Drug Evaluations,* 2nd ed. (Acton, Mass.: Publishing Sciences Group, 1973), p. 403.
9. *Médico Moderno,* Mexican ed., vol. 10, no. 11 (July 1972), cited in *Medical Letter,* as in note 3.
10. Meeting with Mr. Brooks, Mt. Vernon, N.Y., week of 1 April 1974.
11. *Diccionario de Especialidades Farmacéuticas,* Edición Mexicana, 20th ed. (Mexico: P.L.M., 1973), p. 903.
12. Inserts and boxes obtained in Brazil, August 1973 and March-April 1974.
13. Insert obtained in Brazil, March-April 1974.
14. Insert obtained in the Dominican Republic, April 1974.
15. Ibid.
16. Insert obtained in Brazil, March-April 1974.
17. Current package insert as approved by the FDA.
18. *Merck Index,* 1960; FDA letter of 2 August 1974 from Henry B. Packscher, Director, Precedent and Advisory Communications Staff, Bureau of Drugs.
19. World Health Organization (WHO), *Drug Information,* no. 27 (21 August 1964).
20. WHO, *Drug Information,* no. 35 (25 January 1965); no. 39 (31 May 1965).
21. Letter of 20 August 1974 from Frank C. Springer, Manager, Public Relations, Eli Lilly International Corporation. Cf. Lilly DELVEX label, revised 30 June 1964.
22. Packsher, as in note 18.
23. Ibid.
24. Letter of 20 April 1964 from S. Lidsky of Pfizer to George P. Larrick, Commissioner of Food and Drugs.
25. Letter of 31 March 1964 from Larrick to Lidsky.
26. Lidsky to Larrick, as in note 24.
27. Ibid.
28. Insert obtained in Panama, July 1973.
29. Letter of 25 October 1974 from Dr. J. E. Jeffris, Vice President-Medical Director, Pfizer International.
30. Insert obtained in Venezuela, September 1974.
31. *AMA Drug Evaluations,* as in note 8, p. 267; cf. *American Hospital Formulary Service* (Washington, D.C.: American Society of Hospital Pharmacists, 1974), Section 28:08.
32. WHO, *Drug Information,* no. 40 (31 May 1965).
33. The legal basis for this statement is as follows: Section 331 (a) of the Food, Drug, and Cosmetic Act prohibits the introduction into interstate

commerce of any drug which is adulterated or misbranded. Section 352 (f) states that a drug is misbranded unless its labeling bears adequate directions for use and adequate warnings against uses or dosages which are not safe.

34. Current package insert as approved by the FDA.
35. *AMA Drug Evaluations,* as in note 8, pp. 262 and 267.
36. Interviews with Sterling Drug officials, 27 September 1974.
37. *Archivos Dominicanos de Pediatría,* vol. 10, no. 1 (January/April 1974) and vol. 10, no. 2 (May/August 1974).
38. Packet purchased in Brazil, March-April 1974.
39. Ibid.
40. *Index Terapêutico Moderno* (São Paulo: Serpel, 1972), pp. 791f.
41. Ibid.
42. *Mercado Farmacéutico Colombia* (Bogotá: IMS, 1972).
43. BESEROL is marketed in Brazil, Colombia, Venezuela, Mexico; DOLOPIRONA, in Argentina.
44. *Diccionario de Especialidades Farmacéuticas,* 5th ed., Centro-America Dominica (Mexico: P.L.M., 1973), p. 455.
45. *Diccionario . . . Farmacéuticas,* as in note 11, p. 390.
46. *Diccionario . . . Farmacéuticas,* as in note 44, p. 120; *Diccionario de Especialidades Farmacéuticas,* 2nd ed., Colombia-Ecuador (Colombia: P.L.M., 1973), p. 102; *Guia de las Especialidades Farmacéuticas en Venezuela,* 11th ed. (Madrid: A. Spilva de Lehr, 1973), p. 569.
47. *Compêndio Médico,* 15th ed. (São Paulo: Andrei, 1974), p. 193.
48. *Diccionario . . . Farmacéuticas,* as in note 11, p. 213.
49. *Compêndio Médico,* as in note 47, p. 524.
50. *Terapia Vademecum* (Argentina: Terapia, 1972), pp. 39–40.
51. Telephone check with the FDA.
52. *AMA Drug Evaluations,* as in note 8, p. 557.
53. WHO, *Drug Information,* no. 5 (15 January 1964); no. 55 (25 February 1966); no. 32 (20 November 1964); no. 6 (15 January 1964); no. 54 (25 February 1966).
54. Dr. Oree M. Carroll et al., "Stevens-Johnson Syndrome Associated with Long Acting Sulfonamides," *Journal of the American Medical Association,* vol. 195, no. 8 (21 February 1966), pp. 179–181.
55. *AMA Drug Evaluations,* as in note 8, p. 557.
56. Ibid.
57. Inserts obtained in Brazil, March-April 1974; Colombia, April 1974.
58. *Diccionario . . . Farmacéuticas,* as in note 11, p. 569.
59. Ibid., p. 499.
60. Ibid., p. 893.
61. Milton Silverman and Philip R. Lee, *Pills, Profits, and Politics* (Berkeley: University of California Press, 1974), pp. 61–63.
62. W. M. O'Brien, "Indomethacin: A Survey of Clinical Trials," *Clin. Pharmacol. Ther.,* 9, 94 (1968) as cited in *Side Effects of Drugs* (see note 68 below).
63. *AMA Drug Evaluations,* as in note 8, p. 299.

64. Current package insert as approved by FDA.
65. Ibid.
66. Insert obtained in Brazil, Spring 1974.
67. Insert obtained in Venezuela, Spring 1974.
68. *Side Effects of Drugs: A Survey of Unwanted Effects of Drugs Reported in 1968–1971*, vol. 7 in the series *Side Effects of Drugs,* eds. L. Meyler and A. Herxheimer (Amsterdam: Excerpta Medica, 1972).
69. FDA *Requirements,* as in note 2.
70. Current package insert as approved by the FDA.
71. "Medroxyprogesterone Acetate Injectable Contraceptive: Proposed Patient Labeling," *Federal Register,* vol. 38, no. 195 (10 October 1973), pp. 27940-42.
72. Ibid.
73. Ibid.
74. Ibid.
75. HEW Press Release 73-45 (10 October 1973).
76. *Federal Register,* vol. 39, no. 178 (12 September 1974), p. 32909.
77. Ibid., pp. 32907-11.
78. "Upjohn's Marketing of Contraceptive is Stayed by HEW," *The Wall Street Journal,* 10 October 1974.
79. Ad received from Colombia, June 1974.
80. *El Médico,* October 1973; *Revista Colombiana de Obstetricia y Ginecología,* January-February 1972 and March-April 1972.
81. Louis S. Goodman and Alfred Gilman, eds., *The Pharmacological Basis of Therapeutics,* 4th ed. (New York: Macmillan Co., 1970), p. 170.
82. Ibid., p. 173.
83. Ibid., pp. 170f.
84. Current package insert as approved by the FDA.
85. Insert obtained in Brazil, March-April 1974.
86. Letter of 9 October 1974 from Grant Wolfkill, Public Affairs Director, E. R. Squibb & Sons, Inc.
87. Insert obtained in Brazil, March-April 1974.
88. Goodman and Gilman, as in note 81, p. 27.
89. *Drug and Therapeutics Bulletin,* vol. 2, no. 16 (3 August 1973).
90. Current package insert as approved by the FDA.
91. Inserts for ACROMICINA, AUREOMICINA, LEDERMICINA obtained in Brazil, March-April 1974.
92. Inserts for TETREX obtained in Brazil, March-April 1974. Those for BRISTACICLINA-A and BRISTACIN-A obtained in Colombia, April 1974.
93. Inserts for VIBRAMICINA obtained in Colombia, March and April 1974. Those for TETRACYNA, VIBRAMICINA, and TERRAMICINA obtained in Brazil, March-April 1974.
94. *Ginecología y Obstetricia de México,* vol. 35, no. 208 (February 1974).
95. Dra. Martha Romero Orozco, "Valoración de un Nuevo Analgésico en la Dismennorea," *Semana Médica de México,* vol. 74, no. 950 (16 March 1973).
96. FDA *Requirements,* as in note 2.

Sources for Chapter 3 continued

97. *Federal Register,* vol. 39, no. 62 (29 March 1974), p. 11698.
98. Current patient package information as approved by the FDA.
99. Ibid.
100. Insert obtained in Venezuela, April 1974.
101. Insert obtained in Mexico, April-June 1974.
102. Insert obtained in Mexico, April-June 1974.
103. Inserts obtained in Colombia: OVULEN in March and OVULEN 1/2 in April 1974.
104. Insert obtained in the Dominican Republic, Spring 1974.
105. Inserts obtained in Colombia and Brazil, March 1974.
106. Ibid.
107. Letter of 8 November 1974 from John F. Barrett, Sr., Director of Internal Communication, G. D. Searle & Co.
108. Current package insert as approved by the FDA.
109. *Federal Register,* vol. 37, no. 52 (16 March 1972), pp. 5516f.
110. Ibid.
111. Ibid.
112. *Diccionario . . . Farmacéuticas,* as in note 11, p. 746.
113. Ibid.
114. Ibid., pp. 294f.
115. Ibid., pp. 523f.
116. Ibid., p. 524.
117. *Ginecología y Obstetricia de México,* vol. 35, no. 210 (April 1974).
118. Ibid.
119. "Present Status of Cinchophen and Neocinchophen," *Journal of the American Medical Association,* 4 October 1941, pp. 1182f. (part of Reports of the Council on Pharmacy and Chemistry, presented by Theodore G. Klumpp, M.D., Secretary).
120. "Communication on Cinchophen and Cinchophen Derivatives Made Available by Dr. Theodore Klumpp of the Food and Drug Administration," *Journal of the American Medical Association,* 4 October 1941, p. 1183.
121. *AMA Drug Evaluations,* 1st ed. (Acton, Mass.: Publishing Sciences Group, 1971), p. 196.
122. According to FDA letter of 3 August 1974 from Henry B. Packscher.
123. Letter of 16 December 1974 from Gottfried Neuhaus, Director, Administrative Services, International Division, Schering Corp.
124. *Index Terapêutico Moderno,* as in note 40, pp. 748–9.
125. Label obtained in Venezuela, July 1974.
126. Letter of 17 September 1974 from J. L. R. Barlow, M.D., International Medical Director, Abbott Universal Ltd.
127. *Journal of the American Medical Association,* June 1952; 1959; 1967 as cited in *Consumer Reports,* October 1970.
128. Letter of 14 July 1974 from Nina Fritsch SCMM.
129. *New England Journal of Medicine,* vol. 282, no. 14 (1970), pp. 813f.
130. Ibid.
131. Ibid.
132. Ibid.

133. Ibid.
134. Insert obtained in Brazil, March-April 1974.
135. Brochure obtained in Mexico, Spring 1974.
136. *Actualidades Médicas,* February 1974.
137. "Chloramphenicol: Indications and Warnings—An International Survey," work undertaken on behalf of IOCU, 1973 (date submitted), p. 5.
138. *The Lancet,* 3 August 1974, p. 282.
139. Current package insert as approved by the FDA.
140. "The Misuse of Pentazocine: Its Dependence-Producing Potential," Council on Drugs Report in *Journal of the American Medical Association,* vol. 209, no. 10 (8 September 1969), pp. 1515f.
141. Current package insert as approved by the FDA.
142. WHO, *Drug Information,* no. 86 (26 November 1970).
143. Package leaflet obtained in Brazil, March-April 1974.
144. *Diccionario . . . Farmacéuticas,* as in note 11, pp. 779f. SOSIGON (Mexican brand name) labeling: "Su venta requiere receta médica, la que deberá conservarse en la farmacia para su riguroso control," confirmed by letter of 24 July 1974 from Dr. A. Lomeli.
145. *The Lancet,* 21 June 1969, p. 1263.
146. *The Lancet,* 5 July 1969, pp. 56f.
147. Ibid.
148. Ibid.
149. Insert obtained in Colombia, March 1974.
150. Interviews, as in note 36.
151. *Médico Moderno,* vol. 10, no. 12 (August 1972).
152. Interviews, as in note 36.
153. *Médico Moderno,* vol. 11, no. 9 (May 1973).
154. Current package insert as approved by the FDA.
155. Brochure obtained in Brazil, March-April 1974.
156. Norman W. Blacow, ed., *Martindale: The Extra Pharmacopoeia,* 26th ed. (London: The Pharmaceutical Press, July 1972). This work is published by direction of the Council of the Pharmaceutical Society of Great Britain and produced in the Society's Department of Pharmaceutical Sciences.
157. Insert obtained in Colombia, June 1974.
158. Insert obtained in Venezuela, April 1974.
159. *Mercado Farmacéutico Colombia,* as in note 42.

4/Ambivalent Hosts *(text pp. 52–71)*

1. "The American Drug Industry on the World Scene" (Speech by George R. Cain, Board Chairman and President, Abbott Laboratories, before the 18th Annual Convention, Financial Analysts Federation, Sheraton Hotel, Philadelphia, 19 May 1965).
2. Milton Silverman and Philip R. Lee, *Pills, Profits and Politics* (Berkeley: University of California Press, 1974), pp. 178–81 and 336ff. A spot-check

comparison of the U.S. Drug Industry's *Redbook* for January 1974 with the Brazilian *Guia Farmacêutico* for February 1974 and the Argentinean *Manual Farmacéutico* for January 1974 appears to bear this out.
3. Cf. Union Bank of Switzerland, *Prices and Earnings Around the Globe* (Zurich, February 1974), pp. 24f. Also Chapter 2, passim.
4. Examples: for Brazil, see certification of Price Control Council on Pfizer price list; for Colombia, see page 59 of this chapter.
5. International Monetary Fund, *Balance of Payments Yearbook*, as cited in Victor L. Urquidi and Rosemary Thorp, eds., *Latin America in the International Economy* (New York: Halsted Press, 1973), p. 269.
6. Mario Victor de Assis Pacheco, *Indústria Farmacêutica e Segurança Nacional* (Rio de Janeiro: Civilização Brasileira, 1968), pp. 102–106.
7. Ibid.
8. Ibid., pp. 29f.
9. Cf. Philip Siekman, "When Executives Turned Revolutionaries," *Fortune*, September 1964, pp. 147–149+.
10. Personal interview with Dr. Alonso Lucio, Bogotá, 20 June 1974.
11. Ibid.
12. Summaries of evidence prepared by the Dirección General de Aduana of Colombia, copies in the possession of Dr. Lucio.
13. Lucio, as in note 10; confirmed by his letter of 23 January 1975.
14. Summaries, as in note 12.
15. Lucio, as in note 10.
16. Ibid.
17. Ibid.
18. Clippings from Colombian press inspected in files of Lucio.
19. Lucio, as in notes 10 and 18.
20. Ibid.
21. "El Escandalo de las Drogas," *El Tiempo*, 7 February 1970.
22. Lucio, as in note 10.
23. Constantine V. Vaitsos, "The Use of Economic Power by Transnational Corporations and its Effects on Inter-Country Income Distribution" (Doctoral Thesis, Harvard University, 1972). Our information comes from an earlier draft: "Transfer of Resources and Preservation of Monopoly Rents," Economic Development Report No. 168, presented at the DAS Conference, Dubrovnik, Yugoslavia, June 1970 (Cambridge, Mass.: Harvard University Center for International Affairs, Development Advisory Service) (photocopy).
24. Re Argentina: Jorge M. Katz, *La Industria Farmacéutica Argentina: Estructura y Comportamiento* (Buenos Aires: Instituto Torcuato di Tella, 1973), p. 22. Re Chile: Corporación de Fomento (CORFO), División de Productividad y Tecnologia, *Costos Implicitos en la Transferencia de Tecnologia* (mimeo, c. 1972). For other countries see *La Transferencia de Tecnologia hacia los Países del Grupo Andino* (Washington, D.C.: Secretaria General de la Organización de los Estados Americanos, April 1972), pp. 78–81.
25. Richard J. Barnet and Ronald E. Müller, *Global Reach: The Power of the*

Multinational Corporations (New York: Simon and Schuster, 1974).
26. Cf. Raymond Vernon in "An Exchange on Multinationals," *Foreign Policy*, no. 14 (Spring 1974), pp. 84ff.
27. Dirección General de Aduana, as in note 12. Cf. Vaitsos, as in note 23, Appendix A.
28. Vaitsos, as in note 23, p. 34.
29. Ibid., p. 35. Cf. *El Tiempo*, as in note 21.
30. Lucio, as in note 10.
31. Ibid.
32. Ibid.
33. Cf. Barnet and Müller, as in note 25, pp. 157–162.
34. Statement of Gov. Lane Dwinell, Assistant Administrator for Administration, AID, U.S. Department of State, before the Subcommittee on Monopoly of the Senate Select Committee on Small Business, 6 August 1970, pp. 7327ff.
35. Testimony of Mattaniah Eytan, Assistant General Counsel for Procurement and Transportation, AID, before Senate subcommittee, as in note 34, p. 7336.
36. Testimony of Seymour Barondes, Chief of Commodity Eligibility and Price Branch, Office of the Controller, AID, before Senate subcommittee, as in note 34, pp. 7334ff.
37. Dwinell, as in note 34, pp. 7390ff.
38. Ibid., p. 7336.
39. Ibid., pp. 7338f.
40. Department of State, Agency for International Development, "Bulk Pharmaceutical Products, Determination of Commodity Eligibility," 24 December 1970, and Amendments to same, 10 April 1971, *Federal Register*, 30 December 1970 and 9 April 1971.
41. Statement of James F. Campbell, Assistant Administrator for Program and Management Services, AID, before the Subcommittee on Monopoly of the Senate Select Committee on Small Business, in *Competitive Problems in the Drug Industry*, vol. 22, p. 8747.
42. Telephone interview with Jane Jones, Office of Commodity Management, AID, 26 July 1974.
43. Jorge M. Katz, *Patents, the Paris Convention and Less Developed Countries*, Center Discussion Paper No. 190 (New Haven: Yale University Economic Growth Center, November 1973) (mimeo), pp. 6ff.
44. Ibid., pp. 12ff.
45. *Prescription Drug Industry Fact Book* (Washington, D.C.: Pharmaceutical Manufacturers Association, 1973), p. 48.
46. Katz, as in note 43, passim.
47. *Regimen Común de Tratamiento a los Capitales Extranjeros y Sobre Marcas, Patentes, Licencias y Regalías* (Lima: Junta del Acuerdo de Cartagena, August 1971), Article 26, p. 11.
48. Ibid., articles 3, 20f., 25, 37, 41ff.
49. "Andean Nations Face Showdown," *The New York Times*, 9 September 1974, p. 52.

50. Katz, as in note 24, pp. 129ff. Cf., Katz, as in note 43, pp. 30–50.
51. *La Ley (Suplemento Diário)*, 16 February 1971, pp. 1–5.
52. Letter of 26 March 1974 from Jorge M. Katz to author.
53. Unclassified telegram from Secretary of State, Washington, D.C., to U.S. Embassy in San José, Costa Rica, February 1974.
54. Unclassified airgram from U.S. Consul, Rio de Janeiro, to Department of State, 15 June 1973, p. 2. Also "Johnson & Johnson's Research Laboratory Meets Brazilian Demands for Local R&D," *Business Latin America*, 25 November 1971, p. 374.
55. Speech by Deputy Lisaneas Maciel in the Brazilian Chamber of Deputies, 3 May 1973 (photocopy), p. 2.
56. U.S. Consul airgram, as in note 54.
57. "Materia-prima, o ponto frágil dos laboratorios nacionais," *Gazeta Mercantil*, 3 April 1975.
58. This and the following two paragraphs based on the text of the decision by the commission which judged the case: "Decision de la Commission du 14 Septembre 1972," *Journal Officiel des Communautés Européennes*, 31 December 1972, pp. 299/51–299/58.
59. "Insulin dos EUA deve chegar hoje ao Brasil," *O Estado de São Paulo*, 20 May 1975.
60. "Hoechst confirma ser a maior exportadora de pancreas do país," *Gazeta Mercantil*, 12 June 1975.
61. Ibid.
62. "Denunciada manobra com insulina," *O Estado de São Paulo*, 17 May 1975.
63. Figure obtained from CACEX, the Foreign Trade Section of the Banco do Brasil.
64. Dr. Severo Fagundes Gomes, Minister of Industry and Commerce, "Açao do MIC no Setor Farmacêutico" (Report before the Commission on Health of the Brazilian Chamber of Deputies, Brasília, 22 May 1975).
65. *Informe sobre la Industria Farmacéutica en Centroamerica* (Guatemala: Instituto Centroamericano de Investigación y Tecnologia Industrial [ICAITI], December 1971), p. xvii.
66. "A Saúde do Povo uma Nova Prioridade," *Planejamento & Desenvolvimento* (Organ of the Ministry of Planning), December 1973, pp. 43ff. Cf. testimony of Dr. Wilson de Sousa Aguilar before the Brazilian Chamber of Deputies, *Diário do Congresso Nacional*, 12 March 1974, pp. 406–411.
67. Ibid.
68. Ibid.
69. Ibid.
70. "Um diagnóstico da indústria farmacêutica," *Movimento*, 24 August 1975.
71. "País Terá em Cinco Anos Matéria-prima de Remédios," *Jornal do Brasil*, 29 June 1974.
72. Cited by Senator Ferreira in *A Revolução nos Medicamentos* (Separate printing of Senate speech), Brasília, 1971.

73. *Jornal do Brasil*, 27 June 1971.
74. Personal interview with Roberto Schneider at Pfizer plant on São Paulo-Rio highway, 1 April 1974.
75. Photocopy of text of proposed decree along with covering letter to the President signed by João Felicio Scardua, 25 March 1974.
76. Bernardo Kucinski, "Demissionário o conselho da CEME," *Gazeta Mercantil*, 3 April 1975.
77. Photocopy of text of proposed decree along with covering letter to the President signed by L. G. do Nascimento e Silva, Minister of Social Welfare, 20 March 1975.
78. "CEME: Previdencia assume mas a pesquisa fica a cargo do MIC," *Gazeta Mercantil*, 7 April 1975.
79. Carly Batista, "Ministério modifica relação básica proposta pela CEME," *Gazeta Mercantil*, 22 July 1975.
80. Fagundes Gomes, as in note 64.
81. Philippe Guédon, President of ABIF, *Ciencia e Tecnologia na Indústria Farmacêutica* (Statement delivered before the Special Committee on Science and Technology of the Brazilian Chamber of Deputies, 7 November 1972), pp. 10ff.
82. Dr. Geraldo Chaia, testimony before Science and Technology Commission of the Brazilian Chamber of Deputies, *Diário do Congresso Nacional*, 25 August 1973, p. 4841. Cf. *Business Latin America*, as in note 54.

5/Sugar Republic *(text pp. 72–91)*

1. Gulf+Western Industries, Inc. (*hereinafter G+W*), *1974 Annual Report*, p. 12.
2. G+W, *1974 Annual Meeting Report/Report for Three Months Ended October 31, 1974.*
3. USDA figures as reported in *The New York Times*, 3 February 1975, p. 37.
4. G+W, *1974 Annual Report*, as in note 1, p. 13.
5. G+W, Prospectus, 16 January 1973, p. 26.
6. *The Wall Street Journal*, 30 January 1975.
7. *The Sugar Story*, G+W promotional brochure, undated, p. 3.
8. Personal interview with Pedro Caba, who witnessed the events, Santo Domingo, 15 April 1974.
9. Ibid.
10. Except as otherwise noted, all the preceding is based on personal observation on site and conversations with residents of La Otra Banda, 26 May 1974.
11. Re Central Romana's comparative size: G+W's *The Sugar Story*, as in note 7. Re the figure of 30%: as in the following note, p. 11.
12. *Estadísticas Azucareras—1970* (Santo Domingo: Instituto Azucarero Dominicano), pp. 28 and 50.
13. *Comercio Exterior de la República Dominicana—1970* (Santo Domingo: Secretariado Técnico de la Presidencia, Oficina Nacional de Estadística), p.xiv.

14. Banco Central de la República Dominicana, *Boletín Mensual,* vol. 26, nos. 10 12 (October-December 1973), p. 75.
15. Carlos E. Aquino, Secretary of Agriculture, *Breve Análisis de la Situaçión de la Agricultura en República Dominicana* (Address delivered before the American Chamber of Commerce, 21 February 1974) (Santo Domingo: Secretaría de Estado de Agricultura), p. 27.
16. *Estadísticas Azucareras—1970,* as in note 12, p. 8.
17. Ibid., pp. 9f., shows growth in sugar cane production from 410,333 short tons in 1902 to 9,540,100 short tons in 1970. The same source, p. 6, shows that yield per hectare has varied little since 1940. The statement in the text assumes that the same is true back to 1902 as well.
18. *República Dominicana en Cifras,* vol. 6 (Santo Domingo: Oficina Nacional de Estadística, 1971), pp. 54 and 57.
19. *The Wall Street Journal,* 3 December 1974, p. 38.
20. Solon Baraclough, consultant, memorandum to John Robinson, Director USAID, Dominican Republic, on Agrarian Reform Programs for the Dominican Republic, 7 April 1970.
21. According to its 16 January 1973 Prospectus, filed with the Securities and Exchange Commission, G+W owns "about 275,000 acres of which 120,000 are used to grow sugar cane . . . 12,000 are used for related operations." According to Raul E. Perdomo, Agricultural Superintendent, Central Romana Division, in *The Sugar Journal,* October 1973, there are 49,362 acres of *colono* land under contract to G+W. The total area under cultivation in the Dominican Republic in September 1971 (source as in note 18) was 13,209,981 tareas, which is approximately 2,083,600 acres. According to *El Nacional,* 14 June 1973, Dr. Juan Casasnovas Garrido, president of the Land Reform Commission, acknowledged on 13 June 1973, "We still do not know the exact amount of land [G+W] possesses." An article in *El Caribe,* 5 September 1972, cites a figure of 2,000,000 tareas (about 315,000 acres) as G+W's total landholdings. The same paper on 25 November 1972 quotes a government official as saying G+W landholdings amount to 3,000,000 tareas (about 475,000 acres).
22. This estimate is based on two maps. The first outlines landholdings of Central Romana Corp. and was published in *El Caribe,* 25 November 1972, p. 10. The reporter who prepared this chapter saw an identical map on the wall in the office of a company official. The second map is one indicating the productive capacity of land in the Dominican Republic and published in *Reconoscimiento y Evaluación de los Recursos Naturales de la República Dominicana* (Washington, D.C.: Pan American Union, 1967).
23. Cf. Melvin M. Knight, *Los Americanos en Santo Domingo* (Santo Domingo: Universidad de Santo Domingo, 1939), pp. 145f.
24. Re programs: G+W reports, as in notes 1 and 2. Re Dominican law on exchange of export earnings for pesos: see G+W Prospectus, 16 January 1973, p. 26.
25. Personal interview with Alberto Giraldi, Santo Domingo, 27 May 1974.

26. *The Sugar Journal,* October 1973, p. 24.
27. Personal interview with Dr. Raul Perdomo, Chief Agricultural Superintendent, G+W Central Romana Division, La Romana, 31 May 1974.
28. Ibid.
29. Ibid. Also as in following note.
30. Interviews with residents of La Otra Banda and La Florida, May 1974.
31. Ibid. Also, Knight, as in note 23.
32. Personal interviews, as in note 30.
33. Knight, as in note 23. Cf. "Strange Bedfellows from Labor, Business Own Dominican Resort," *The Wall Street Journal,* 25 May 1973.
34. Personal interview, as in note 27.
35. Personal interviews, as in note 30.
36. Existence of plantation stores, factories, repair shops verified by personal observation of reporter.
37. *The Sugar Story,* as in note 7, p. 3.
38. *La Romana Industrial Free Zone,* G+W promotional brochure, p. 6.
39. Personal interview with Pablo Fernandez, former cane cutter with G+W. Cf. Baraclough to Robinson, as in note 20; personal interviews, as in note 30.
40. Personal interviews with cane cutters in the fields, 26 May 1974.
41. Personal interview with Dr. Enrique Garcia Godoy, attorney for G+W, La Romana, 31 May 1974.
42. Baraclough to Robinson, as in note 20.
43. Ibid.
44. Personal interview, as in note 39.
45. Ibid.
46. Baraclough to Robinson, as in note 20. Also, *Encuesta sobre los Ingenios Azucareras de la República Dominicana* (Santo Domingo: Centro de Investigación y Acción Social) as cited in Carlos M. Vilas et al., *Imperialismo y Clases Sociales en el Caribe* (Buenos Aires: Cuenca, 1973), p. 17. Cf. Arismendi Días Santana, "Papel de los Braceros Haitianos en la Producción de Azúcar Dominicana" (Paper presented before the First Latin American Seminar on the Role of Ethnic Minorities [African and Asian] in the Socio-Political Development of Latin America, Panama, 1974) (photocopy).
47. The increased wage rate during 1963–64 is evident from wage figures in *Estadística Industrial de la República Dominicana 1969* (Santo Domingo: Oficina Nacional de Estadística), p. 74.
48. Ibid.
49. *Poor's Register of Corporations, Directors, and Executives—1967* (New York: Standard and Poor's Corp., 1967), pp. 1450 and 1916.
50. Chris Welles, "Close Up/Charles Bluhdorn, Collector of Companies: Multimillion Reach of Wall Street's 'Mad Austrian'," *Life,* vol. 62 (10 March 1967), p. 43.
51. "Senalan Caso Gil Noticia del Este," *El Nacional,* 28 December 1967;

"Entregan Informe Caso Gil," *El Nacional,* 16 January 1968; "Se Cumple Primer Año Desaparición Guido Gil," *El Caribe,* 17 January 1968; "Recuerdan Desaparición de Guido Gil," *El Nacional,* 18 January 1973.

52. Personal interview with Julio de Peña Valdez, union leader, Santo Domingo, 3 June 1974. Also, personal interview with Mario Sandoval (pseudonym), La Romana, May 1970.
53. Ibid.
54. Decision of the Court of Appeals of San Pedro Marcoris, 23 March 1972. The court upheld the bank's action.
55. Personal interviews, as in note 40.
56. Personal interview, as in note 39. Cf. *El Nacional,* as in note 51; Baraclough to Robinson, as in note 20.
57. "Autorizaran Aumentar Siembras de Caña," *Azúcar y Diversificación* (Santo Domingo: Dominican Sugar Institute), vol. 1, no. 4 (October 1972), p. 7.
58. Export figures: *Comercio Exterior . . . 1970,* as in note 13, pp. xiv ff. and pp. 235–254. Total production figures: *Boletín Mensual,* as in note 14, p. 146.
59. *Comercio Exterior . . . 1970,* as in note 13, p. xiv.
60. *Boletín Mensual,* as in note 14, p. 113.
61. The following paragraphs are based on interviews with members of this family, La Romana, 31 May 1974. Names have been fictionalized.
62. Personal interviews, as in note 55.
63. Dr. Garcia Godoy, as in note 41.
64. Personal interviews, as in note 40.
65. Ibid.
66. Ibid.
67. Personal experience of the reporter.
68. Personal interview with Carlos Logroño, attorney for G+W, May 1970.
69. "Estado Nutricional en la República Dominicana: Informe sobre la Encuesta Nacional de Nutrición (1969)," *Archivos Dominicanos de Pediatría*, April 1970, pp. 147–165.
70. Ibid.
71. Ibid.
72. Secretaría de Estado de Agricultura, Departamento de Economía Agropecuaria, *Area, Producción, Consumo, Costos, Productividad y Precios de Productos Agrícolas* (Santo Domingo: 4 January 1974) (typescript copy).
73. Cf. Speech by President Balaguer to U.S. Chamber of Commerce of Santo Domingo, 30 April 1971, excerpted in Appendix 3 of Carlos María Gutiérrez, *The Dominican Republic: Rebellion and Repression* (New York: Monthly Review Press, 1972), p. 167.
74. Personal interview with Lic. Marino Vinicio Castillo, 30 May 1974.
75. *La Noticia*, 20 August 1973, p. 11.
76. G+W reports, as in notes 1 and 2.

77. *La Noticia*, as in note 75.
78. *El Caribe*, 23 March 1974, editorial.
79. *El Caribe*, 22 March and 5 April 1974.
80. *La Romana Industrial Free Zone*, G+W promotional brochure, p. 3.
81. Ibid., pp. 4–5.
82. Ibid., p. 6.
83. *La Romana, Zona Franca Industrial*, G+W promotional brochure, November 1973. This figure is based on the brochure's projections to the end of 1974.
84. Ibid., p. 8.
85. *La Romana Industrial Free Zone*, as in note 80, p. 6.
86. Personal interview with Sr. Santoz, General Secretary of the Confederacíon General de Trabajo, 29 May 1974.
87. *La Romana, Zona Franca Industrial*, as in note 83. Cf. Special Advertising Supplement to the Sunday edition of *The New York Times*, 28 January 1973, p. 6.
88. Robert D. Crassweller, *Trujillo: The Life and Times of a Caribbean Dictator* (New York: Macmillan Co., 1966), pp. 39–72.
89. Cf. "The Man Behind Our Latin American Action," *Look*, 15 June 1965.
90. Knight, as in note 23, pp. 145–147.
91. Re negotiations for acquisitions: *Poor's Register*, as in note 49; *Life*, as in note 50. Re AID program: *U.S. Overseas Loans and Grants and Assistance from International Organizations: Obligations and Loan Authorizations July 1, 1945–June 30, 1972* (Washington, D.C.: Statistics and Report Division, Office of Financial Management, Agency for International Development, May 1973), p. 46.
92. AID report, as in note above, p. 46.
93. List obtained from Export-Import Bank, July 1974. Re Eximbank interest rates: see "The Eximbank and Export Subsidies," editorial in *The Wall Street Journal*, 28 June 1974.
94. Overseas Private Investment Corporation, *Cumulative Political Risk Insurance Issued from Inception (1948) to Date—June 30, 1973* (Washington, D.C.: OPIC, 1973).
95. "A.I.D. Assistance to the Agricultural Sector," 12 March 1974, portion of a mimeographed report obtained from the U. S. Embassy in Santo Domingo, March 1974.
96. William E. Beach and C. James Murphrey, *Agricultural Development in the Dominican Republic—April 1965 to June 1973: Texas A & M University Participation* (Final Report of Technical Assistance to the Government of the Dominican Republic) (USAID and Texas A & M University, August 1973), pp. 18–24.
97. "A.I.D. Assistance . . . ," as in note 95.
98. Personal interview with James Stone, Agricultural Section, U.S. Embassy, Santo Domingo, June 1974.
99. Cf. "Text of President Ford's Address at U.N. Assembly," *Washington Post*, 19 September 1974, p. A 10.

6/One Man's Meat *(text pp. 92–98)*

1. Lyle P. Schertz, "Nutrition Realities in the Lower Income Countries," *Nutrition Reviews,* vol. 31, no. 7 (July 1973), p. 206.
2. Re U.S. government emphasis on production: "Address of U.S. Secretary of State Henry A. Kissinger to the United Nations, at the Seventh Special Session of the U.N. General Assembly (delivered by Daniel P. Moynihan, U.S. Representative to the United Nations), 1 September 1975 (Washington, D.C.: Bureau of Public Affairs, Office of Media Services, U.S. Department of State, 1 September 1975). Re spokesmen for multinational agribusiness: See, for example, Roger E. Anderson, chairman and chief executive officer of Continental Illinois Corp., "A Race Against the Clock on Food," *The New York Times,* 16 June 1974, p. F-14.
3. Alan Berg, *The Nutrition Factor: Its Role in National Development* (Washington, D.C.: The Brookings Institution, 1973), p. 72.
4. Ibid., p. 48.
5. Ibid., p. 72.
6. "Social Ills Tied to Malnutrition," *The New York Times,* 26 August 1975.
7. Berg, as in note 3, p. 59.
8. Gae A. Bennett, *Agricultural Production and Trade of Colombia,* ERS–Foreign 343 (Washington, D.C.: USDA Economic Research Service, February 1973).
9. Ibid.
10. Letter of 11 March 1975 from Eduardo Diaz Calderon, President of Cooperativa Agropecuaria de Ginebra, Ltda.
11. Ibid.
12. Ibid.
13. For Mexico: *Avicultura Organizada,* March 1974 and June/July 1973, p. 32. For Colombia: Nilson Lopez S., Alfredo Carrasco, "Situación Actual de la Industria de Alimentos para Animales en Colombia," *Agricultura Tropical,* vol. 24, no. 10 (October 1968), p. 743. Also "Los Concentrados y su Papel en la Avicultura," *El Tiempo,* 29 September 1974.
14. Personal interview with Dr. Jorge Alberto Gonzalez, former president of ACOFAL (Asociación Colombiana de Fabricantes de Alimentos para Animales), Bogotá, 25 June 1974.
15. *Ralston Purina Company Annual Report 1957.*
16. Gonzalez, as in note 14.
17. Personal interview with Dr. Gabriel Misas, Departamento Administrativo Nacional de Estadística, Bogotá, 10 June 1974. Also, Gonzalez, as in note 14.
18. Gonzalez, as in note 14.
19. Personal interview with Bernardo de la Pava, ex-president of FEDERAL (federation of animal food producers) and Dr. Jairo Garzón of PROSA (Promotores, S.A.), Bogotá, 24 June 1974. Also, Misas, as in note 17.
20. Telephone interview with Carlos Arbelaez, Director of Latin American Operations, Ralston Purina, Coral Gables, Florida, 5 September 1974.

Also, Gonzalez, as in note 14. Cf. Wayne G. Broehl, Jr., *The International Basic Economy Corporation* (Washington, D.C.: National Planning Association, 1968), p. 240.

21. Ibid. Also, personal interview with Gabriel Mejia, Bogotá, 25 June 1974. Mejia, a former employee of Purina, is now a competitor.
22. Garzón, as in note 19.
23. Ibid.
24. Ibid.
25. Personal interview with Drs. Consuelo Baez, Miguel Chacon and Roberto Arce, economists of ASOHUEVO, PROPOLLO and INCUBAR (poultry and egg industry associations) in joint offices, Bogotá, 18 June 1974. Figures are from Dr. Baez.
26. United Nations *Yearbook of National Accounts Statistics* 1972, vol. 3: International Tables (ST/STAT/Ser.0/2/Add.2).
27. Hollis Chenery et al., *Redistribution With Growth*: A Joint Study by the World Bank's Development Research Center and the Institute of Development Studies at the University of Sussex (London: Oxford University Press, 1974), p. 12.
28. Ministerio de Agricultura, *Precios Promedios a Nivel Mayorista de los Huevos y la Carne de Pollo Registrados en los Principales Centros de Consumo en el País, Período: 1970–1971–1972–1973–Primero Cinco Meses de 1974* (Bogotá: Instituto de Mercado Agropecuario [IDEMA], 29 July 1974).
29. Baez et al., as in note 25.
30. Misas, as in note 17.
31. Giovanni Acciarri, Dean H. Wilson and Victoria E. Cuartas, *Producción Agropecuaria y Desnutrición en Colombia: El Problema de la Desnutrición visto bajo el Enfoque de Sistemas* (Cali: Universidad del Valle, División de Ingeniería, Depto. de Información y Sistemas, 1973), p. 11 and chart no. 7.
32. Ibid., charts no. 6 and 11.
33. Ibid. Population figures from United Nations *Monthly Bulletin of Statistics*, vol. 28, no. 3 (March 1974) (ST/ESA/STAT/Ser.Q/15).
34. Arbelaez, as in note 20.

7/The Protein Business *(text pp. 99–110)*

1. See John B. Cordaro, "An Inquiry into the Agency for International Development's Commercial Studies High Protein Food Program" (M.A. thesis, Cornell University, 1972). Also Elizabeth Orr, *The Use of Protein-Rich Foods for the Relief of Malnutrition in Developing Countries: An Analysis of Experience* (London: Tropical Products Institute, August 1972).
2. Cordaro, as in note 1, p. 34. Cf. Davis, as in note 15 below; Klein, as in note 36 below.
3. Alan Berg, "Industry's Struggle with World Malnutrition," *Harvard*

Business Review, January-February 1972, pp. 130, 133. Cf. Cordaro, as in note 1, pp. 129–135.
4. Berg, as in note above.
5. Orr, as in note 1, p. 17.
6. Ibid., p. 34.
7. Cordaro, as in note 1, pp. 23–26; Orr, as in note 1, pp. 28f.
8. Cordaro, as in note 1, pp. 103–105; Orr, as in note 1, p. 35. Also personal interview with J. B. Cordaro, Washington, D.C., 12 June 1974; telephone interview with Rod Crowley, Nutrition and Agribusiness Group, July 1974.
9. Cordaro, as in note 1, pp. 59ff. Cf. Davis, as in note 15 below.
10. Orr, as in note 1, pp. 7–11, 17–19.
11. Ibid., p. 34.
12. Ibid., pp. 18f., 67. Cf. Davis, as in note 15 below; interviewees, as in note 22 below.
13. Orr, as in note 1, pp. 18, 69.
14. Ibid.
15. Personal interview with Alan G. Davis, President, Productos Quáker, S.A., Cali, Colombia, 17 June 1974. Also telephone interview with Pearson Oliver, Vice-President of Productos Quáker, S.A., 12 June 1974.
16. Davis, as in note 15.
17. Ibid.
18. Ibid.
19. All information in this paragraph is from Davis, as in note 15.
20. Ibid.
21. Ibid.
22. Personal interviews with Consuelo Cardona Llano, home economist; Lady Perea Valea, nutritionist and dietician; and Luis Francisco Lopez, communications specialist, at Government Rural Development Project, Santander de Quiliachuan, Cauca, Colombia, 17 June 1974.
23. Personal interview with Dr. Teresa Salazar de Buckle, Instituto de Investigaciónes Tecnologicas, Bogotá, 26 June 1974.
24. Orr, as in note 1, p. 19.
25. Ibid.
26. Ibid. Cf. Davis, as in note 15.
27. Davis, as in note 15.
28. Ibid.
29. Ibid.
30. Ibid.
31. Ibid.
32. All information in this and preceding paragraph is from Davis, as in note 15.
33. Orr, as in note 1, pp. 9f.
34. Ibid., p. 19.
35. Davis, as in note 15.
36. Personal interview with Wolfgang Klein, Assistant Manager, Maizena, S.A., Cali, Colombia, 20 June 1974.
37. Davis, as in note 15.

38. *CPC International Almanac*, 1971 ed.
39. Agency for International Development, *Status of Loan Agreements as of December 31, 1973* (Washington, D.C.: Office of Financial Management, AID, 1974), p. 20.
40. Personal observations of the reporter.
41. Personal interviews with Dr. Renato Woiski, Chief of Pediatrics, Santa Casa de Misericordia Hospital, São Paulo, August 1973 and April 1974.
42. Interviews as in note 22.
43. Woiski, as in note 41.
44. Personal interview with Dr. Moises Behar and Ivan Beghin, Institute of Nutrition of Central America and Panama (INCAP), Guatemala City, 6 July 1973.
45. Personal interview with Dr. Max Milner, formerly Director of Secretariat, Protein Advisory Group of the United Nations System, New York, 29 May 1974.
46. Allegation by Davis, as in note 15; denial by Klein, as in note 36.
47. Klein, as in note 36.
48. Ibid.
49. Orr, as in note 1, p. 20.
50. Klein, as in note 36.
51. Ibid.
52. Ibid.
53. Orr, as in note 1, p. 20 and Appendix Table VI, p. 70.
54. de Buckle, as in note 23.
55. Initial spot checks by the reporter confirmed in March 1975 through survey of Bogotá stores by Maria Conseulo Restrepo de Melo.
56. Cordaro, as in note 1, pp. 59f.
57. Klein, as in note 36.
58. Ibid.
59. de Buckle, as in note 23.
60. Telephone conservation with Enrique Martinas, South American Liaison, CPC International, 1 October 1975.
61. Orr, as in note 1, p. 15.
62. Ibid., p. 16.
63. Ibid., pp. 29f.
64. Personal interview with Coca-Cola chemist, Rio de Janeiro, 9 April 1974.
65. Personal interview with Gerald Shaw, Director of Coca-Cola in Brazil, Rio de Janeiro, 11 April 1974.
66. Cordaro, as in note 1, p. 131.
67. Ibid.
68. Ibid.
69. Ibid. Cf. Orr, as in note 1, p. 15.
70. Orr, as in note 1, pp. 15f.
71. Cordaro, as in note 1, p. 131.
72. Telephone conversation with Ferdinand G. Meyer, Manager of Research, Technology Department, New Enterprise Division, Monsanto Chemical Corp., 21 September 1974.
73. Cordaro, as in note 1, p. 131.

74. Confidential source. Cf. Orr, as in note 1, Appendix Table III, p. 67.
75. Confidential source, as in note above.
76. Cordaro, as in note 1, p. 131.
77. Ibid.
78. Ibid.
79. Personal interview with Stul Beckman, Rio de Janeiro, 4 April 1974.

8/I'd Like to Buy the World a Coke *(text pp. 111–126)*

1. Interview with Alan G. Davis, President of Productos Quáker, S.A., Cali, Colombia, 17 June 1974.
2. Cf. Fortune 500 list for the years 1964–1974.
3. "Invasión Monopolista," *Tiempo*, 4 March 1974.
4. Ibid.
5. Personal communication from Rev. Crisoforo Florencio, parish priest of Olinala, Guerrero, Mexico, June 1974.
6. *Tiempo*, as in note 3.
7. Ibid.
8. Per capita consumption in Mexico: *Tiempo*, as in note 3. Per capita consumption in Brazil: from personal interview with José Roberto Orsi, São Paulo, 22 March 1974.
9. Personal interview with Charles Rais, marketing manager for Antartica, São Paulo, 20 March 1974. Rais said that cola drinks have 30% of the market and orange-lemon drinks have 25%. Since Coca-Cola and Pepsi produce the only cola drinks and most of the orange drinks, they hold among them at least 40% of the market.
10. U.S. Department of Agriculture, Foreign Agricultural Service, *Citrus Processing in Brazil*, March 1970, p. 1.
11. Re figure of 97.5%: *Brazilian Bulletin* (London), April 1974. Re foreign buyers: personal interview with João Sapienza, director of Sanderson do Brasil, wholesale marketer of citrus fruits, 26 March 1974. Cf. Coca-Cola advertisement in *Visão*, 28 August 1972.
12. "Crianças e Adolescentes, os que Consomem," *Jornal do Brasil*, 28 October 1971.
13. *Nivel Alimentar da População Trabalhadora da Cidade de São Paulo*, Departamento Intersindical de Estatística e Estudos Sócio-econômicos: Estudos Sócio-econômicos no. 1, July 1973, p. 14.
14. Leoncio Basbam, *História Sincera da República*, 3rd ed. (Editôra Fulgor), vol. 3, p. 122.
15. *A Vanguarda*, 28 October 1948, p. 7.
16. Ibid.
17. Ibid.
18. *O Estado de São Paulo*, 10 October 1973.
19. *Federal Register*, vol. 39, no. 169, 8 October 1974.
20. Personal interview with Prof. Leon Fiker, Instituto A. Lutz, São Paulo, 21 March 1974. (The Institute is a food and drug control agency for the State of São Paulo.) We preferred to quote this more conservative recent figure of

one third given by Fiker rather than the average of one fifth presented in 1950 by Peregrino, as in note 56 below.

21. Personal interview with Dr. Luiz Piragibe, Laboratório Bromatológico, Rio de Janeiro, 10 April 1974. Also Sapienza, as in note 11.
22. Rais, as in note 9, says that guaraná has 40% of the market. Our figure allows for some possible exaggeration on his part.
23. *A Vanguarda*, as in note 15.
24. Ibid.
25. Noé Azvedo, *O Caso Coca-Cola* (brochure), Emprêsa Gráfica Revista dos Tribunais Ltda., 1955.
26. Ibid.
27. Personal interview with Coca-Cola chemist, Rio de Janeiro, 9 April 1974.
28. Rais, as in note 9.
29. Personal interview with Stul Beckman, Rio de Janeiro, 4 April 1974.
30. Ibid.
31. Personal interview with Ralph Cruz, Coca-Cola's Advertising Director, Rio de Janeiro, 6 April 1974.
32. "How Coke Runs a Foreign Empire," *Business Week*, 25 August 1973, p. 41.
33. "Refrigerantes," *Visão*, 12 April 1971.
34. Ibid.
35. Julio Pimentel, marketing director of Pepsi-Cola, interview in *Expansão*, 23 August 1972.
36. Ibid.
37. Rais, as in note 9; Beckman, as in note 29. Cf. personal interview with João Santos, official of the Associação dos Fabricantes de Refrigerantes, Rio de Janeiro, 4 April 1974.
38. Personal interview with Dr. Julio Raja Gabaglia, Commissioner, CADE (Conselho Administrativo de Defensa da Economia), Rio de Janeiro, 5 March 1974.
39. Figures for 1971: *Visão*, as in note 33. Figures for 1974: Beckman, as in note 29; Cruz, as in note 31.
40. Juarez Bahia, "Entre uma Guerra e Outra," *Jornal do Brasil*, 13 November 1972.
41. "Bebidas: Quem Compra no Sul," *Veja*, 17 January 1973, p. 78.
42. Date: Rais, as in note 9. Re motive: interviewer verified exclusivity in retail outlets, e.g. "Lojas Americanas" in São Paulo.
43. Personal interview with Gerald Shaw, Director of Coca-Cola in Brazil, Rio de Janeiro, 11 April 1974.
44. Ibid. Cf. Rais, as in note 9.
45. Shaw, as in note 43.
46. Raja Gabaglia, as in note 38.
47. *Jornal do Brasil*, 15 May 1973.
48. Billings of Mauro Salles for 1973: *Brazilian Gazette*, Special Supplement (London & New York), March 1974. Size of Pepsi-Cola account: based on figures in *Visão*, 12 April 1971.
49. Orsi, as in note 8.

50. Ibid.
51. Rais, as in note 9.
52. Shaw, as in note 43.
53. Orsi, as in note 8, gives 1974 national consumption of soft drinks at 240 million cases (24 bottles per case). From Rais, as in note 9, Coca-Cola and Pepsi have about 40% of the market. Coca-Cola's share is about five times that of Pepsi.
54. Preliminary results of survey given in personal interview with nutritionist Wilma Durano, Instituto de Nutrição Anne Dias, Rio de Janeiro, 7 March 1974, and telephone follow-up, 9 March 1974.
55. Shaw, as in note 43.
56. Armando Peregrino, Introduction to Mozart de Cunto, *Refrigerantes Populares* (Rio de Janeiro: Serviço de Alimentação Pública, 1950), pp. 5 and 9.
57. Juarez Bahia in *Jornal do Brasil*, 27 October 1971, p. 15; 30 October 1971, p. 13.
58. *Jornal do Brasil*, as in note 12.
59. *Nivel Alimentar,* as in note 13.
60. The legislation is contained in Law No. 5-823 of 14 November 1972 *(Atos do Poder Legislativo,* November 1972, pp. 64f.) and Decree No. 73.267 of 6 December 1973 (*Vox Legis,* vol. 60, December 1973, Seção 1, pp.13-49).
61. Paulo Cesar, "Muito tarde e muito pouco," *Movimento,* 25 August 1975.
62. Ibid.
63. Ibid.
64. Ibid. Also Shaw, as in note 43.
65. Cesar, as in note 61.

9/Formula for Malnutrition *(text pp. 127–145)*

1. Protein Advisory Group of the United Nations System, *Promotion of Special Foods (Infant Formula and Processed Protein Foods) for Vulnerable Groups*, PAG Statement No. 23, revised 28 November 1973.
2. Derrick B. Jelliffe and E. F. Patrice Jelliffe, "An Overview," in *The Uniqueness of Human Milk*, eds. D. B. Jelliffe and E. F. P. Jelliffe, Symposium reprinted from *The American Journal of Clinical Nutrition*, vol. 24 (August 1971), p. 1014.
3. D. B. Jelliffe, "Commerciogenic Malnutrition?" *Nutrition Reviews,* vol. 30, no. 9 (September 1972), p. 200; *The National Food and Nutrition Survey of Barbados*, Scientific Publication No. 237 (Washington, D.C.: Pan American Health Organization, 1972), p. 53.
4. Alan Berg, *The Nutrition Factor* (Washington, D.C.: The Brookings Institution, 1973), p. 90.
5. Emergency Committee for American Trade, "The Role of Multinational Corporations in the United States and World Economies," in *Multinational Corporations: A Compendium of Papers Submitted to the Subcommittee on International Trade of the Committee on Finance of the*

Sources for Chapter 9 continued

United States Senate (Washington, D.C.: U.S. Government Printing Office, 1973), p. 839.
6. Harry F. Schroeter, quoted in "Why Food Processors are Starving for Profits," *Business Week*, 1 December 1973, p. 89.
7. Figures from Bureau of the Census, U.S. Department of Commerce.
8. Ibid.
9. Roy J. Harris, Jr., "The Baby Bust," *The Wall Street Journal*, 4 January 1972.
10. "The Bad News in Babyland," *Dun's Review*, December 1972, p. 104.
11. Ibid.
12. The Population Council, "Population and Family Planning Programs: A Factbook," *Reports on Population/Family Planning*, no. 2 (September 1973), p.19.
13. *The Wall Street Journal*, as in note 9; *Dun's*, as in note 10.
14. Population Council, as in note 12.
15. Abbott Laboratories, *1973 Annual Report*, pp. 3, 7, 9.
16. American Home Products Corp., *Annual Report/1973*, p. 4f.
17. Bristol-Myers Company, *Annual Report for 1973*, pp. 7, 18f.
18. "Finding His Feet," *Forbes*, 1 November 1974, p. 78.
19. Information obtained by author on tour of Latin America, July–August 1973.
20. Ibid.
21. Protein Advisory Group, as in note 1.
22. Mike Muller, *The Baby Killer* (London: War on Want, 1974).
23. Ruth Rice Puffer and Carlos V. Serrano, *Patterns of Mortality in Childhood*, Scientific Publication No. 262 (Washington, D.C.: Pan American Health Organization, 1973), p. 161.
24. Ibid., p. 268.
25. D. B. Jelliffe, as in note 3.
26. John McKigney, "Economic Aspects," in *The Uniqueness of Human Milk*, eds. D. B. Jelliffe and E. F. P. Jelliffe, Symposium reprinted from *The American Journal of Clinical Nutrition*, vol. 24 (August 1971), p. 1009.
27. V. G. James, "Household Expenditure on Food and Drink by Income Groups" (Paper delivered at Seminar on National Food and Nutrition Policy of Jamaica, Kingston, 27–31 May 1974) (photocopy).
28. *National Food and Nutrition Survey of Barbados*, as in note 3.
29. D. B. Jelliffe, as in note 3.
30. Dr. R. G. Hendrikse, Director of the Tropical Child Health Course at Liverpool University, quoted in "The Baby Food Tragedy," *New Internationalist*, vol. 7 (1973), p. 10.
31. Berg, as in note 4, p. 95.
32. J. M. Gurney, "PCM in Trinidad and Tobago: Its Prevalence, Causes and Effects," in *Food and Economic Planning in Trinidad and Tobago: The Proceedings of a Seminar, 27–30 November 1972* (National Nutrition Council/Caribbean Food and Nutrition Institute, 1973), p. 13.
33. Puffer and Serrano, as in note 23, p. 179.

34. Hendrikse, as in note 30, p. 11.
35. O. Ballarin, "Effect of Introduction of Infant Foods in Developing Countries: The Viewpoint of Industry" (Paper presented at the PAHO/WHO-UNICEF Conference of Pediatricians and Representatives of the Food Industry on Infant Feeding in Latin America and the Caribbean, Bogotá, 5–6 November 1970).
36. Muller, as in note 22, p. 6.
37. Cf., ILO *Statistical Yearbook of Labour Statistics*, 1973.
38. Cf., S. J. Plank and M. L. Milanesi, "Infant Feeding and Infant Mortality in Rural Chile," *Bulletin of the World Health Organization*, vol. 48, no. 2 (1973), p. 204.
39. *Report of an Ad-Hoc Committee on Young Child Feeding* (New York: Protein Advisory Group, 1971).
40. M. D. Samsudin et al., "Rational Use of Skim Milk in a Complete Infant Formula," *American Journal of Clinical Nutrition*, vol. 20 (1967), p. 1304.
41. McKigney, as in note 26.
42. David O. Cox, "Economics of Feeding Infants and Young Children in Developing Countries" (Paper presented at the Protein Advisory Group Ad-Hoc Working Group Meeting on Feeding the Preschool Child, Geneva, 11–13 December 1972).
43. Cf., Economic Commission for Latin America, *Income Distribution in Latin America* (New York: United Nations, 1971), p. 76.
44. Back-cover advertisement for OSTERMILK and FAREX in *You and Your Baby* (Family Doctor Caribbean Special), published by the British Medical Association circa 1965; slogan also used in *The Ostermilk Book About You and Your Baby*, July 1969, obtained in Jamaica in 1974.
45. Ibid., *You and Your Baby*, back-cover advertisement.
46. D. B. Jelliffe, as in note 3, pp. 200f.
47. Protein Advisory Group, as in note 1.
48. *The Ostermilk Mother and Baby Book*, October 1971, obtained in Jamaica in 1974.
49. *The Mead Johnson Family of Formula Products Provides the Answer to Every Infant Feeding Need*, promotional brochure obtained in Jamaica in 1974.
50. *Cow & Gate Babycare Booklet*, obtained in Jamaica in 1974, p. 5.
51. Nestlé's *Your Baby and You,* obtained in Jamaica in 1974, pp. 43 and 45.
52. Nestlé's *A Life Begins*, obtained in Jamaica and the Dominican Republic in 1974 and in Colombia in 1973, p. 34.
53. Benjamin Spock, M.D., *Baby and Child Care* (New York: Pocket Books, 1968), p. 90.
54. *The Womanly Art of Breastfeeding*, 2nd ed. (Franklin Park, Ill.: La Leche League International, 1963), p. 54.
55. Spock, as in note 53, pp. 92f.
56. *National Food and Nutrition Survey of Barbados*, as in note 3, p. 52.
57. *La Poterie Nutrition Survey, 1972, Grenada, W.I.* (Caribbean Food & Nutrition Institute, May 1972), pp. 2.3 and 2.7.
58. Gurney, as in note 32, p. 13.

Sources for Chapter 9 continued

59. The information on milk nurses is all taken from a letter dated 28 October 1974, written by Miss Patricia Maynard, a nurse specializing in nutrition education, who was hired by the Caribbean Food & Nutrition Institute to conduct a study on the use of milk nurses in Jamaica.
60. Report no. 1 from journalist Eunice Lluberes (*El Sol*), Santo Domingo, July 1974, p. 3.
61. Report no. 2 from Eunice Lluberes, Santo Domingo, 11 September 1974, pp. 1f.
62. Ibid.
63. Letter from confidential source, Guatemala City, 2 August 1974, pp. 3f.
64. Lluberes, report no. 2, as in note 61, p. 1.
65. Confidential source, as in note 63, p. 3.
66. Lluberes, report no. 1, as in note 60, p. 2.
67. Information obtained from Eileen Cox of the Guyana Consumers Association, October 1974.
68. Questionnaire completed by Sheryl Shapiro, La Leche League representative in Rio de Janeiro, September 1974.
69. Lluberes, report no. 1, as in note 60, p. 2.
70. Maynard, as in note 59, p. 4.
71. Samples obtained from the Dominican Republic and Brazil, 1974.
72. Maynard, as in note 59, p. 4.
73. Observations by the author during tour of Latin America, July-August 1973. Cf. questionnaire completed by Emily T. Rapp, August 1974.
74. Confidential source, as in note 63, p. 5.
75. Ibid.
76. Various sources including Maynard, as in note 59; Lluberes, report no. 2, as in note 61; Shapiro, as in note 68.
77. Maynard, as in note 59.
78. Nestlé's *A Life Begins*, as in note 52; *The Ostermilk Book About You and Your Baby*, as in note 44.
79. Spock, as in note 53, p. 81.
80. Nestlé's *A Life Begins*, as in note 52; *The Ostermilk Book About You and Your Baby*, as in note 44.
81. Nestlé's *A Life Begins*, as in note 52.
82. Spock, as in note 53, p. 97; *The Womanly Art*, as in note 54, pp. 98f.
83. D. B. Jelliffe and E. F. P. Jelliffe, "The Effect of Famine on the Family and the Community," in *Proc. Swedish Nutr. Found. Conf.* cited in "An Overview," in *The Uniqueness of Human Milk*, as in note 2, p. 1014.
84. Jelliffe and Jelliffe, "An Overview," as in note 2.
85. Ibid.
86. *The Womanly Art*, as in note 54, p. 120.
87. Nestlé's *A Life Begins*, as in note 52, p. 39.
88. *Cow & Gate Babycare Booklet*, as in note 50, inside back cover.
89. *The Ostermilk Mother and Baby Book*, as in note 48, section entitled "Baby's Growing Diet."
90. Ross Laboratories, *Caring for Your Baby*, obtained in Trinidad in 1973, inside front cover.

91. Ross Laboratories, *Your Baby is Coming Soon!*, obtained in Jamaica in 1974, inside front cover.
92. Samples obtained in Brazil in 1974.
93. Maynard, as in note 59, p. 4.
94. Lluberes, report no. 1, as in note 60, p. 2.
95. Ibid., p. 1.
96. Cf., courses listed at back of *ANAIS NESTLÉ*, Fasc. No. 72. Also Shapiro, as in note 68; Rapp, as in note 73.
97. Ibid.
98. Sample obtained in Brazil in 1974.
99. Shapiro, as in note 68, p. 2.
100. Ibid.

10/The U.S. Government's Helping Hand *(text pp. 146–157)*

1. Cf. Paul Griffith Garland, *Doing Business in and with Brazil* (São Paulo: Banco Lar Brasileiro, associated with the Chase Manhattan Bank, 1971), pp. 125-140. Also Chapter 4, p. 57; *Syntex: A Commitment to the Life Sciences: Annual Report 1973*, p. 32.
2. *G. D. Searle & Co. Annual Report 1973*, p. 29.
3. "Tax Bill Summary," *Tax Notes*, vol. 3, no. 2 (31 March 1975), p. 10. For estimated $620 million tax expenditure, see *Estimates of Federal Tax Expenditures*, prepared by the staffs of the Treasury Department and Joint Committee on Internal Revenue Taxation (Washington, D.C.: Committee on Ways and Means, 8 July 1975), p. 8.
4. "The Numbers Game: Bringing Home the Tax Bacon," *Forbes*, 1 December 1974, pp. 66-72.
5. Personal interview with James Byrne, editor, *Tax Notes*, July 1974.
6. "A Tax Worry for Multinationals," *Business Week*, 2 March 1974, p. 52.
7. Telephone interview with Thomas Field, Tax Analysts and Advocates, 26 December 1974.
8. *Panel Discussion before the Committee on Ways and Means, House of Representatives, 93rd Congress, First Session, on the Subject of General Tax Reform*, part 2, 23 February 1973. Quote is from statement of Stanford G. Ross, p. 1732. Concurring opinions: Jay W. Glassman, p. 1713; Thomas E. Jenks, p. 1745; Peggy B. Musgrave, pp. 1757ff.; Lawrence M. Stone, p. 1840.
9. *The Operation and Effects of the Domestic International Sales Corporation Legislation—1972 Annual Report* (Washington, D.C.: Department of the Treasury, April 1974), p. 4.
10. "Possessions Exemption, Foreign Credit Reduce Drug Company Taxes," *Tax Notes*, vol. 2, no. 29 (22 July 1974), pp. 11f.
11. "Tax Bill Summary," *Tax Notes*, vol. 3, no. 13 (31 March 1975), p. 11.
12. *Operation and Effects*, as in note 9, p. 13. Re 1974-75 losses: Statement by Senator Muskie, *Congressional Record*, 24 June 1974, p. S 11302. For

updated figures see *Budget of the United States, Fiscal 1976,* Chapter F, "Special Analyses."

13. Jenks, in *Panel Discussion,* as in note 8, pp. 1746f. Cf. Ross, also as in note 8, p. 1730.
14. Philip M. Stern, *The Rape of the Taxpayer* (New York: Random House, 1973), p. 261.
15. "Tax Problems for the Drug Industry???" *Washington Research Associates,* 5 March 1973, pp. 8f.
16. *Tax Notes,* as in note 10.
17. Jenks, in *Panel Discussion,* as in note 8, p. 1748.
18. Ibid., p. 1749.
19. *Tax Notes,* as in note 10.
20. "Tax Expenditure Tables by Function," *Tax Notes,* vol. 3, no. 6 (10 February 1975), pp. 4f.
21. "Tax Bill Summary," as in note 3.
22. *An Introduction to OPIC* (Washington, D.C.: Overseas Private Investment Corporation, July 1971), p. 2.
23. For the preceding paragraphs see *The Overseas Private Investment Corporation Amendments Act,* Report of the Committee on Foreign Relations, United States Senate, on S. 2957 (Washington, D.C., 1974), pp. 15ff.
24. Telephone interview with Buck Jordan, Public Affairs Officer, OPIC, July 1974.
25. *OPIC Amendments Act,* as in note 23, pp. 25ff.
26. Re multiple users: *U.S. Overseas Loans and Grants and Assistance from International Organizations: Obligations and Loan Authorizations July 1, 1945-June 30, 1972* (Washington, D.C.: Statistics and Report Division, Office of Financial Management, Agency for International Development, May 1973), p. 46. Re direct loans: Overseas Private Investment Corporation, *Active Direct Investment,* Report no. C.1.B., 11 July 1974, p. 7.
27. Executive Office of the President, Office of Management and Budget, *Commercial and Economic Representation Abroad,* Staff Report, January 1973, pp. 67ff.
28. Unclassified telegram from Secretary of State, Washington, D.C., to U.S. Embassy in San José, Costa Rica, February 1974.
29. Telephone interview with Byron Byron, Foreign Economic Reporting Division, Bureau of Economic and Business Affairs, U.S. Department of State, April 1974.
30. Statement of Daniel Parker, Administrator, AID, before the Senate Subcommittee on Foreign Agricultural Policy, 4 April 1974 (typescript), p. 8.
31. For a convenient explanation of how P.L. 480 works see *P.L. 480 Concessional Sales,* Foreign Agricultural Economic Report no. 65 (Washington, D.C.: USDA Economic Research Service, September 1970), p. 4.
32. Re 75%: Statement of Carroll G. Brunthaver, Assistant Secretary, USDA, before the House Committee on Agriculture, 4 April 1973, p. 4.

Re $16 billion: *Title I, Public Law 480: Total Amounts Shipped Through June 30, 1973 by Country and Commodity* (Washington, D.C.: USDA Export Marketing Service, October 1973), p. 164.

33. Telephone interviews with Daniel Tierney, Director, Program Operations Division, Title I, USDA, 6 June 1974 and 3 July 1974.
34. Ibid.
35. According to *P.L. 480, 1973 Annual Report,* Tables 1 and 8, the U.S. has exported a total of $121.8 billion in agricultural commodities since the passage of P.L. 480 in 1954 through the end of 1973. Of those, $22.5 billion, or 18%, were shipped under P.L. 480. Assuming that P.L. 480 transactions have not displaced normal commercial sales [which, according to Section 103(c) of the Act, they are not supposed to do], that $22.5 billion represents an average of over $1 billion a year in extra business.
36. Tierney, as in note 33.
37. "The Incredible World of Michel Fribourg," *Business Week,* 11 March 1972, p. 84. Cf. Seth S. King, "Five Grain Dealers Dominant in a Hungry World," *The New York Times,* 10 November 1974.
38. *P.L. 480, 1973 Annual Report,* Table 8.
39. United States Department of Agriculture, Commodity Credit Corporation, "Twenty Largest Exporters of Grains Under Title I, P.L. 480, Sales for Foreign Currencies from Inception through December 31, 1969" (photocopy).
40. Total grain shipments through 1973 were worth nearly $15 billion, according to *P.L. 480, 1973 Annual Report,* Table 8.
41. Tierney, as in note 33.
42. Dale W. Adams et al., *Public Law 480 and Colombia's Economic Development* (Michigan State University, Dept. of Agricultural Economics, and Universidad Nacional de Colombia, Facultad de Agronomía, March 1964), pp. 105, 120, 140ff. Also telephone interview with Mr. Durnan, Title I Office, Food for Peace, AID, 15 July 1974.

11/Conclusion *(text pp. 158–164)*

1. *The International Regulation of Pharmaceutical Drugs:* A Report to the National Science Foundation on the Application of International Regulatory Techniques to Scientific/Technical Problems (Washington, D.C.: RANN/Office of Exploratory Research and Problem Assessment, 1975), p. 43.
2. Ibid., pp. 57-64.
3. Ibid., pp. 74-77.
4. United Nations, *The Impact of Multinational Corporations on the Development Process and on International Relations,* Report of the Group of Eminent Persons to Study the Role of Multinational Corporations on Development and on International Relations (E/5500/Add. 1 [Part I]), 24 May 1974.

Sources for Chapter 11 continued

5. *A Review of the Report of the Group of Eminent Persons to Study the Role of Multinational Corporations on Development and on International Relations* by the USA-BIAC Committee on International Investment and Multinational Enterprise, November 1974, p. 41.
6. *Prophylactic and Therapeutic Substances,* Report by the Director-General, World Health Organization, to the 28th World Health Assembly, 3 April 1975 (a28/11).
7. "Address of U.S. Secretary of State Henry A. Kissinger to the United Nations, at the Seventh Special Session of the U.N. General Assembly" (delivered by Daniel P. Moynihan, U.S. Representative to the United Nations), 1 September 1975 (Washington, D.C.: Bureau of Public Affairs, Office of Media Services, U.S. Department of State, 1 September 1975).

INDEXES

Generic Drugs

Brand Names

Corporations

AUTHOR

Born in New York City in 1933, Robert J. Ledogar served for five years as professor of theology and liturgy at the Maryknoll Seminary in Ossining, New York. He holds master's and doctoral degrees (the latter *maxima cum laude*) from the Institut Catholique de Paris. After leaving the Roman Catholic priesthood in 1969, he worked for a brief time with the United Nations, then, on a fellowship from the Loula D. Lasker Foundation, studied at the Massachusetts Institute of Technology, where he received a master's degree in urban planning.

It was while serving as a consultant to Consumers Union that he made his third visit to Latin America and conceived the idea for this book. After completing it, he returned to the United Nations, where he currently serves with the Department of Economic and Social Affairs.

COLLABORATORS

Laurie M. Kramer

A graduate of Smith College, Ms. Kramer was Robert Ledogar's assistant on the Consumers Union international desk during the year this book was written. She is now a writer in the Broadcast/Film Division of Consumers Union.

Bernardo Kucinski

A Brazilian journalist, Mr. Kucinski has just joined the staff of *Movimento,* a new weekly journal of news and opinion published in his country, after having most recently reported for *Gazeta Mercantil,* a Brazilian business weekly. Prior to these assignments, he shuttled for several years between Brazil and England, serving as the London correspondent for the weekly *Opinião,* published in Rio de Janeiro. While in England, he was also associated with the Brazilian Service of the BBC. For several months during 1973, he worked with a BBC television crew in Brazil as researcher and consultant on a film on the Transamazon Highway, directed by Richard Taylor, then returned to London to provide general assistance to the director and to write the film's commentary. Before his London assignment, Mr. Kucinski had been a member of the editorial staff of *Veja,* the Brazilian weekly news magazine.

Susan Gross

A political science graduate of Mount Holyoke College, Ms. Gross is currently Director of Communications for The Council of Public Interest Law in Washington, D.C. Her previous positions have included those of Director of

Research and Education for the Center/Project on Corporate Responsibility (Washington, D.C.); Washington editor of *Business and Society Review,* a quarterly magazine based in New York City for which she wrote the column "Washington Watch"; press consultant and researcher for the Center for Law and Social Policy (Washington, D.C.); and reporter for the Washington-based *Antitrust and Trade Regulation Report,* a weekly news publication.

Alan Howard

A graduate of Hamilton College, Mr. Howard went as a Fulbright Scholar to San Carlos University in Guatemala City in 1964. While in Guatemala, he wrote two articles for *The New York Times* magazine, "Petronillo Learns to Write His Name" (February 1965) and "With the Guerrillas in Guatemala" (June 1966). Returning to the United States, he was an International Fellow at Columbia University in 1966, specializing in journalism and international politics.

Since then he has worked as a freelance writer and has recently completed the manuscript for a book on politics in Latin America. Research for this project involved two years of travel throughout Central and South America and the Caribbean, during which time he was a correspondent for Liberation News Service. He also wrote the one-hour program "Chile: A Special Report," which appeared on WNET in New York in October 1973. He has served as adjunct professor in Latin American affairs at Ramapo College in Mahwah, New Jersey, and is currently staff coordinator for the New York Chile Solidarity Committee.

Rick Edwards

An ordained minister of the United Methodist Church, Mr. Edwards received a B.A. with honors in history from the University of North Carolina at Chapel Hill in 1965 and the Master of Divinity degree from Union Theological Seminary in New York City in 1971.

As a Peace Corps volunteer, he worked as a

community action organizer in the Tolima area of Colombia and later coordinated a research and planning team for rural development programs, which brought him in contact with several organizations of the food and agricultural industries in that country. He also served parttime in the Peace Corps volunteer training school in Buga. Back in the United States, he worked for four years as a staff member of the North American Congress on Latin America (NACLA).

Mr. Edwards is now a campus minister at Columbia University; associate pastor of the Church of St. Paul and St. Andrew (UMC), specializing in young adult work on Manhattan's Upper West Side; and a senior staff member of Church Research & Information Projects (CRIPS), a group focusing on the critical study of U.S. religious institutions.

IDOC PROJECTS AND PUBLICATIONS

A public foundation incorporated as a nonprofit religious and educational institution, IDOC/North America is part of a cooperative network of individuals and groups in more than 40 countries who regularly exchange documentation, surveys, reports, and ideas on issues of human and religious renewal. The acronym IDOC is derived from "international documentation."

Since its incorporation in New York State in 1969, IDOC/North America has sponsored projects, conferences and symposia, and publications focusing on trends within contemporary theology; issues of responsibility and accountability within the worlds of organized religion, government, and business; international crises involving the denial of dissent, civil and religious liberties, and basic human rights; and ethical issues in economic and human development. Further information on IDOC/North America and its monographic series *IDOC/International Documentation* (of which this book is a part) is available from IDOC/North America, 235 East 49th Street, New York, New York 10017.

IDOC/International in Rome, publishes the monthly *IDOC Bulletin* (in English); two bimonthly series (in English), *The Future of the Missionary Enterprise* and *Europe: Churches in Their Environment;* and *IDOC/Internazionale,* a fortnightly documents review (in Italian). Further information on these series and other IDOC offices may be requested from IDOC/International, Via S. Maria dell'Anima 30, 00186 Rome, Italy.

IDOC publications topically related to *Hungry for Profits,* and available from the New York office and selected bookstores, are listed on the following two pages.

LATIN AMERICA

Chile: Under Military Rule

Edited by Diana Calafati-Coben and Gary MacEoin

More than one hundred documents and analyses in eight sections, prefaced by MacEoin's "Chile to the Third Circle": Counterrevolution • Life Under the Junta • Human Rights and Justice • Critics and Defenders • Chile in the U.S. Congress • The International Response • The Church and Chile • The Economic Dimension • Epilogue: "The Phoenix and the Albatross." With source list, selected bibliography, index of names.

"A volume of extreme usefulness to students, professors, journalists, clergymen—to all persons interested in humanitarian causes . . . Clearly, in posing the need for Christian social action, it can serve as a corrective, or at least a complement, to the inadequate coverage of the Chilean crisis in the American press."—*Perspective*

1974, PAPER, 8½ X 11, 164 PP., $4.95
(COMBINED EDITION OF IDOC NOS. 62 AND 64)

Chile: The Allende Years, The Coup, Under the Junta
Documents and Analysis

Edited by Laurence Birns

"Beyond rhetoric to accessible, well-documented evidence. . . . An excellent start on the consciousness-raising that will be needed to counter our new style of war . . . a much-needed corrective to the myths promoted by the Nixon administration."—*Village Voice*

1973, PAPER, 8½ X 11, 78 PP. $2.95 (IDOC NO. 58)

Freedom and Unfreedom in the Americas
Toward a Theology of Liberation

Edited by Thomas E. Quigley
Introduction by Harvey Cox

1971, PAPER, 5½ X 8½, 140 PP. $1.95

Poverty, Environment, and Power
Papers on Issues of Justice in the Americas
1973, PAPER, 8½ X 11, 64 PP., $2.95 (IDOC NO. 53)

The Gospel and Violence: Bolivia
1974, PAPER, 8½ X 11, 106 PP., $3.95 (FME NO. 11–12)

DEVELOPMENT ETHICS

The Myth of Aid
The Hidden Agenda of the Development Reports
By Denis Goulet and Michael Hudson
Prepared by the Center for the Study of Development and Social Change
1971, PAPER, 5 X 8, 144 PP., $2.95

Asia, Oil Politics, and the Energy Crisis
The Haves and Have-Nots
By Leon Howell and Michael Morrow
1974, PAPER, 8½ X 11,180 PP., $5.95 (IDOC NO. 60–61)

The Philippines: American Corporations, Martial Law and Underdevelopment
1973, PAPER, 8½ X 11, 78 PP., $2.95 (IDOC NO. 57)

An Ethical Primer on the Multinational Corporation
By Severyn T. Bruyn, Norman J. Faramelli, and Dennis A. Yates
1973, PAPER, 8½ X 11, 48 PP., $2.95 (IDOC NO. 56)

Aid and Development: Indochina
1976, PAPER, 8½ X 11, 160 PP., $3.95 (FME NO. 16)